Wordsworth and
the Cultivation of Women

Wordsworth and the Cultivation of Women

Judith W. Page

UNIVERSITY OF CALIFORNIA PRESS
Berkeley · *Los Angeles* · *London*

University of California Press
Berkeley and Los Angeles, California

University of California Press, Ltd.
London, England

© 1994 by
The Regents of the University of California

Library of Congress Cataloging-in-Publication Data

Page, Judith W., 1951–
    Wordsworth and the cultivation of women / Judith W. Page.
       p.   cm.
    Includes bibliographical references (p.) and index.
    ISBN 0-520-08493-4 (alk. paper)
    1. Wordsworth, William, 1770–1850—Political and social views.
    2. Feminism and literature—England—History—19th century.
    3. Women and literature—England—History—19th century.   I. Title.
    PR5892.F45P34 1994
    821'.7—dc20
                                                  93-34121
                                                   CIP

Printed in the United States of America
9 8 7 6 5 4 3 2 1

The paper used in this publication meets the minimum requirements of
American National Standard for Information Sciences—Permanence of Paper
for Printed Library Materials, ANSI Z39.48-1984. ⊗

*To my parents, with gratitude, and
to Bill, in love and friendship*

Contents

Illustrations

Preface

Writing a book is both a solitary activity and a collaborative effort. In my work on this project I have benefited immeasurably from much excellent Wordsworth criticism, as well as from the generosity of other scholars. The idea for this project grew out of a conversation with my friend and former colleague Nona Fienberg (although she may not remember it). Catherine Burroughs, Anne Mellor, Bradford Mudge, and William Page all read and commented on one or another version of the manuscript; William Page read far more than one version. (Better not count!) I thank them all, as well as the following people who read parts of the manuscript, or discussed their ideas with me, or responded to my letters in ways that have enriched my work: Laurie Brown, James Chandler, Frances Ferguson, Lorne Fienberg, Mary Ellis Gibson, Bruce Graver, Sandra Grayson, Anthony Harding, Elizabeth Helsinger, Theresa Kelley, T. W. Lewis, Dennis McGucken, Anne MacMaster, Peter Manning, Greg Miller, Alan Richardson, David Simpson, Elise Smith, Steven Smith, Kathleen Spencer, and Cammy Thomas. Despite this rich collaboration, all responsibility for the book, of course, rests with me.

I would also like to thank the members of the NEH seminar "Gender and English Romanticism" (University of California, Los Angeles, 1989) for far-reaching discussions on the subject and for responding to and encouraging my work at an earlier stage. In addition, audiences at the Wordsworth Summer Conference (Grasmere, 1990) and the MLA (Chicago, 1990) responded helpfully to my work on "Laodamia" and "The Banished Negroes," respectively.

More thanks are in order. I appreciate the directness and enthusiasm of Doris Kretschmer, acquisitions editor at the University of California Press, as well as the expertise of Erika Büky and Jane-Ellen Long. At Millsaps, Buddie Louise Hetrick and Virginia Salter have helped with preparing the manuscript and have given much support along the way. Dean Robert King, Professor Robert Padgett, and the Faculty Development Committee of Millsaps have supported my work in numerous ways, for which I am most grateful. I thank the staff at the Millsaps Library, particularly Floreada Harmon, for responding to what must have seemed to her my endless requests for interlibrary loans, and James Parks, for bending the rules for me (although perhaps I should not say this in print). Finally, Carol Cox assisted with proofreading.

I have been fortunate also to work at other libraries and collections. In the Rare Book Room at the Boston Public Library, I read first editions of several of Wordsworth's texts and consulted other nineteenth-century works familiar to Wordsworth. My biggest debt is to the staff at the Wordsworth Library and to its registrar, Jeff Cowton. On my two research trips to Grasmere in 1990 and 1992, Jeff Cowton opened files and boxes of Dora Wordsworth's letters, journals, and other materials to me, even though on the second trip I showed up at a most inconvenient time. I thank the entire staff and the Wordsworth Trust for their generosity and hospitality. The Wordsworth Trust has kindly given me permission to quote from Dora Wordsworth's unpublished texts; they have also been most accommodating in supplying and giving me permission to reproduce many of the illustrations for this book.

Through the 1989 seminar, a summer grant in 1990, and a travel grant in 1992, the NEH helped to make this project possible.

I would also like to thank the editors of *Criticism* and of *Texas Studies in Literature and Language* and their respective presses, Wayne State University Press and the University of Texas Press, for permission to reprint portions of chapters that were previously published in their journals. A version of part of chapter 3 was published as "'The weight of too much liberty': Genre and Gender in the Calais Sonnets," *Criticism* (Spring 1988): 189–203, and a version of part of chapter 4 was published as "'Judge her gently': Passion and Rebellion in Wordsworth's 'Laodamia,'" *Texas Studies in Literature and Language* (Spring 1991): 24–39.

This book is lovingly dedicated to my parents, Mollie and Mayer Wallick, whose support and confidence have always sustained me, and to my husband Bill, who alone knows the extent of my debt to him. I could not close without thanking our daughters Rebekah and Hannah for their love, which has helped me keep everything else in perspective, and for forgiving me for all the softball games I missed while I was completing this project.

Highlands, North Carolina
June 1993

Abbreviations

LY	*The Letters of William and Dorothy Wordsworth. The Later Years, 1821–1853.* 4 parts. Ed. Ernest de Selincourt. Revised by Alan G. Hill. Cited as *LY by part.*
Moorman	Mary Moorman. *William Wordsworth: A Biography.* Volume 1: *The Early Years, 1770–1803.* Volume 2: *The Later Years, 1803–1850.* Identified as *Moorman* by volume.
MY	*The Letters of William and Dorothy Wordsworth.* Ed. Ernest de Selincourt. 2 parts. Part 1: *The Middle Years, 1806–1811.* Revised by Mary Moorman. Part 2: *The Middle Years, 1812–1820.* Revised by Mary Moorman and Alan G. Hill. Cited as *MY* by part.
PrW	*The Prose Works of William Wordsworth.* 3 vols. Ed. W. J. B. Owen and Jane Worthington Smyser. Cited as *PrW* by volume. When not noted otherwise, references to Wordsworth's prose are to this edition.
PW	*The Poetical Works of William Wordsworth.* Ed. Ernest de Selincourt and Helen Darbishire. 5 vols. When not noted otherwise, references to Wordsworth's poetry are to this edition.
R&F	Anne K. Mellor, ed. *Romanticism and Feminism.*

Introduction

Milton and Ben Jonson had a dash too much of the male in them. So had Wordsworth and Tolstoi.
Virginia Woolf, A Room of One's Own, *1929*

The instinct to stand guard over its boundaries, to assert its distinctness, Coleridge considered the first indication of a masculine mind, and one supremely obvious in Wordsworth's.
John Jones, The Egotistical Sublime, *1954*

Wordsworth is never too masculine. The most male is the Miltonic sublime. The most female is the languishing pathos of the story-poems, where the sufferings of women, children, and animals are dwelt upon at excruciating length.
Camille Paglia, Sexual Personae, *1990*

My interest in Wordsworth dates back to my senior year in college, when I literally heard "Tintern Abbey" for the first time. I remember being moved by the sheer beauty of the language and rhythm, but feeling surprised when the speaker turns to his sister, the silent auditor who stands beside him on the banks of the Wye. The poem had seemed to my responsive ear so much a monologue that the sister's presence gave me a jolt, but it also pleased me, although I did not realize then how fully I identified with her.

It was not until several years later that I began to consider the sister's role in terms of the burdens as well as the blessings laid on her both in this poem and in others by Wordsworth. When in the fall of 1987 I began thinking about this project on Wordsworth and women, I found a body of feminist criticism and theory that could help me analyze the sister's role, although very little had been written specifically on Romanticism and feminism. With the publication of the anthology with that title in the spring of 1988, as well as several publications since then, feminist studies of Romanticism entered a new and productive phase, in which scholars have focused on both canonical and non-canonical writers, on questions of authorship and identity, and on the constructions of gender in the early nineteenth century.[1]

Although feminist criticism of Wordsworth over the past decade has contributed energetically to this crucial revisionary work, it has often been hampered both by an adherence to a strict ideological approach and by an almost exclusive focus on the long-accepted canonical texts of the Great Decade. This perspective has shaped the interpretation of Wordsworth in a predictable way, as an exploiter of nature in his poetry and a domestic tyrant in his life. Wordsworth, like the other male Romantics, is seen as an appropriator of women and the feminine for an exclusively male poetic enterprise which ultimately denies women their subjectivity and value. The poet, according to these readers, is alternately figured as a rapist, a conqueror, a cannibal, or a capitalist.

But Wordsworth and his poetry are more complicated than the assumptions behind these metaphors would suggest. If we assume from the beginning that an interpretive grid fits Wordsworth, then we lose the richness, variety, and complexity of his poetry. While it is true that in some poems Wordsworth reveals this male desire to control and to appropriate the feminine and to objectify female characters, in others he identifies both with women and with qualities conventionally associated with the feminine. Contradictions abound: in "Nutting," Wordsworth tells of a boyhood transgression, but in that poem he turns away from the boy's violence. In his prefaces Wordsworth does liken the poet to such great conquerors as Hannibal among the Alps, but he also describes the poet as being attuned to the most basic human affections, and when he dramatizes himself in *The Prelude* as crossing the Alps, it is as an ordinary hiker disappointed by the experience. Furthermore, Wordsworth was aware of the dangers of imaginative transgression and solipsism; he continuously shows himself pulling back from or being shocked out of his egotism. In "Resolution and Independence," for instance, the poet laughs himself to scorn with Chaucerian humor for being so obtuse with the old leech-gatherer. Mary Wordsworth finally found a way to interrupt her husband's poetic reveries: she is reported to have once broken a china plate outside the door of his study to rouse him to everyday life.[2]

Rather than assume that the poet simply appropriates women and the feminine, I shall ask what other configurations were possible for a male poet living from 1770–1850 and what configurations are revealed in Wordsworth's poetry. In so doing, my approach to Wordsworth is as a resisting but reconstructive reader.[3] While I would no longer project pure adoration onto the sister in "Tintern Abbey," reading the poem without critical distance, I am not prepared to see her simply as a victim of her brother's narrative. Nor do I deny the pleasure I continue to derive from reading Wordsworth, despite my critique of his relationships with women.

No one can contemplate women and the feminine in Wordsworth's poetry without considering the women in his life. As is well known, Wordsworth's household was filled with devoted women who not only did the laundry but took dictation and labored to make fair copies of manuscripts. Dorothy Wordsworth's journals and family letters attest to the roles played by Dorothy, Mary Wordsworth, Mary's sister Sara Hutchinson, and later the Wordsworths' daughter Dora and her friend Isabella Fenwick. But beyond mere domestic and editorial help, these women made the poetry possible by providing emotional and intellectual contexts in which Wordsworth could write.

Furthermore, although the Wordsworths subscribed to many of the gender stereotypes of their age, their lives belie any easy notion of an ideology of separate spheres, because in the Wordsworth family the home was everyone's workplace and the focus of value. That is, the home was for Wordsworth a place of refuge not *from* work but *to* work. Also, to view these women as mere supporters of male genius, as some recent readers have done, is to deny the complicating point that the women themselves valued their domestic work and their lives in different ways, during both the early and later years. They related to Wordsworth as more than mere female devotees, and they come alive as individuals when we read what they say about themselves and each other. It is too simplistic to look at these talented women merely as slaves to male poetic genius. Sara Hutchinson smuggles *Blackwood's Magazine* into the house against her brother-in-law's wishes in order to read bad reviews of his poetry, and Mary Wordsworth refuses to work with her husband on revisions until his mood improves. Isabella Fenwick, perhaps Wordsworth's closest friend during his last decade, has been reduced to "Fenwick notes" in most Wordsworth criticism. My research will begin to restore both this friend and Wordsworth's daughter Dora to their rightful places in the history of Wordsworth's career.

I assume in this study that the Wordsworths' journals, letters, and other prose works can be read as inter-texts, pre-texts, and contexts for understanding the poetry. I make use of both published and unpublished materials, having benefited from access to manuscripts housed at the

Wordsworth Library in Grasmere. Together, these published and un-published texts weave a detailed tapestry of the Wordsworths' lives for more than half a century, revealing the interconnections between private and political concerns, imaginative and economic matters, intellectual conversation and smoking chimneys.

My interest in Wordsworth's life, furthermore, led me to the later po-etry, not the other way around. Having read and written about only the poetry of the Great Decade, and having been firmly indoctrinated in the idea that after 1807 he had written nothing worth reading, I, like most students, had neglected most of Wordsworth's career. But the contex-tual reading opened up a new Wordsworth. My study thus asks what happens when we redefine Wordsworth as a poet who wrote for about sixty-five or seventy years (if we count schoolwork) and whose life reached well into the Victorian period. The most basic answer is that we get a picture of Wordsworth that fits none of the prefabricated images of our mythology, but the picture is also surprisingly unified with his ear-lier "self" and attitudes. And we discover a body of interesting and en-gaging poetry. By focusing on three major periods in his career (poems written in the 1790s and early 1800s, poems published in 1814 and 1815, and poems written and published in the 1820s and 1830s), I in-tend both to redefine what we think of as "Wordsworth" and to demon-strate the centrality of Wordsworth's attitudes toward gender in under-standing the conflicts, compromises, and resolutions of his career. Wordsworth was neither a feminist nor a misogynist, but he did not es-cape the gender ideologies of his time.

In *The Egotistical Sublime*, John Jones pointed out that in Words-worth's poetry the family was a microcosm of the world.[4] Although Jones did not extend this insight as far as he might have, the importance of his assertion should not be obscured by its simplicity. From our vantage point, we might say that the sexual conflicts and configurations of gen-der within the family reveal both Wordsworth's personal and his polit-ical anxieties. Wordsworth writes of fathers who cannot function in the family, of women driven to madness by despair, of parents who tyran-nize over their children, of children left on their own in time of war and famine. Wordsworth knows as well as his contemporaries Blake and Wollstonecraft that questions of power, authority, passion, and rebel-lion apply both to the family and to the larger society. We see, too, the intricate plot of the family romance of Wordsworth's life—his love af-fair in France, his loss of loved ones, his possessive and fearful love of his daughter Dora—imposed on his poetry. Wordsworth shows the family in both metonymic and metaphorical relationship to society: the family both represents the workings of the society and is analogous to that society. In focusing on various familial relationships, Wordsworth inevitably raises questions of sex and gender, even though he may do so in such oblique ways that readers have seen him as uninterested in and prudish about sex (as in Shelley's "moral eunuch" from *Peter Bell the Third*) and rigid in his thinking about gender.

By creating the fiction in "Tintern Abbey" of composing the poem in the presence of his sister and turning to her as his most receptive and intimate audience, Wordsworth raises (for us if not for himself) questions about women as readers of his poetry. Throughout Wordsworth's lifetime, as we shall see, women comprised both Wordsworth's most reliable first readers and (later) the popular audience for his poetry. In this century, several noted Wordsworth scholars have been women, including Wordsworth's biographer, Mary Moorman, and one of his editors, Helen Darbishire, as well as others such as Alice Comparetti and Edith Batho. Important as these scholars have been to textual and biographical studies, they are united in having read Wordsworth without critical distance when it comes to intersections of his life and art: they are latter-day versions of the Dorothy whom Wordsworth imagines in "Tintern Abbey," and they defend the poet most strongly in his relationships with women. After reading their commentaries, I am left with the feeling that the ladies do protest too much.

Moorman, for instance, takes the attitude that the affair with Annette Vallon was genuine but transitory, that "There was in her nothing that could have 'reciprocated him' (to use Coleridge's phrase) in all the deepest springs of his being" (*Moorman* 1:181). Darbishire simply accepts that there was a "gradual drifting apart,"[5] and Comparetti balks at George McLean Harper's suggestion that *The White Doe of Rylstone* had anything to do with Wordsworth's meditating on the fate of women in his life.[6] In these pre-feminist works, women scholars refuse to read Wordsworth's experiences with Annette Vallon as having a major effect on his life and work, and they reject all criticism of his relationship with Dorothy. They read Wordsworth completely on his own terms and see themselves as his defenders.

Some recent feminist readers—both women and men—err, I believe, not in emphasizing the importance of Wordsworth's affair with Annette Vallon, but in reducing Wordsworth to a conventional patriarchal villain. Wordsworth's responses to his experiences in revolutionary France reveal his continued (if unacknowledged) anxieties about both the political excesses and the sexual license. Wordsworth's abandonment of Annette Vallon and their daughter Caroline is finally connected in his imagination to his feelings of abandonment by his mother (who died when he was eight) and to his lifelong fear of further loss. He thus experiences abandonment not just from the perspective of having abandoned Annette and Caroline but, paradoxically, with an understanding of what it means to be left behind. The grieving or abandoned women in his poetry—in the *Lyrical Ballads*, in "Laodamia," in *The Excursion*—can be seen, then, as expressions of guilt *and* empathy.

In his recent book on Wordsworth and contemporary critical theory, Don Bialostosky uses an essay of mine (an early version of part of chapter 3) to represent the feminist approach to Wordsworth. Bialostosky criticizes my article for being "more judicial than judicious" in reaching the conclusion that Wordsworth abandoned his illegitimate daughter and her mother and for emphasizing the "biographical situation" over the "poetic situation."[7] I hope in this book, not to place Wordsworth on trial under a single set of standards, but to view his career and work from multiple perspectives in order to avoid a dualistic approach to the poet as either hero or villain. Furthermore, my commitment to what might be called feminist "new biography" assumes the interrelation of the text and the world, of the "poetic situation" and the "biographical [or historical] situation." This perspective unites the many voices of feminist theory and practice, including those that could be considered much more hard-line than my own.

Whereas recent feminist readers critique Wordsworth as a poet of egotistical sublimity, I see in Wordsworthian sublimity a paradoxical yearning for relationship, a tension that in the later poetry resolves itself in images of beauty and domesticity constructed from a masculine point of view. I argue in my first chapter that we can see this conflict even in the early poetry. Readers have noted, for instance, that in *The Prelude* Wordsworth organizes his early experiences into the aesthetic terms of the sublime and the beautiful; the highly schematic two-part *Prelude* of 1799 reveals that Wordsworth also follows Edmund Burke in aligning these categories in terms of gender.[8] Here he dramatizes an inner conflict between sublime impulses, associated with masculinity and solitude, and the attractions of the beautiful, associated with feminine nurturing and community.

While the narrator's view of the feminine in the 1799 *Prelude* is positive—even idealized—in other contexts Wordsworth is not as much at ease with gendered relationships, especially when he thinks of his public audience. In my second chapter I argue that in the 1800 Preface to *Lyrical Ballads* Wordsworth tries to disassociate himself from women writers and from what he regards as feminine weaknesses at the same time that he defends writing about figures on the margins of society—including, of course, forsaken women and mad mothers. He carefully frames his argument in terms of class and not of gender, in order to avoid any association with "frantic" and "sickly" (*PrW* 1:128) literary trends, some of which were being set by hundreds of women writers. In the rhetoric of the Preface Wordsworth establishes himself as "a man speaking to men," a man writing in the tradition of a great brotherhood of poets from Catullus to Pope. Wordsworth's argument neglects to mention women writers such as Joanna Baillie, who may very well have influenced the Preface. But despite this public pose both in the Preface and in poems such as "Michael," Wordsworth also depends on a supportive private audience (composed largely of women), as both his letters and his great poem "Tintern Abbey" make clear. Wordsworth continues to cultivate women, even as he ignores the possibility that women authors are among those who have cultivated him.

The third chapter focuses on Wordsworth's experiences in revolutionary France and on how these experiences continued to shape his poetry. As Wordsworth looks back on the personal and political excesses of this period, he wants to control both the sexual and the political passions that led to illegitimacy. In the poetry written during the mid to late 1790s and beyond, we see Wordsworth linking revolutionary ardor and sexual passion, revising and rethinking his own past in such poems as the sonnets he wrote in Calais in 1802, at the time of his final separation from Annette Vallon and just before his marriage to his childhood friend Mary Hutchinson. I argue that in confronting his own transgressions, Wordsworth spiritualizes or silences women so that he does not have to come to terms with them as sexual Other. I consider closely the group of sonnets that Wordsworth wrote while in Calais, as well as the multiple revisions of a sonnet commemorating an African woman he encountered on his return voyage.

In chapter 4 I consider two poems published in 1815, both of which center on conflicts between rebellion and order, passion and restraint. In *The White Doe of Rylstone*, Wordsworth celebrates "female patience winning firm repose," while in "Laodamia" he censures a woman's "rebellious passion."[9] Both poems end in silence and death, one woman sainted for her passivity and the other condemned for her passion. In *The White Doe*, Wordsworth invokes spirituality and renunciation as a way of avoiding the haunting history of revolution. And although Wordsworth finally condemns Laodamia, his revisions reveal that into the 1840s he continued to agonize over her fate. I believe that Wordsworth was ambivalent here, as in *The White Doe*, because he identified with Laodamia's rebellious passion as he continued to re-imagine the consequences of his own past. We see similar tensions in several narratives from the sixth book of *The Excursion*, written during the same years.

In my fifth chapter I focus on a series of poems about Dora Wordsworth and other young women which show Wordsworth making the transition from rebellious son to Victorian father. I believe that Wordsworth's daughter Dora, who has thus far been an object of little critical interest, holds the key to understanding Wordsworth's later life and poetry. Wordsworth's later poetry is marked by a need to control and circumscribe women and the feminine, often represented by a daughter. Although Wordsworth acknowledges powers and talents that defy culturally prescribed roles, in his late writing he endorses an ideology of womanhood that limits and contains women's achievements by emphasizing virtues associated with home and hearth. The daughter who assumes the role of "my Antigone" in "A Little Onward" (1816) is in her father's later writing playfully transformed into a domestic angel who ministers to weary men. Both Wordsworth's letters and such poetry as "The Egyptian Maid" (1835), a fanciful romance, and "The Triad," written in 1828 for a popular Christmas annual, provide us with his views of feminine duty. In the 1820s and 1830s Wordsworth reshapes his poetry according to the increasingly ceremonious vision of female piety and virtue he has cultivated—a view that almost destroys his relationship with Dora when she marries at the age of thirty-seven without her father's wholehearted approval.

I conclude this book on Wordsworth as a "reader" of women with a discussion of Dora Wordsworth's letters and her unpublished travel journal as records of one remarkable woman's loving but ambivalent reading of Wordsworth. The journal, a Dove Cottage manuscript entitled "Dora Wordsworth's Journal of a Tour of the Continent" (1828), reveals Dora's humanity and intelligence; one particular letter, written a decade later, reveals her difficulty in playing the daughter's part. In this crucial letter to Isabella Fenwick, written on her first visit to "Tintern

Abbey" at the age of thirty-four, Dora Wordsworth contemplates the gulf between her father's poem and her own life. In reconstructing the history of her relationship, I show the significance of Dora's visit forty years after her father and aunt stood on the banks of the Wye.

This study, ranging as it does over Wordsworth's long career, is representative rather than comprehensive. It would be virtually impossible to discuss every poem in which Wordsworth explicitly celebrates or struggles with images of women and the feminine, much less every poem in which these concerns implicitly appear. Although I have focused on some of his best-known poetry—reference to "Tintern Abbey," for instance, serves both as a frame for this book and as a marker along the way—I have deliberately worked with lesser-known or now-neglected works as a way of opening up the Wordsworth canon. But this does mean that some standard works, such as the Lucy poems, get less attention than might be expected. Still, the problem has been one of abundance and not scarcity, even though when I began this project one skeptical friend quipped, "Wordsworth and *women*—that will be a short book."

A word about my title. I am aware that the word *cultivation* may strike the reader as both odd and ambiguous. I intend the word to refer to Wordsworth and to women, to suggest Wordsworth's attraction to women and the feminine *and* to highlight the roles of women and the feminine in the shaping of his life and career. I also want to link women in Wordsworth's poetry and life to culture as well as to nature—in fact, to show that culture and nature are not necessarily oppositional terms.

In *Keywords*, Raymond Williams traces the various meanings of the word *culture* and its relatives such as *cultivation*, revealing that the words went through a "metaphorical extension from a physical to a social or educational sense" in the seventeenth century.[10] In their earliest uses the words were associated with husbandry: "Culture in all its early uses was a noun of process: the tending of something, basically crops or animals. . . . From [the early sixteenth century] the tending of natural growth was extended to a process of human development, and this, alongside the original meaning in husbandry, was the main sense" until the late eighteenth or early nineteenth century (77). The history of the word reveals the connection between the concrete and the metaphorical meanings, as well as the progressive emphasis on the various metaphorical developments. We can speak of cultivation as a process of forming, fostering, or nurturing someone else's growth, development, or education. Given the standard gender roles in the 1790s as well as the 1990s, this meaning of cultivation would be identified with the feminine gender and with women's roles.

I use the term *cultivation*, then, both to refer to a certain quality associated with women and the feminine and to suggest a process by which Wordsworth was formed, fostered, and nurtured by women and his ideas of the feminine. I shall also argue that Wordsworth himself cultivated women, that he increasingly sought out their company and friendship, even though he defined himself as a poet by distinguishing himself from women. Increasingly, too, as Wordsworth moves metaphorically from ruined cottages to well-appointed houses, he associates the cultivation of women with the creation of domestic happiness, which depends on familial cohesion. His later poetry, as we shall see, inscribes the gender ideology associated with such cultivation, but—like his life—it also reveals what can happen when cohesion confines individuals within the family circle.

CHAPTER ONE

From the Sublime to the Beautiful

Solitude and Community in the 1799 Prelude *and Beyond*

[T]hough it is impossible that a mind can be in a healthy state that is not frequently and strongly moved both by sublimity and beauty, it is more dependent for its daily well-being upon the love & gentleness which accompany the one, than upon the exaltation or awe which are created by the other.—
Hence, as we advance in life, we can escape upon the invitation of one more placid & gentle nature from those obtrusive qualities in an object sublime in its general character; which qualities, at an earlier age, precluded imperiously the perception of beauty which that object if contemplated under another relation would have been capable of imparting.
Wordsworth, *"The Sublime and the Beautiful,"*
probably 1811–12

According to most feminist readers, Wordsworth appropriates the feminine (often associated with nature) for the great masculine tradition in which women cannot participate.[1] This way of reading Wordsworth sees the poet as a violator or conqueror of a feminized nature which first nurtures the male child and then is forced by him to yield up her secrets. This reading of Wordsworth, though provocative, simplifies the role of gender and the meaning of nature in his poetry by presenting nature simply as a victim of male desire (as in "Nutting"). But Wordsworth also presents nature as a punitive force representing patriarchal authority. In fact, nature in the two-part *Prelude* seems to be the site in which the child acts out *both* his desire for and fear of transgression *and* his need for love and relationship. Nature is the punishing father and the nurturing mother, as well as the lover. In this early version of *The Prelude*, based on memories of childhood and adolescence, Wordsworth stages a drama in which the feminine continuously transforms masculine experiences and questions the feelings upon which they are based. The poet interprets the experiences of childhood through these gendered aesthetic categories. Countering Wordsworthian solitude and self-absorption (Keats's "egotistical sublime") is a paradoxical yearning for relationship.[2] Both of these impulses animate Wordsworth's life and his poetry.

I want to revise the assertion that Wordsworth attempts to transcend the feminine, associated with nature and youth.[3] Perhaps this is the case in "Tintern Abbey," but in the two-part *Prelude*, where Wordsworth is not thinking of the work as public and thus vulnerable to the whims of its audience, he creates a positive space for the feminine. His view of the feminine in the 1799 *Prelude* is idealized and conventional, but he embraces rather than transcends its associated values: nurturing, community, beauty. As I argue in the next chapter, only when he thinks of rhetorical strategies and the fickle taste of readers of poetry does Wordsworth identify the feminine with the fickleness of the marketplace and with a corrupt taste for the sensational.

The so-called two-part *Prelude* is a particularly interesting text for studying the origins of Wordsworth's understanding of aesthetic categories in terms of conventions of gender. Only for about the last twenty years (since it was published in the third edition of *The Norton Anthology of English Literature*) has it been possible to think of this early version of *The Prelude* as a text in itself. But because the poem was written at such a crucial time in Wordsworth's life and because he focuses on his development from child to adolescent, the two-part *Prelude* provides both a pre-text for chapters that follow through on Wordsworth's life and work and a context for thinking about the culture in which Wordsworth grew up.

WORDSWORTH'S AESTHETICS:
DANGER AND DOMESTICITY

In the two-part *Prelude* Wordsworth introduces the struggle between contrary impulses toward solitude and toward community, revealing the direction in which his poetry will move in the years to come: from a valuing of the sublime, solitary moments in nature to a celebration of more communal experiences. The poet of the egotistical sublime and of visionary moments ("when the light of sense / Goes out": 1805 *Prelude* 6:334–35) will become a more ceremonial and pictorial poet of Victo-

rian scenes, complete with the props of home, hearth, and tea urn. Both
the visionary intensity of the sublime and the pictorial balance of the
beautiful (the familiar aesthetic categories of the eighteenth century,
highlighted in the two-part *Prelude*) are aligned with gendered roles in
Wordsworth's poetry. The two-part *Prelude* dramatizes in microcosm
the tension and direction of Wordsworth's career.

As is well known, Wordsworth began this earliest version of *The Prelude* during the winter of 1798–99, when he was living with Dorothy
Wordsworth in Goslar, Germany, and he completed it at the end of 1799,
when he was back in England. The poem reflects this movement: the first
part is linked to Goslar and to Wordsworth's partly self-imposed alienation from the local community, the second to a more communal existence when William and Dorothy were reestablishing old friendships
with the Hutchinsons, who were living in Sockburn-on-Tees. This was
a difficult time for Wordsworth: the winter in Germany was bitterly cold
and the culture inhospitable to the Englishman and his sister who did
not speak the language and who soon gave up the attempt to learn.
Wordsworth complained of the gruff natives and stingy landlords in
Goslar, but he did not find his situation in England much of an im-
provement: he was in his thirtieth year, financially insecure, and without an established home. Not until he and Dorothy settled at Dove Cottage in December 1799 did William in fact begin to feel at home. But the
earliest version of *The Prelude* predates the domestic stability of Dove
Cottage.

In the two-part *Prelude* the poet records the origins of his vocation in
the major events and habitual experiences of his early life. The poem al-
ternates between excited narrative passages referring to impressive
events of childhood and more subdued discursive passages reflecting on
the narrative events that have shaped the poet's imaginative experience.
These narrative "spots of time" (1:288) often involve the child in a solitary confrontation with a powerful and impressive natural object, a conventionally sublime experience. The child feels frightened or chastened
as he returns to the more comforting world of human society and habitual tasks. By turning these often disturbing events into narrative, the
poet can read them and interpret their meaning for his life.

The two-part *Prelude* introduces a dialectic between these sublime
"spots of time" and more contained and domesticated experiences, usually of later childhood. Like Edmund Burke, to whom he was indebted,
Wordsworth links the sublime with patriarchal authority and with other
qualities, such as power and strength, conventionally ascribed to mas-

culinity.[4] Wordsworth explicitly refers to the more comforting domestic and natural scenes as beautiful. He associates the category of beauty with a Burkean delicacy, but also with nurturing. While the sublime experiences have startling and lasting effects, Wordsworth claims in *The Prelude* that his mind was shaped by both fear and love, terror and beauty. He celebrates the severe interventions of nature, the "huge and mighty forms that do not live / Like living men" (1:127–28) and "the babe who sleeps / Upon his mother's breast" (2:270–71), "Subjected to the discipline of love" (2:281). Paradoxically, without that steady discipline the mind would not have been fully receptive to sublime moments—to the visionary insights that Wordsworth both values and questions in later versions of the poem.[5] But for now, the poet implies that "rival claims demand / Grateful acknowledgment" (1:247–48).

The chronological development of the two-part *Prelude* reveals that the more sublime and solitary encounters with nature are associated with the earlier years of childhood, whereas adolescence is a time of greater community and shared feeling in nature. In the two-part *Prelude*, experiences of sublimity and solitude, often involving theft and transgression, give way to such diversions as card games (in part 1) and picnics (in part 2). Even though there is a progression from solitude to community, Wordsworth chooses to highlight the opposition between the sublime and the beautiful by continually circling back to it in his narrative.

In emphasizing this opposition Wordsworth follows Burke, who contrasts the two terms in his theory and links them to gender. But whereas Burke's dichotomy favors the sublime, and hence the masculine (his descriptions of the beautiful are relatively insipid), for Wordsworth scenes of the beautiful are attractive and inviting. Whereas Burke develops the binary opposition (so it seems) to construct his aesthetic model, Wordsworth embraces both ways of experiencing the world. In the early *Prelude* he dramatizes a conflict within himself over the "rival claims" (1:247) of his imaginative perception of the natural world. Wordsworth, then, uses a binary model associated with masculine Romanticism, but he is not as sure of the primacy of the sublime as twentieth-century critics have taken him to be. In addition to representing the psychological conflict, Wordsworth's binary scheme underscores the mythic and religious dimension. The sublime inspires awe; the beautiful suggests more comforting and familiar piety. In religious terms, sublime awe is associated with transcendent experiences and with feelings of fear and dread, whereas piety is associated with familial devotion and dutiful conduct.

Wordsworth's geological theory in the *Guide to the Lakes* (1810) parallels these ideas of the sublime and the beautiful: "Sublimity is the result of Nature's first great dealings with the superficies of the earth; the general tendency of her subsequent operations is toward the production of beauty; by a multiplicity of symmetrical parts uniting a consistent whole."[6] When Wordsworth describes landscapes in the *Guide*, he speaks of the sublime and beautiful together, revealing both cataclysmic processes and the softening influences of time and human life. He is especially interested in the margins of lakes as sites that reveal both "rugged steeps, admitting of no cultivation," and "gently-sloping lawns and woods, or flat and fertile meadows [which] stretch between the margin of the lake and the mountains" (36). The contrasts between the two types of aesthetic experience are even more marked in the two-part *Prelude*, where Wordsworth is concerned with personal rather than geological history.

ULLSWATER AND CONISTON

Two scenes from the two-part *Prelude* demonstrate the dialectic of the sublime and the beautiful. The first is the boat-stealing episode on Ullswater, from part 1, and the second is a very different boating scene on the lake of Coniston, from part 2. The one commemorates a critical moment in the narrator's life, the other a typical outing. The first refers to the time of childhood; the second, adolescence. Furthermore, Ullswater, with its rugged cliffs coming down to the water, and Coniston, with its more gradual rises, are appropriate geological sites for this drama.

In part 1, Wordsworth describes the child alone in a stolen (actually, borrowed) boat on a moonlit lake:

> . . . It was an act of stealth
> And troubled pleasure. Not without the voice
> Of mountain echoes did my boat move on,
> Leaving behind her still on either side
> Small circles glittering idly in the moon,
> Until they melted all into one track
> Of sparkling light. A rocky steep uprose
> Above the cavern of the willow-tree,
> And now, as suited one who proudly rowed
> With his best skill, I fixed a steady view
> Upon the top of that same craggy ridge,
> The bound of the horizon—for behind
> Was nothing but the stars and the grey sky.

> She was an elfin pinnace; twenty times
> I dipped my oars into the silent lake,
> And as I rose upon the stroke my boat
> Went heaving through the water like a swan—
> When from behind that rocky steep, till then
> The bound of the horizon, a huge cliff,
> As if with voluntary power instinct,
> Upreared its head. I struck, and struck again,
> And, growing still in stature, the huge cliff
> Rose up between me and the stars, and still,
> With measured motion, like a living thing
> Strode after me. With trembling hands I turned,
> And through the silent water stole my way
> Back to the cavern of the willow-tree.
> There in the mooring-place I left my bark,
> And through the meadows homeward went with grave
> And serious thoughts; and after I had seen
> That spectacle, for many days my brain
> Worked with a dim and undetermined sense
> Of unknown modes of being. In my thoughts
> There was a darkness—call it solitude,
> Or blank desertion—no familiar shapes
> Of hourly objects, images of trees,
> Of sea or sky, no colours of green fields,
> But huge and mighty forms that do not live
> Like living men moved slowly through my mind
> By day, and were the trouble of my dreams.
>   (1:90–129)

This episode has the marks of a sublime experience: it is an act of "troubled pleasure" made exciting by potential danger. The boy's terror grows out of his guilt, of course, which causes him to invest the cliff with the punitive powers of a primitive god. The boy's transgression (with the obvious sexual implications of dipping the oars in the lake and rising upon the stroke) is punished by his own imagination, which creates a monstrous figure who establishes the limits of the child's autonomy. Even as the insistent iambs of the repeated "I struck, and struck again" emphasize the child's action, they also underscore his powerlessness. The child's romantic quest in his "elfin pinnace" is cut short by the striding form, and he is forced to recognize powers that he cannot control. Although the avenging form is not explicitly identified as male, its attributes fit the conventional qualities, and the boy is haunted by "huge and mighty forms that do not live / Like living *men*" (my emphasis). Perhaps more important, this experience obliterates known categories. Whereas the "elfin pinnace" is identified as female, the poet refers to the cliff as "it."

In a notable passage in his *Enquiry*, Burke comments on a passage in Job as being sublime because terrifyingly unfamiliar:

> There is a passage in the book of Job amazingly sublime, and this sublimity is principally due to the terrible uncertainty of the thing described. *In thoughts from the visions of the night, when deep sleep falleth upon men, fear came upon me and trembling, which made all my bones to shake. Then a spirit passed before my face. The hair of my flesh stood up. It stood still,* but I could not discover the form thereof; *an image was before mine eyes; there was silence; and I heard a voice.*[7]

The sublime fear described here, like that in the boat-stealing episode, depends on the dissolution of known categories of seeing and comprehending experience. The terror is ungendered, "a spirit." The indistinct image is followed by silence and then by sound; in this passage from Job, as in Wordsworth, there are no visual details or particulars.

Wordsworth's narrator boldly outlines the landscape and scene—the moon, the cliff, the horizon. There are no moderating details either in the initial description or in the boy's memory of the event. In fact, Wordsworth characteristically uses a series of negatives—"no familiar shapes . . . [no] images of trees, . . . no colours of green fields"—to make the absence of the familiar world palpable. The effect of the experience is a "dim and undetermined sense / Of unknown modes of being," a sublimity dependent on darkness and absence. Only in narrating the event, in composing the poem many years later, does the poet seem to recognize the way such experiences have shaped his being, and in fact only now does he actually recognize the experience as sublime. As he meditates later, in part 2, he recognizes these "fleeting moods / Of shadowy exaltation" (361–62) because the soul "retains an obscure sense / Of possible sublimity" (366–67).

It is interesting to speculate on just how much of Wordsworth's memory of this event was colored by his knowledge of the many guidebooks to the Lake District that had been written in the years before his composition of the 1799 *Prelude*. Several of these guides also follow Burke in distinguishing sharply between sublime and beautiful elements of landscape, identifying particular scenes with particular emotions. For instance, Thomas West, in his *Guide to the Lakes* (1784), regularly sets the sublime in opposition to the beautiful: Levens Park is beautiful; Borrowdale is sublime; Coniston is beautiful, and so on. Surely Wordsworth must have been thinking of this description when he framed the boat-stealing episode: "Picture the mountains rearing their majestic heads with native sublimity; the vast rocks boldly projecting their terrible craggy points."[8] Wordsworth, I would argue, not only remembers the events but also reproduces the conventional language associated with the sublime. In other words, he has turned his past into a story which he then reads with the help of this critical vocabulary.

By using the word *spectacle* in the boat-stealing episode and throughout the two-part *Prelude*, Wordsworth emphasizes the aesthetic context. Burke uses the same word in analyzing the aesthetics of the sublime in his *Enquiry*, and, as Ronald Paulson has shown, in a more pejoratively theatrical sense in *Reflections on the Revolution in France*.[9] According to Burke in the *Enquiry*, we view painful spectacles with what Wordsworth might call "troubled pleasure" because "terror is a passion which always produces delight when it does not press too close" (46). The act of stealing the boat produced "troubled pleasure," which threatened to become unmitigated terror before the child returned safely to the mooring-place. As Wordsworth explains in his later fragment on "The Sublime and the Beautiful," "it cannot be doubted that a Child or an unpractised person whose mind is possessed by the sight of a lofty precipice, with its attire of hanging rocks & startling trees, &c., has been visited ·by a sense of sublimity, if personal fear & surprize or wonder have not been carried beyond certain bounds" (*PrW* 2:253). Like Burke, Wordsworth emphasizes the psychological need for distance, for not pressing too close to the spectacle.

The poet indeed recognizes the sublimity at a safe distance, from the mooring-place of memory. The mediating power of memory functions, in other words, as a kind of aesthetic distance. With the vocabulary of adult experience, the poet has the tools for ordering and interpreting the events on Ullswater. Perhaps there is a parallel to Wordsworth's life in 1798–99, for the anxiety that biographers and critics have seen in Wordsworth at this time may be related to those authority figures in the Wordsworth family who did not think of poetry as much of a profession.[10] Huge, craggy cliffs may have haunted the poet's dreams in childhood, but his waking hours were now filled with other kinds of fears.

Sublime scenes such the boating adventure on Ullswater contrast with those that evoke feelings of sociability and community, scenes that celebrate bonds rather than challenge boundaries. These experiences derive from the familiar and the domestic, qualities explicitly absent from the sublime. In fact, in "The Sublime and the Beautiful," Wordsworth explains that "Familiarity with these [natural] objects tends very much to mitigate & to destroy the power which they have to produce the sensation of sublimity" (*PrW* 2:253). If objects are too familiar, in other

words, they cannot create the unsettled feeling associated with the sublime, although they inspire love and devotion:

> Yes, I remember when the changeful earth
> And twice five seasons on my mind had stamped
> The faces of the moving year, even then,
> A child, I held unconscious intercourse
> With the eternal beauty, drinking in
> A pure organic pleasure from the lines
> Of curling mist, or from the level plain
> Of waters coloured by the steady clouds.
>
> (1:391–98)

Wordsworth here sees himself as a child laden with unconscious sexuality, drinking in pleasure from the breast of nature as "the infant babe"
(2:267) drinks in nourishment from his mother. He also describes the
objects of nature as conventionally beautiful, with gently curving lines
in scenes of repose. These experiences are associated with gradual sea-
sonal change and with gentle processes of nature, not with huge and
mighty forms. In writing about them here, Wordsworth seems also to
remember the scenes through the lens of art: specifically, the prints and
watercolors of beautiful Lake District scenes, as well as guidebook descriptions. He uses an artistic vocabulary of "lines" and color to com-
pose the scene. In his representation of the beautiful in the two-part *Prelude*, Wordsworth also consistently invests the beautiful scene with
feminine images: the nursing child is half in love with his mother's body,
which is suggested by the "lines / Of curling mist."

Although, according to his later theory, Wordsworth might have
found Ullswater at a moment other than that of a moonlit adventure to
be a stage for the beautiful, he moves to other locations to inscribe the
beautiful in the two-part *Prelude*. He describes a typical day on the lake
of Coniston in terms very different from the heightened adventure of the
boat-stealing episode:

> There was a row of ancient trees, since fallen,
> That on the margin of a jutting land
> Stood near the lake of Coniston, and made,
> With its long boughs above the water stretched,
> A gloom through which a boat might sail along
> As in a cloister. An old hall was near,
> Grotesque and beautiful, its gavel-end
> And huge round chimneys to the top o'ergrown
> With fields of ivy. Thither we repaired—
> 'Twas even a custom with us—to the shore,

And to that cool piazza. They who dwelt
In the neglected mansion-house supplied
Fresh butter, tea-kettle and earthenware,
And chafing-dish with smoking coals; and so
Beneath the trees we sate in our small boat,
And in the covert eat our delicate meal
Upon the calm smooth lake.

(2:140–56)

This ruin inspires not a sublime awe but rather a pleasing sense of natural processes, of familiar joys. The impulsiveness of the boat-stealing episode becomes a celebration of the habitual—of custom and ceremony, in this case the ritual of tea-drinking. The hall seems to have become part of the landscape, in which the long boughs of trees stretching over the water form a gloomy cloister, a refuge from which the light of the setting sun is visible. Any awe that a "neglected mansion-house" might inspire is domesticated by the homey details.

Although Wordsworth prefers explicitly to appeal to the sublime/beautiful dichotomy in the two-part *Prelude*, this description of the "old hall" is perhaps more closely aligned with the picturesque, which Uvedale Price associated with the passage of time in *An Essay on the Picturesque* (1794), a book admired by Wordsworth:

Observe the process by which Time (the great author of such changes) converts a beautiful object into a picturesque one: First, by means of weather stains, partial incrustations, mosses, &c. it at the same time takes off from the uniformity of the surface, and of the color; that is, given a degree of roughness, and variety of tint. Next, the various accidents of weather loosen the stones themselves; they tumble in irregular masses upon what was perhaps smooth turf or pavement, or nicely-trimmed walks and shrubberies, now mixed and overgrown with wild plants and creepers, that crawl over, and shoot among the fallen ruins . . . while the ivy mantels over other parts, and crowns the top.[11]

Time thus transforms the regularity and smoothness of beauty into a picturesque scene. For Price, variety and intricacy are the primary characteristics of the picturesque. An old mansion that is neglected but not in a state of ruin is a perfect example of the picturesque. Perhaps Wordsworth's introduction of the word *grotesque* is meant to convey the "picturesquely irregular" (as suggested by the *OED*). The hall is not just beautiful, it is "Grotesque and beautiful," almost a contradiction in terms. Wordsworth may also have had Milton's description of Paradise in mind, where *grotesque* is clearly associated with wild and irregular vegetation:

> As with a rural mound the champaign head
> Of a steep wilderness, whose hairy sides
> With thicket overgrown, grotesque and wild.
>   (*Paradise Lost* 4:134–36)

Perhaps Wordsworth's description of the beautiful here also suggests the picturesque because he introduces into the poem the human community, and thus necessarily a kind of variety and irregularity not found in the misty visual images of the beautiful. And although Wordsworth does not identify the scene on Coniston as picturesque, he notes what time has done to it: the "ancient trees, since fallen"—the "old hall"—"the top o'ergrown / With fields of ivy." Natural processes act upon the human lives associated with the "neglected mansion-house"; the scene suggests the gradual processes of change—death, reversal of family fortunes, and such—that have allowed nature to take over and make the hall, if not a complete ruin, then at least overgrown and neglected. We wonder what has happened over the years, but no story fills in the gaps as it does in "The Ruined Cottage." Nevertheless, the scene is made human here in a way that it is not in the narratives of the sublime. On Coniston Water Wordsworth represents people in daily contact with nature. The ruins, too, are placed in a human context, as they are not in "Tintern Abbey," where there is no mention of the ruins themselves, much less of the beggars and vagrants who inhabited them, as recent criticism has emphasized.[12]

Rather than the lone "I" of the boat-stealing episode, in the Coniston scene the narrator uses the plural pronoun to indicate that this event is shared among friends. Only after the initial description of Coniston does the narrator use the singular pronoun to reflect on personal insights derived from the custom of stopping to enjoy the lake. Whereas the first part of the scene identifies the experience as nurturing and maternal, this second part figures nature as a remembered lover:

> . . . It was a joy
> Worthy the heart of one who is full grown
> To rest beneath those horizontal boughs
> And mark the radiance of the setting sun,
> Himself unseen, reposing on the top
> Of the high eastern hills. And there I said,
> That beauteous sight before me, there I said
> (Then first beginning in my thoughts to mark
> That sense of dim similitude which links
> Our moral feelings with external forms)
> That in whatever region I should close

My mortal life I would remember you,
Fair scenes—that dying I would think on you,
My soul would send a longing look to you,
Even as that setting sun, while all the vale
Could nowhere catch one faint memorial gleam,
Yet with the last remains of his last light
Still lingered, and a farewell lustre threw
On the dear mountain-tops where first he rose.
                                        (2:156–74)

Wordsworth shifts to the first person singular here because he looks away from the old house and the shared meal to the "high eastern hills," away from the "covert" or refuge and toward eternity. He records a special moment in which he recognizes that the "beauteous sight before me" will be linked to his "moral feelings." The boat-stealing episode would haunt Wordsworth's unconscious mind with "unknown modes of being," whereas this insight implies a conscious effort to memorialize and recognize the influence of nature's beauty. The youth imagines that "fair scenes" such as the "radiance of the setting sun" over the hills of Coniston will become a memory for him like the memory of a lost love: "My soul would send a longing look to you." He sees himself lingering over the fair scenes as the setting sun lingers lovingly over a landscape. Although he feminizes the landscape here as a lover, the tone is wistful rather than proprietary.

In the two-part *Prelude* Wordsworth traces the boy's development from a primitive "naked savage in the thunder-shower" (1:26) to a civilized, more cultivated young man. He uses different modes of representation to convey the emotions associated with the experiences that have shaped his life. The boat-stealing episode evokes the structure of a Gothic tale, with psychological rather than supernatural explanations; the scene on the lake of Coniston remains pictorial and ritual-like, rather than a dramatically plotted narrative. The beautiful is framed and contained as a memorial scene, whereas the sublime intrudes itself into the unconscious memory. There is no conflict in the Coniston passage, as there certainly is in the boat-stealing. The boy leaves the protected cavern of the willow tree for his adventure on Ullswater, but the adolescent remains "in our small boat," "in the covert," on "the calm smooth lake" of Coniston.

Although Wordsworth emphasizes the duality of the sublime and the beautiful, he acknowledges that certain events and occupations defy classification:

> . . . It were a song
> Venial, and such as—if I rightly judge—
> I might protract unblamed, but I perceive
> That much is overlooked, and we should ill
> Attain our object if, from delicate fears
> Of breaking in upon the unity
> Of this my argument, I should omit
> To speak of such effects as cannot here
> Be regularly classed, yet tend no less
> To the same point, the growth of mental power
> And love of Nature's works.
>
> (1:248–58)

This passage seems to be presented as a justification for including a memory that has neither the thrilling quality of Ullswater nor the beauty of Coniston—neither romance nor pastoral. If anything, the scene introduces a Cowperesque mock-heroic dimension into the narrative. I am referring to the card game that immediately precedes this discursive passage:

> I would record with no reluctant voice
> Our home amusements by the warm peat fire
> At evening, when with pencil and with slate,
> In square divisions parcelled out, and all
> With crosses and with cyphers scribbled o'er,
> We schemed and puzzled, head opposed to head,
> In strife too humble to be named in verse;
> Or round the naked table, snow-white deal,
> Cherry, or maple, sate in close array,
> And to the combat—lu or whist—led on
> A thick-ribbed army, not as in the world
> Discarded and ungratefully thrown by
> Even for the very service they had wrought,
> But husbanded through many a long campaign.
> Oh, with what echoes on the board they fell—
> Ironic diamonds, hearts of sable hue,
> Queens gleaming through their splendour's last decay,
> Knaves wrapt in one assimilating gloom,
> And kings indignant at the shame incurred
> By royal visages.
>
> (1:206–25)

Using the mock-heroic form here seems to be another way for Wordsworth to order his past. Whereas memory mediates the "danger and desire" (1:195) of the sublime, the mock-heroic provides a distance from the "home amusements." The poet, in fact, turns the innocent childhood card game into an allegory of genre, gender, and class. This is an old, patched-together deck of cards, "husbanded through many a long campaign." The children have replaced worn-out cards with others, perhaps letting a Ten serve as a King in order to fill out the deck. And through long use the cards all begin to look alike, so that the children have to use their imagination to distinguish among them.

Part of the joke, of course, is that the place of the dying royalty will be usurped by plebeians, and, perhaps before that, kings by queens and by "hearts of sable hue." In literary terms, the children change the rules by allowing cards to play various roles, to "represent" other "persons." Wordsworth prefigures both the generic experimentation and blending of the longer versions of *The Prelude* and the themes of legitimacy/illegitimacy in which both genre and gender are implicated. The mock-heroic also gives Wordsworth an avenue for political commentary. From the perspective of the 1790s, this is a subversive passage both in its violation of hierarchies and in the knowledge that in England soldiers *are* "Discarded and ungratefully thrown by / Even for the very service they had wrought."[13]

WORDSWORTH'S RESOLUTION

In recognizing and memorializing other modes of perception, Wordsworth begins to question the arrogance and autonomy of the sublime. Especially since he, like Burke, came to associate the sublime with the unbridled energies of the Revolution and the Terror, Wordsworth looked toward the habitual and customary—values associated with "patriotic and domestic love" (2:229)—to contain that violence in its energy. The beautiful in the two-part *Prelude*, centered on sociability and community, underscores the dangers of the sublime and also sets it in high relief.

The aesthetic categories of the sublime and the beautiful, associated by Wordsworth with his earliest imaginative life, are also linked to the thoughts of his more mature years and to his representation of gender and his relationships with women. In fact, it is possible to look at the poetry of Wordsworth's later years, as well as the mode of his domestic life, as a feminization of the impulses of the sublime. Interestingly, too, in the description of the picnic on Coniston Wordsworth associates the grace and hospitality of the beautiful mansion with the feminine. "They who dwell / In the neglected mansion-house" are never named, but they seem to be women, since they perform conventionally feminine duties. The young boaters depend on their hospitality and care in setting up a "delicate meal." "They" supply "Fresh butter, tea-kettle and earthen-ware," a rustic feast perhaps prefiguring the more refined teas of Rydal Mount, the "manor house" that Wordsworth would inhabit from 1813 until his death.[14] In 1799 Wordsworth anticipates the nineteenth-century notion of the feminine—home and hearth—as a refuge from the public sphere. The conditions of the Wordsworths' household as it was coming into existence in 1799 and as it would establish itself in the coming years replicate these aesthetic categories. As we shall see, Wordsworth's interest in women and conventional feminine values in his poetry is paralleled by the circumstances of his life, in which Dorothy Wordsworth, Mary Wordsworth, and Sara Hutchinson played nurturing and supportive roles that first made his sublime poetry of solitary visions possible, and then rechanneled the direction of that poetry.

Significantly, in Wordsworth's poetry there is no female sublime, and hence no female identity apart from male perception. The poet in "Tintern Abbey," as we shall see, meditates on his sublime experiences, but his sister inhabits the beautiful as seen from the male perspective.[15] Wordsworth constructs both the sublime and the beautiful, then, from a perspective that excludes the agency of the female. This exclusion haunted Dora Wordsworth in 1838, when she visited Tintern Abbey for the first time and tried to find her place between her father's "sense sublime" (95) and the "lovely forms" (140) that he attributes to her aunt.

Much has been written recently about Wordsworth and the archetypal Romantic female, the silenced object of male desire. As gendered narratives of development, what is interesting about the Lucy poems—in contrast to the heroic story of the growth of the poet's mind—is that Lucy is always shaped or controlled by someone else. Whereas the boy of The Prelude seeks out adventures, learning his limitations through experience or being nurtured by "gentle visitation[s]" (1:73), the archetypal girl Lucy is also the archetypal stepchild. In "Three Years She Grew," for instance, a personified (mother) nature decides her fate:

> The stars of midnight shall be dear
> To her; and she shall lean her ear
> In many a secret place
> Where rivulets dance their wayward round,
> And beauty born of murmuring sound
> Shall pass into her face.
>
> (PW 2:25–30)

Emptied of drama and tension, the girl's narrative is one of passive sur-
render and early death in which a feminine nature is implicated. While
the boy is fostered by both fear and beauty, Lucy is perceived only as an
object of the beautiful, both by her lover and by nature.

It could be argued that when the women Wordsworth wrote about
chose to write or to draw, they composed in a mode best described as
picturesque, the aesthetic category that seemed to open up a space for
women as writers, painters, and observers. Dorothy Wordsworth's style
has been described as picturesque,[16] and both Sara Hutchinson's sketch
The Mill—Grasmere and Dora Wordsworth's watercolor *Dove Cottage,
Town End* demonstrate picturesque features in the raggedness of the
edges, the roughness of nature (figures 1 and 2). Uvedale Price particularly identifies a mill as having "the greatest charm to the painter" of the
picturesque, because of "the extreme intricacy of the wheels and the
wood work; the singular variety of forms, and of lights and shadows, of
mosses and weather stains from constant motion" (52–53). In a more
recent essay, "The Picturesque Moment," Martin Price notes that the
picturesque expresses itself best in scenes "in which form emerges only
with study or is at the point of dissolution. It turns to the sketch, which
precedes formal perfection, and the ruin, which succeeds it."[17] I would
add that the sketch, like the journal, makes no claim to be a completed
object in terms of genre or expectation. Thus, both the sketch and the
journal were genres that the women of the Wordsworth circle—who
voiced no ambitions toward artistic or literary careers—could nonetheless work within. As we will see in the case of Dora Wordsworth and
her travel journal of 1828, she regularly writes and sketches in this picturesque tradition.

But whereas the picturesque, in which nature is not terrifying but does
need human care, opens up possibilities for women as creators and observers, Wordsworth moves in the direction of the beautiful—a more
idealized conception of nature and gender. By 1815, when Wordsworth
recognizes his audience in the "Essay, Supplementary to the Preface" as
those few who are appreciative of his genius, he constructs images of female piety and domesticity at the center of his poetry—or in the case of
"Laodamia," an image of failed piety. Far from transcending the feminine in his later poetry, he retrieves the ideal images of the beautiful and
resituates them in the transitional culture of the 1820s and 1830s. It is
not such a far leap from the Coniston scene of the two-part *Prelude*
or "She was a Phantom of Delight" (composed 1803–4) to the domesticated and conventional images of "The Triad" (1828), where Words-

Figure 1. *The Mill—Grasmere*. Pencil sketch by Sara Hutchinson. By permission of the Wordsworth Trust, Dove Cottage, Grasmere, England.

Figure 2. *Dove Cottage, Town End*. Watercolor by Dora Wordsworth after Amos Green. By permission of the Wordsworth Trust, Dove Cottage, Grasmere, England.

worth's ideas about womanhood converge with religious and political orthodoxy.

But Wordsworth's evocation of the beautiful in his later poetry has something of the mock-heroic playfulness found in the early card game from the two-part *Prelude*. Although the images of female beauty are often distanced and ideal, the contexts in which they are presented are just as often playful, as if to suggest that Wordsworth is conscious of his own exaggerations. Accordingly, in chapter 5 I shall replace the stereotype of the somber and stodgy poet of Rydal Mount with a more subtle picture.

What I wish to emphasize here is that in 1798–99 Wordsworth already prefigures the gendered values and conventions of his later life. The gendered landscapes of the two-part *Prelude* set the stage for what is to come. Whereas many readers of Wordsworth have seen little connection between the Wordsworth of 1799 and the Wordsworth of 1835, I see the earlier work as containing—to borrow Wordsworth's own agricultural metaphor from *The Prelude*—the germ of the later Wordsworth. But the question remains: what role do women and the poet's ideas about women play in the husbandry of Wordsworth's imagination?

CHAPTER TWO

Wordsworth and the Poetic Vocation

A Man Speaking to Men

But it is not necessary to *invent* a literary tradition for
women, only to rewrite the records and to put in what men
have left out.

> *Dale Spender,* Mothers of the Novel, *1986*

When Wordsworth wrote the fragmentary passages that would form the
two-part *Prelude* in 1798–99, he was not thinking specifically in terms
of audience or publication. Rather, as he says in his letter, he wrote in
the isolation of the German winter "in self-defence."[1] In thinking back
to the striking events of childhood and youth, Wordsworth embraced
both the sublime and the beautiful, both the terrifying and the nurturing capacity of the natural world. Especially in the second part, Wordsworth evokes the beautiful, associated with the feminine, and describes
its influence on his life.

But by the time he composed the Preface to *Lyrical Ballads* (1800),
Wordsworth was considering his relationship with his audience. Now
Wordsworth presents himself as a poet with a vocation; he specifically
stakes his claim to being a serious male poet who sees himself in the company of poets from Catullus to Pope (*PrW* 1:122). In the Preface
Wordsworth reiterates his claim to this male vocation at the same time
that he defends writing about abandoned women and mad mothers and
focuses his poetics on emotion. Furthermore, Wordsworth's dependency
on women as responsive readers of his work grew even stronger in the
first decade of the nineteenth century. But in the Preface Wordsworth
makes no direct connection between his writing, in which women figure
prominently as subjects, and women readers or writers.

There is also an interesting discrepancy between Wordsworth's public
pose in the Preface to *Lyrical Ballads*, his aim of reforming the reading

29

public of the nation, and the way that so many poems in the volume construct a more intimate and reassuring audience: the "dear Sister" in "Tintern Abbey," the "few natural hearts" of "Michael." Several recent commentators, such as Jon Klancher, have seen a shift in Wordsworth (by the time of the "Essay, Supplementary to the Preface" of 1815) toward a much more ideal conception of his reader and from a model of an audience based on "consumption" to a model based on "reception."[2] In both the "Essay, Supplementary" and in letters of the period Wordsworth draws a distinction between the reading "Public" and the "People" who one day will appreciate his poetry.[3] But in the rhetoric of the Preface Wordsworth focuses on the corrupt taste of the public readership: he still hopes to wake them from their torpor, and in his emphasis on taste he presumes that his poetry is written for consumption (even though he protests against any analogy between a taste for poetry and a taste for sherry). In the *Lyrical Ballads*, Wordsworth paradoxically wants to reach his audience by replicating the intimacy of a private reading, imagining his audience in place.

Furthermore, contrary to Klancher's argument that Wordsworth moves from a concern with "consumption" to a preoccupation with "reception," I believe that Wordsworth never fully abandons the consumption model and, in fact, he rephrases it in the late 1820s and 1830s. Klancher assumes a Wordsworthian decline after 1815 and stops there; he reads the "Essay, Supplementary" as if it were Wordsworth's last word on readers and poetic tradition. But for thirty-five more years, as his correspondence reveals, Wordsworth was intensely involved in new editions of his poetry, in revising poems for publication, and in the debate over the laws of copyright. He thought and wrote constantly about how his poetry was presented to the public and who was reading it. In fact, he thought even more intensely about himself as a publishing poet because he *was* a poet in an age of popular novel-reading, an activity he steadfastly disparaged.

In an essay that precedes the more recent historicist arguments (and that Klancher particularly critiques), Morris Eaves theorizes that in one phase of an expressive theory the artist not only expresses the work of art but also expresses and personalizes his audience.[4] The Romantic expressive artist, in Eaves's formulation, reaches out to his audience in a gesture of love and intimacy and requires the same commitment from his readers: "The assumption is that acts of imagination, to be complete, must be mutual; and the conditions for them are the same as for any profound human relationship, the forgiveness and love that assure mutual commitment and engagement, because complete human relationships are also imaginative acts" (793). For Blake the ultimate model for the relationship between artist and audience is that of Jesus to his disciples (794–95); for both Wordsworth and Blake, Eaves claims, the basis of the mutual love relationship between artist and audience is equality: "An art that assumes a worthy audience of equals is the only authentically democratic art" (797).

Both Eaves's elegant argument and Klancher's critique of its Romantic idealism omit the category of gender. But, as I shall argue, gender anxiety was at the heart of Wordsworth's formulations in the Preface to *Lyrical Ballads*. Wordsworth imagined as gendered the marketplace he must enter, the literary tradition to which he aspired, and the role of the poet he wished to fill. As we shall see, from this point of view a love based on the prophet/disciple model—no matter how great the intimacy or what theological sanction it has—presumes inequality: Wordsworth never imagines his "man speaking to men" to be in fact a woman.

If in 1800 Wordsworth imagines that he is above the frantic and fickle marketplace and the tastes of uncultivated readers, and in the "Essay, Supplementary" (1815) he seems to give up on the reading public altogether, by around 1830 he redefines his relationship to his contemporary audience. Although Wordsworth always complained about how little money he made from his publications—not enough to buy his shoestrings, according to one story—he did achieve popularity in the 1830s. And when he perceived of himself as a known and popular poet, he wanted to enter the marketplace on his own terms: in carefully planned editions of poems. His involvement with gift annuals, as we shall see in chapter 5, gave him great anxiety because they were financially tempting but robbed him of at least some control over the production and distribution of his own work. He resented not so much entering the market as entering the market on someone else's terms and in the mixed, feminized company of the anthologies that were finding their way into middle-class drawing rooms and into literary hearts across England.

THE COMMON INHERITANCE OF POETS

In the first years of the nineteenth century, however, Wordsworth inhabited a different literary world. In the Preface to *Lyrical Ballads* he couches the bond between the poet and tradition in terms that are familial but that exclude women from the genealogy:

> I have at all times endeavored to look steadily at my subject, consequently I
> hope it will be found that there is in these Poems little falsehood of descrip-
> tion, and that my ideas are expressed in language fitted to their respective im-
> portance. Something I must have gained by this practice, as it is friendly to
> one property of all good poetry, namely good sense; but it has necessarily cut
> me off from a large portion of phrases and figures of speech which from *fa-*
> *ther to son* have long been regarded as the common inheritance of Poets.
>
> (*PrW* 1:132, my emphasis)[5]

Wordsworth wants to preserve the ideal of inheritance from father to
son, but he also wants to change the terms of that inheritance. What
should be passed on from father to son, he implies, are not phrases and
figures of speech (which can be reproduced by any imitator) but a universal, permanent and philosophical language (1:124) that goes back to
the King James Bible and beyond, to the origins of the modern English
language.[6] This is the language of Chaucer, Shakespeare, and Milton—
the language of the poetic as well as the biblical patriarchs. This is not
the language of "sickly and stupid German Tragedies" or that of "frantic novels" (*PrW* 1:128), that is, of popular gothic fiction such as that of
Ann Radcliffe. Wordsworth contrasts the philosophical language to
which he aspires with the artificial language of writers who "separate
themselves from the sympathies of men, and indulge in arbitrary and
capricious habits of expression in order to furnish foods for fickle tastes
and fickle appetites of their own creation" (1:124).

Wordsworth's rhetoric in the Preface privileges the stable and the permanent over the fickle and the fashionable. It would have been usual at
the time to link such terms as *universal* and *permanent*, on the one hand,
and such qualities as capriciousness, fickleness, fashion, and appetite, on
the other hand, with gender categories. The universal is masculine, of
course, and everything uncertain or fickle is feminine. Mary Wollstonecraft, for instance, speaks in the *Vindication of the Rights of
Woman* (1792) of the "frippery of dress" (75), "the varnish of fashion"
(99), and "luxury and appetite" (137) as the vices to which women are
most subject.[7] Wordsworth claims universal terms as a "man speaking
to men"—and he really does speak as a *man* and a male poet who sees
himself as an inheritor of a tradition of male poets. And for all the apparent modesty in the "man speaking to men" euphemism, Wordsworth
goes on to claim that the poet is greater than ordinary mortals:

> a man, it is true, endowed with more lively sensibility, more enthusiasm and
> tenderness, who has a greater knowledge of human nature, and a more com-
> prehensive soul, than are supposed to be common among mankind; a man

pleased with his own passions and volitions, and who rejoices more than other men in the spirit of life that is in him; delighting to contemplate similar volitions and passions as manifested in the goings-on of the Universe, and habitually impelled to create them where he does not find them.

(*PW* 1:138, 1850)

The poet Wordsworth describes here is not just the author of the *Lyrical Ballads*; this is also the poet whom Coleridge has urged to write the great philosophical poem of the age, *The Recluse*. His "comprehensive soul" distinguishes him not only from other "men" but also, by inference, from inferior poets and authors of "frantic novels."

Whereas in his life and poetry Wordsworth may cultivate the feminine, in the Preface his gendered rhetoric associates the feminine with contemptible qualities in both authors, with their false refinements, and in the reading public, with its degenerate taste. Although Wordsworth does not name them, he implicitly denigrates popular women writers as well as any readers who respond to them:

> For a multitude of causes unknown to former times are now acting with a combined force to blunt the discriminating powers of the mind, and unfitting it for all voluntary exertion to reduce it to a state of almost savage torpor. The most effective of these causes are the great national events which are daily taking place, and the encreasing accumulation of men in cities, where the uniformity of their occupations produces a craving for extraordinary incident which the rapid communication of intelligence hourly gratifies. To this tendency of life and manners the literature and theatrical exhibitions of the country have conformed themselves. The invaluable works of our elder writers, I had almost said the works of Shakespear and Milton, are driven into neglect by frantic novels, sickly and stupid German Tragedies, and deluges of idle and extravagant stories in verse.

(*PrW* 1:128)

The political importance of this passage has been noted in recent years, but its gendered rhetoric deserves equal attention. In Wordsworth's analysis of the corrupt state of society, the increasingly urban, industrial, and commercial world is driven by cravings and desire for instant gratification. According to this view, society is corrupted by what it thinks of as progress, and literature by the same craving, the public's desire to be entertained and teased by gothic plots (often fashioned by women writers) when they could be reading Shakespeare—or Wordsworth. In contrast to the extravagance of these writers, Wordsworth argues for the elegant simplicity of the *Lyrical Ballads*. And in contrast to the instant gratification of appetite, Wordsworth wants readers to cultivate a taste for literature, "for an *accurate* taste in Poetry and in all the other arts, as Sir Joshua Reynolds has observed, is an *acquired* talent, which can only be produced by thought and long continued intercourse with the best models of composition" (*PrW* 1:156). This intercourse, according to neoclassical standards, should be governed by a sense of propriety. The extended sexual metaphor suggests that legitimate forms of intercourse are sanctioned by custom and thought, not debased by instant gratification of desire. The admirable writer, in Wordsworth's terms, does not prostitute himself to gratify the reader, nor does he want to tease the reader. Wordsworth instead subscribes to an ideal, universal view of the male artist working in a male tradition: an exclusive, patriarchal, but non-Freudian (non-Bloomian) model of literary relationship.[8]

Wordsworth's view of contemporary society and the reading public sounds remarkably like another writer's critique:

> These are the women who are amused by the reveries of the stupid novelists, who, knowing little of human nature, work up stale tales, and describe meretricious scenes, all retailed in a sentimental jargon, which equally tend to corrupt the taste, and draw the heart aside from its daily duties. I do not mention the understanding, because never having been exercised, its slumbering energies rest inactive, like the lurking particles of fire which are supposed universally to pervade matter.[9]
>
> (183)

Mary Wollstonecraft's rhetoric in the *Vindication* of 1792 echoes through the Preface of eight years later: "stupid novelists"/"stupid German Tragedies" and "frantic novels," "slumbering energies"/"savage torpor," "meretricious scenes"/"deluges of idle and extravagant stories," and so on. A strange alliance, perhaps, but both writers distrust the trends in literature and the manners that such trends follow. Wollstonecraft wants to wake middle-class women's energies from their moral and imaginative slumber; Wordsworth wants to awaken a feminized reading public to the powerful simplicity of his own poetry.

Wordsworth disparages the gothic tradition as a low and feminized form that caters to the base instincts of the reading public. Gothic fiction seems almost below comment in Wordsworth's immediate circle, but their dislike extends to the novel in general. The Wordsworths maintained (judging from correspondence) a lifelong dislike of the novel as a genre. Typical comments from Dorothy Wordsworth include the letter she wrote to William on 23 April 1812: "We have not been sufficiently settled to read anything but Novels. Adeline Mowbray [1804, by Mrs.

Opie] made us quite sick before we got to the end of it" (*MY* 2:7). Nor did William ever show much interest in novels, to say the least. He had some eighteenth-century favorites and had some respect for Scott as a novelist, but he remained ambivalent about the genre. Wordsworth was even reported to have said of Dickens: "a very talkative, vulgar young person—but I dare say he may be clever. . . . I have never read a line he has written."[10] Whether this quote is accurate or not, Wordsworth's omission of the novel from his serious discourse on literary traditions supports this position.

Bradford Mudge has recently argued that Wordsworth's disparagement of the gothic in particular and the novel in general can be seen in the context of male anxiety about the popularity of novels, the explosion of women as readers, and the threat of women writers.[11] Mudge's argument links this anxiety about the gothic with the hysteria over prostitution that arose in the middle of the nineteenth century, a response to the threat of disruptive female sexuality. Wordsworth, as we have seen, anticipates this midcentury discourse by connecting "frantic novels" with illicit sex and by implying that some women authors—never named—are engaging in literary prostitution.[12]

One of the great paradoxes of Wordsworth's stance against popular gothic fiction is that he seems to be drawing the line between high (masculine) and low (feminine) culture, but the core of the Preface and of his program for poetry explodes hierarchies, lifting and ennobling the simple, the lowly, and the rustic. Wordsworth accomplishes this through experimentation with a popular form, the ballad. But in the Preface Wordsworth frames his argument by emptying the ballad of its folk heritage and lifting it up to the level of a literary genre. In this inventive approach to the origins of ballads, Wordsworth in effect erases a part of women's literary tradition. As Virginia Woolf muses in *A Room of One's Own*: "I would venture to guess that Anon, who wrote so many poems without signing them, was often a woman. It was a woman Edward Fitzgerald, I think, suggested who made the ballads and the folk-songs, crooning them to her children, beguiling her spinning with them, or the length of the winter's night."[13] We can imagine many of the women in the *Lyrical Ballads* spinning and crooning, but in Wordsworth's invention of literary history women are neither authors nor transmitters of folk culture.

As a male poet, too, Wordsworth can emphasize the importance of "pleasure" without fear of criticism, for pleasure had been sanctioned by theorists from Aristotle to Burke:

Nor let the necessity of producing immediate pleasure be considered as a degradation of the Poet's art. It is far otherwise. It is an acknowledgment of the beauty of the universe, an acknowledgment the more sincere, because not formal, but indirect; it is a task light and easy to him who looks at the world in the spirit of love: further, it is a homage paid to the native and naked dignity of man, to the grand elementary principle of pleasure, by which he knows, and feels, and lives, and moves. We have no sympathy but what is propagated by pleasure.

(1:140, 1850)

So, at the same time that he condemns the fickle taste of the reading public, Wordsworth builds his poetics on the idea that the true pleasures of poetry are akin to those of legitimate and well-regulated sexual passion. He argues that "the direction of our sexual appetite, and all the passions connected with it" derive from "the perception of similitude in dissimilitude" (148). With the authority of a male tradition, Wordsworth claims that the poet is "a man pleased with his own passions and volitions" (138) as he imparts pleasure to the reader.[14] Wordsworth idealizes pleasure as the "spirit of love" and the "naked dignity of man," a sanctioned response to the reading experience when there is the proper (marriage) contract between author and reader.

Although Wordsworth and other male writers may be nervous about female passions, Wordsworth is certainly not shy about constructing his poetics on an extended sexual analogy. In fact, he explicitly describes meter as both adding a charm to poetry and tempering the power of poetic passion so that it does not exceed proper bounds. The metrical form of poetry is thus for Wordsworth the perfect medium *both* for expressing the overflowing passions *and* for keeping those passions in check, presumably so that his poetry never sinks to the level of mere gratification of appetite. Meter, "the exponent or symbol held forth . . . in different areas of literature" (1:122), is basic both to the poet's relationship to poets of the past—from Catullus to Pope—and to his contemporary audience.

Marlon Ross has argued that Wordsworth and other Romantic poets "subliminally" identify with two related nineteenth-century masculine roles: those of "the scientist and the industrial capitalist."[15] Ross offers many insights into the gendered Romantic imagination, but in this case, I think, he misrepresents Wordsworth's attitudes. Wordsworth has much more uncertainty—both subliminal and spoken—about the role model of the poet as masculine conqueror than Ross acknowledges. Rather than a masculine empire, Wordsworth sees the industrial and commercial world as feminized (fickle and transitory), opposed to the enduring forms of nature that fill the mind of the poet who has "thought long and deeply." Wordsworth has to maintain himself in the face of what he sees as the industrial and commercial degradation of nature and the arts; he seeks, not conquest, but renewal.

J. G. A. Pocock argues that the view of economic man as a conquering hero is a nineteenth-century fantasy, very different from the eighteenth-century conception:

> His eighteenth-century predecessor was seen as on the whole a feminized, even an effeminate being, still wrestling with his own passions and hysterias and with the interior and exterior forces let loose by his fantasies and appetites, and symbolised by such archetypically female goddesses of disorder as Fortune, Luxury, and most recently Credit herself. . . . Therefore, in the eighteenth-century debate over the new relations of polity to economy, production and exchange are regularly equated with the ascendancy of the passions and the female principle.[16]

Pocock's insight helps to clarify Wordsworth's position, which is in this case more in tune with the eighteenth century. Wordsworth's anxieties about the contemporary world in the 1800 Preface lead him to disassociate himself from "effeminate" displays of appetite, sensation, and over-refinement in culture and society. Wordsworth feminizes the fickle audience—and the marketplace he must enter. In the place of capriciousness and corruption, Wordsworth urges his readers to cultivate a taste based on a particular tradition; hence the allusion to classical writers and to Sir Joshua Reynolds's standard of a taste that must be acquired through the contemplation of excellent models.

Without considering gender, David Simpson has argued that Wordsworth's theory of poetic diction, appended to the 1802 Preface, is also an economic and political statement.[17] According to Simpson, Wordsworth sees excesses of literary refinement as "literary manifestations of negative changes in the condition of England" (63). By extension, both the poetic diction of the neoclassical period and the literary excesses of the contemporary gothic are associated with corruptions on two extremes of the spectrum: with over-refinement, on the one hand, and with appetite, on the other. In eighteenth-century discourse, both of these are associated with the feminine, with the inability to find a middle ground between the two extremes.

Paradoxically, Wordsworth's own language implicates both poetic diction and the gothic, both high and low, in the same corruption of language and taste:

In process of time metre became a symbol or promise of this unusual language, and whoever took upon him to write in metre, according as he possessed more or less of true poetic genius, introduced less or more of this adulterated phraseology into his compositions, and the true and the false were inseparably interwoven until, the taste of men becoming gradually perverted, this language was received as a natural language: and at length, by the influence of books upon men, did to a certain degree really become so. Abuses of this kind were imported from one nation to another, and with the progress of refinement this diction became daily more and more corrupt, thrusting out of sight the plain humanities of nature by a motely masquerade of tricks, quaintnesses, hieroglyphics, and enigmas.

(Appendix, *PrW* 1:161–62)

This is an extraordinary passage, in which Wordsworth uses the charged language of adulteration, perversion, and corruption to condemn poetic diction. Furthermore, the image of the "motely masquerade of tricks" suggests both illicit pleasures and a carnivalesque inversion of appropriate relationships, with the degraded masquerades usurping the "naked dignity of man."

Perhaps Wordsworth expended so much rhetorical energy in the Preface disassociating himself from the feminine in art and culture because he knew that his subject matter (forsaken women, mad mothers, and other marginalized figures) and his reverence for emotion would in fact associate him with women and with women writers. Like the other male Romantics, Wordsworth feared the charge of feminization as leveled by contemporary critics. In his infamous review of the 1807 poems, which also includes comments on the *Lyrical Ballads*, Francis Jeffrey implies that Wordsworth has feminized poetry with his "namby-pamby," his "prettyisms," his "babyish" verse. Jeffrey's attack on Wordsworth's lack of decorum reveals gendered standards. Although Jeffrey implies that serious male poets do not write poems on daisies or daffodils, he approves of a few poems (such as "The Character of the Happy Warrior") as being "manly."[18] In none of Jeffrey's reviews is Wordsworth the conquering hero; he comes across more as the fool who wastes his talents on unworthy, womanish subject matter. Nor, it might be added, does the liberal Jeffrey object to Wordsworth's defense of the lower classes per se: his critique is motivated by anxiety about gender, not class. In fact, Jeffrey and Wordsworth share a deep anxiety about gender, an anxiety that lies at the heart of both Jeffrey's rejection of low (hence, feminized) subjects and Wordsworth's distrust of the novel. They just do not agree on what is unworthy.

SHAKESPEARE'S SCOTTISH SISTER

Despite Wordsworth's implicit denial of his connection with women writers, the Preface belongs in the context of the rise of women poets in the later eighteenth and early nineteenth centuries. Because scholars have only recently begun to rediscover the women writers of this period, Wordsworth's Preface has been read in isolation from this tradition. The first issue of the *Women Writers Project Newsletter*, however, includes the astounding claim that over five hundred women published at least one volume of verse between 1770 and 1830.[19] Wordsworth, writing his Preface smack in the middle of this period, was, of course, aware of many of these writers and, as Stuart Curran has argued, was influenced by them.[20] But Wordsworth defines himself against them, instead claiming kinship with a male tradition, that is, with Catullus and Pope, Milton and Shakespeare, rather than Charlotte Smith or Joanna Baillie. He does not even mention women writers in the Preface, because he does not want to be placed in their company. Indeed, one could—and many of us have—read the Preface as if there were no women writers to be considered. As Marlon Ross suggests, patriarchal tradition viewed women as dabblers in verse, not as poets with careers to found and maintain.[21] But the absence of women in the Preface is remarkable for the poet whose first poem, published in 1787, was entitled "Sonnet on Seeing Miss Helen Maria Williams Weep at a Tale of Distress."

As recent scholarship has demonstrated, Virginia Woolf's story of Shakespeare's sister from *A Room of One's Own* has to be revised. The question is no longer, Why were there no female Shakespeares? but, rather, Why and how were Shakespeare's sisters excluded from the canon? In Wordsworth's case, patronizing attitudes toward the careers of women writers and the refusal to take women writers seriously when discussing the "common inheritance of Poets" perhaps begin to explain the absence of women from the Preface. Wordsworth, I think, particularly felt the need to distance himself from popular contemporary women writers, who were, after all, his competitors. He deliberately constructs a view of literary history without women, mentioning gothic novelists only to dismiss them. By his silence he completely omits poets such as Charlotte Smith, whose *Elegiac Sonnets* (1784) was among the many well-known volumes by women. In fact, Wordsworth not only read *Elegiac Sonnets* at Cambridge, but he also called on Smith in Brighton in November 1791 on his way to France. As Mary Moorman explains, Smith not only received Wordsworth warmly, but she also "gave him a

letter of introduction to Miss Helen Maria Williams, who had been living in Orleans, the very city in France to which he was now making his
way" (*Moorman* 1:170). Despite this interest in both writers, neither
finds her way into the Preface.

By 1815, in the "Essay, Supplementary to the Preface," Wordsworth
could safely praise the natural imagery of Anne Finch's poetry in the context of denigrating other eighteenth-century writers.[22] But in the Preface
to *Lyrical Ballads*, only male writers may be heirs to the tradition. One
of the many ironies of Wordsworth's position in the Preface is that in
his later years he began to advocate the inclusion of women poets of the
seventeenth and eighteenth centuries in various anthologies of British
verse. In a letter dated 12 January 1829 to Dionysius Lardner, for instance, Wordsworth complains that "neither Dr Johnson, nor Dr Anderson, nor Chalmers, nor the Editor I believe of any other Corpus of
English Poetry takes the least notice of female Writers—this, to say nothing harsher, is very ungallant. The best way of giving comprehensive interest to the subject would be to begin with Sappho and proceed down-
wards through Italy antient and Modern, Spain, Germany, France, and
England" (*LY* 2:4). On 16 October of the same year he writes to the editor Alexander Dyce concerning Dyce's *Specimens of the British Poet-
esses*, congratulating him on the publication but asking to be consulted
if there is to be a second edition, specifically so that he can include the
poems of Anne Finch (*LY* 2:157). Granted, in 1829 Wordsworth sees
his mission as a kind of gallantry, but he is nonetheless quite familiar
with female poets and he has a sense of a female tradition that begins
with Sappho. Perhaps Wordsworth was more generous and less defensive in his correspondence because there he was not considering his own
reputation and readership—or perhaps he was feeling secure enough in
1829 to be generous.

In the Preface, however, the popularity of women writers is an unacknowledged influence on (and subtext of) Wordsworth's attempt to define his career. One work in particular, Scottish writer Joanna Baillie's
"Introductory Discourse" to *A Series of Plays, in Which It Is Attempted
to Delineate the Stronger Passions of the Mind*, only recently even linked
to Wordsworth, may be an important pre-text for Wordsworth's Preface.[23] Baillie's "Discourse" was first published in 1798, with the first
volume of her plays. As Stuart Curran and Marlon Ross indicate in
separate articles, this anonymous publication made a much greater im-
pression on the reading public of London and Edinburgh than another
anonymous publication of 1798, the first edition of the *Lyrical Ballads*,

and had a lasting influence on the theory of Romantic drama.[24] Baillie's until recently neglected "Discourse" may be seen as a precursor to Wordsworth's analysis of the literary and cultural environment of 1800, thus linking Wordsworth's theory closely to that of one of his female contemporaries.

But although Baillie's preface resembles Wordsworth's, her anonymity and her tone reveal crucial differences in how she views her role. Wordsworth claims that as a poet he is not different in kind from other men, but only in degree—he feels and thinks more intensely. He "detains" the reader because of the importance of his subject and his authority in presenting it. Baillie acknowledges, "I am not possessed of that confidence in my own powers, which enables the concealed genius, under the pressure of present discouragement, to pursue his labors in security, looking firmly forward to other more enlightened times for his reward" (17). Baillie asks for helpful criticism and apologizes for any appropriations she may unconsciously have made from other writers. Whereas Wordsworth both appeals to tradition and claims originality, Baillie says, "There are few writers who have sufficient originality of thought to strike out for themselves new ideas upon every occasion" (17). In feminist terms, Baillie sees herself as a collaborator, not as a solitary original genius. She is not so much interested in founding a career or attaining fame in posterity as she is in teaching the people of her own time.

Baillie is concerned with the effect that literature has on the mind of the reader, or that drama has on the audience. She states that "there is no mode of instruction they will so eagerly pursue, as that which lays open before them, in a more enlarged and connected view than their individual observations are capable of supplying—the varieties of the human mind" (4). For Baillie, the best literature leads to greater understanding of "human nature," not as an abstraction, but as an idea that encompasses diversity. Unlike Wordsworth, who states that his purpose is to trace "the grand and simple affections of our nature" (*PrW* 1:126) in the stories of common folk, Baillie wants to discover how those affections change in different circumstances. She is not as confident as Wordsworth is of the universality and permanence of the affections, although she does state that "The highest pleasure we receive from poetry, as well as from the real objects which surround us in the world, are derived from the sympathetic interest we all take in beings like ourselves" (6). For Baillie, pleasure is grounded in sympathy and identification rather than in the tension between similarity and dissimilarity.

Despite her more modest self-presentation, Baillie anticipates Wordsworth in arguing for simplicity and naturalness in literary representation
and in her critique of gothic and romance. Wordsworth, however, is
more dismissive than she of "frantic novels" as a mark of corrupt taste,
and, as we have seen, his comments about genre are also about gender.
Baillie wants to analyze the impulse toward the marvellous, but she does
not impose negative gendered terms on the argument:

> Our desire to know what men are in the closet as well as in the field; by
> the blazing hearth and at the social board, as well as in the council and the
> throne, is very imperfectly gratified by real history. Romance writers, there-
> fore, stept boldly forth to supply the deficiency; and tale writers and novel
> writers, of many descriptions, followed after. If they have not been very skil-
> ful in their delineations of nature; if they have represented men and women
> speaking and acting as men and women never did speak or act; if they have
> caricatured both our virtues and our vices; if they have given us such pure
> and unmixed, or such heterogeneous combinations of character, as real life
> never presented, and yet have pleased and interested us; let it not be imputed
> to the dulness of man in discerning what is genuinely natural in himself. There
> are many inclinations belonging to us besides this great master-propensity of
> which I am treating. Our love of the grand, the beautiful, the novel, and,
> above all, of the marvellous, is very strong; and if we are richly fed with what
> we have a good relish for, we may be weaned to forget our native and favourite
> aliment. Yet we can never so far forget it but that we shall cling to, and ac-
> knowledge it again, whenever it is presented before us. In a work abounding
> with the marvellous and unnatural, if the author has any how stumbled upon
> an unsophisticated genuine stroke of nature, we shall immediately perceive
> and be delighted with it, though we are foolish enough to admire, at the same
> time, all the nonsense with which it is surrounded. After all the wonderful in-
> cidents, dark mysteries, and secrets revealed, which [sic] eventful novel so lib-
> erally presents to us; after the beautiful fairy-ground, and even the grand and
> sublime scenes of nature with which descriptive novel so often enchants us;
> those works which most strongly characterise human nature in the middling
> and lower classes of society, where it is to be discovered by stronger and more
> unequivocal marks, will ever be the most popular.
>
>   (5–6)

Rather than simply dismiss the appeal of the marvellous, Baillie places
it in the context of a desire to know more about personal and domestic
life, and not just the military and social chronicles of "real history." Baillie also uses the metaphor of taste and appetite, but rather than seeing
the reader's taste as a corrupted craving for incident and event, Baillie
uses a metaphor of maternal nourishment: readers have been weaned
from their "native and favourite aliment" by their relish for the more
refined products. But they never lose their taste for what is native and

natural. Baillie goes on to imply that this appeal is most strongly associated with the "middling and lower classes of society," thus anticipating Wordsworth's theory. Even the inclusiveness of Baillie's language— "men and women speaking"—suggests the wider possibilities of human discourse.

To conclude the paragraph Baillie introduces the familiar pairing of art and nature, using the metaphor of landscape to underscore the value she places on the natural and native as opposed to artful cultivation of the unknown plants:

> For though great pains have been taken in our higher sentimental novels to interest us in the delicacies, embarrassments, and artificial distresses of the more refined part of society, they have never been able to cope in the public opinion with these. The one is a dressed and beautiful pleasure-ground, in which we are enchanted for a while, among the delicate and unknown plants of artful cultivation: the other is a rough forest of our native land; the oak, the elm, the hazel, and the bramble are there; and amidst the endless varieties of its paths we can wander forever. Into whatever scenes the novelist may conduct us, what objects soever he may present to our view, still is our attention most sensibly awake to every touch faithful to nature; still are we upon the watch for every thing that speaks to us of ourselves.

(6)

Whereas Wordsworth sees the reading public as so sated with extravagance that it may be incapable of appreciating tales of common life and basic human affections, Baillie seems to have faith that readers will respond with sympathy to "natural" writing. She does not construct a resisting or negligent reader as a defense for the possibility that her works will not be well received. Instead, she implies that failure will mean that her works lack the human appeal of that "native and favourite aliment."

Wordsworth's uneasiness in the Preface—uneasiness with the direction his society is taking and with what he regards as the corrupted taste of his readership—is compounded by his uneasiness with the role of the poet: "there is a numerous class of critics who, when they stumble upon these prosaisms as they call them, imagine that they have made a notable discovery, and exult over the Poet as over *a man ignorant of his profession*" (132, my emphasis). Wordsworth fears the judgment of other professionals, the critics. He is less concerned in this passage with poetic diction per se than he is with rhetorical strategy and with his own status as a professional who is not a hack writer. He worries about what his so-called prosaisms reveal about himself and the kind of poetic ambitions he holds. Wordsworth's preoccupation is all the more intense because in the 1800 Preface he is no longer presenting himself as a collaborator in an anonymous volume, but as a poet named W. Wordsworth who has been encouraged by friends to write this preface to his volumes.

Perhaps Wordsworth reveals such anxiety in the Preface and the letters of the period because he was unsure of himself as an actor in the prescribed middle-class male script: his brothers were following the conventional paths into law (Richard), the East India Company (John), and the clergy (Christopher), but at thirty William was still a little-acknowledged poet. In a later letter, Mary Wordsworth revealed that the elders in her family had regarded William as a "Vagabond" at the time: "My father's Bachelor Brother Henry,—upon whom we were, as Orphans, in some measure dependent . . . had no high opinion of Young Men without some Profession, or Calling."[25] Wordsworth's task in the years following his trip to Germany in 1798–99 was to establish himself as a poet. He felt compelled to justify this choice to his formidable elders and to the world; he could not be a man ignorant of his profession.

"TINTERN ABBEY": THE SISTER'S LOST NARRATIVE

In 1798, in the poem strategically placed at the end of the first edition of the *Lyrical Ballads*, Wordsworth had meditated on his vocation as poet, this time by addressing his hopes and dreams to Dorothy Wordsworth. John Barrell and David Simpson have (in separate pieces) recently written on the place of Dorothy in "Tintern Abbey" and in William's poetry generally.[26] Simpson underscores Barrell's argument that the language of "Tintern Abbey," the abstract language of educated males of Wordsworth's time, would preclude a female as a reader because she would not have had access to the education needed to use and understand such language. Therefore, according to this argument, Wordsworth addresses Dorothy in "Tintern Abbey" in a language that she cannot understand. In Simpson's words, "it may be that Wordsworth and Coleridge's joint entry into the literary marketplace of 1798 is in fact prefigured (in the preparation of the volume) and concluded (as one reads through it) by the marginalization of the exemplary female, who may be a worshipful or proleptic companion but who can never be a reader" (550).

Leaving aside the irony of this comment when we think of Wordsworth's female readership, I would suggest that the emphasis on language here misses the point. It is not so much that Dorothy Wordsworth is excluded by William's language (even though she herself might have used a more concrete language); the main point is that William turns to her in "Tintern Abbey" and sees, in her "wild eyes," *himself*. He describes both her past and her future in terms he has invented. She may embody "nature and the language of the sense" (108) to him, but he has defined her in terms of his own story. She is present as the poet composes himself and his poem, and she assists in the processes leading to its publication in the *Lyrical Ballads*. Nevertheless, the core of "Tintern Abbey" is Wordsworth's narrative of a young man's life: his progression from the "glad animal movements" (74) of his "boyish days" (73) through the "dizzy raptures" (85) and "aching joys" (84) of eroticized adolescence to the present time of subdued thoughts about humanity.

There is nothing new in seeing "Tintern Abbey" as a familiar Wordsworthian "scene of instruction," with the brother projecting his sense of reality and his morality onto the devoted sister.[27] But I would argue not that the sister lacks the necessary language to form her life but that she is denied her own narrative in the context of Wordsworth's masculine narrative of loss and desired restoration. Carolyn Heilbrun clarifies this distinction between language and narrative in *Writing a Woman's Life*:

> If I had to emphasize the lack either of narrative or of language to the formation of new women's lives, I would unquestionably emphasize narrative. Much, of a profound and perceptive nature, has been written about the problem of women coping with male language that will not say what they wish: we remember Woolf's enigmatic statement that Jane Austen was the first to write a woman's sentence. Some part of us responds to this, as to the words of Anne Elliot in *Persuasion*—"Men have had every advantage of us in telling their story. Education has been theirs in so much higher a degree; the pen has been in their hands."—and of Bathsheba in Thomas Hardy's *Far from the Madding Crowd*—"It is difficult for a woman to define her feelings in language which is chiefly made by men to express theirs." But what we speak of here . . . is not so much women's lack of a language as their failure to speak profoundly to one another.[28]

Or, as Heilbrun goes on to argue, the failure to invent new narratives, new life patterns for themselves. In 1798—and, as Austen's Anne Elliot knew, a few years later—this was much easier for a man than for a woman to do. But if women were—and are—to have their own narratives, they must be more than good listeners, muses, or footnotes.

Wordsworth plotted his life against convention (he did not enter the clergy or the bar), and in *The Prelude* he attempts to justify his choice to himself and eventually to the world. He uses the archetype of the romantic quest to dramatize not how he conquered the world but how he formed himself. Wordsworth presents himself as the typical Englishman who has lived through the failure of revolutionary hope and who needs to reestablish his life. But while Wordsworth describes himself here and in "Tintern Abbey" as suffering through the revolution and its aftermath, Dorothy remained in England, viewing events from afar and dependent on relatives for her home. Until she set up a household with William in 1795, Dorothy lived the life of an orphan, shuttled from one family to another.

Wordsworth makes no mention of Dorothy's real circumstances or possibilities in "Tintern Abbey." But the records of history and literature make clear that her culture placed limitations on her life. Seen in the light of Heilbrun's theory, the two plots Dorothy Wordsworth might have learned from literature were the marriage plot and the plot of abandonment and death. Historians such as Lenore Davidoff and Catherine Hall have taught us that another familiar middle-class plot—and the one, of course, that Dorothy Wordsworth chose—had the unmarried sister or daughter live in the household of a brother or her father; such a sister contributed immeasurably to the economy of the household and helped to raise the children.[29] In the fiction of "Tintern Abbey," this life is not considered, although in the years to come Wordsworth was to praise such a domestic mission. In 1798, however, before settling at Grasmere, Wordsworth did not yet envision his vocation in relation to his sister's work.

In "Tintern Abbey" the beloved sister silently serves as a mirror in which the poet can gaze into his past and hope for his future. It is fitting that when Shelley critiques Wordsworthian visionary egotism in "Alastor," he endows the visionary with Dorothy's wild eyes, and as the visionary approaches death, those eyes eerily "seemed with their serene and azure smiles / To beckon him" (491–92) into the caverns of selfhood and death. But in "Tintern Abbey" Wordsworth sees Dorothy's reflective and subsidiary role as potentially redemptive—as a way that he can avert the finality of death. He imagines that in redeeming him she will be able to save herself, but he does not acknowledge the differences in their experiences of the momentous events of the 1790s and in their daily lives when they were apart. What if Dorothy had gone to London or Paris like Mary Wollstonecraft or Helen Maria Williams? What if she had taken her literary talents seriously? What if *she* had borne an illegitimate child?

Instead of posing such disruptive questions, Wordsworth frames his narrative so that Dorothy, representing the possibilities of the beautiful, tempers and calms his unsettling memories:

> . . . and, in after years,
> When these wild ecstasies shall be matured
> Into a sober pleasure; when thy mind
> Shall be a mansion for all lovely forms,
> Thy memory be as a dwelling-place
> For all sweet sounds and harmonies
>   (137–42)

Theresa Kelley has read "Tintern Abbey" as a poem in which the beautiful subdues the sublime and revolutionary passions.[30] Once again, this movement to the beautiful is subtly gendered: the image of the inner mansion, a place of refuge from the world, prefigures the ideal of Victorian domesticity. This image of mental harmony and refuge, Wordsworth's version of Milton's "paradise within," is related both to "the neglected mansion-house" (two-part *Prelude* 2:151) on Coniston and to Rydal Mount, the comfortable house of later years.

But what of the disruptive questions that do not fit into this version of Wordsworth's life story? If we are to be other than resisting readers of Wordsworth, then we must explain why "Tintern Abbey" continues to hold appeal for readers, in spite of the poet's blindness. It is true that the male poet denies his sister her own story, but he does bless her life with the highest love he can imagine:

> . . . Therefore let the moon
> Shine on thee in thy solitary walk;
> And let the misty mountain-winds be free
> To blow against thee . . .
>   (135–38)

Also, in focusing on the transference of his hopes and joys to his sister, Wordsworth demonstrates his dependence on her, even as he constructs his myth of male development. In this poem that closed the 1798 edition of the *Lyrical Ballads*, the poem in which Wordsworth frames his own narrative of loss and recovery, he acknowledges his "dear, dear Sister" (122) as his most valued audience and his dearest friend. In comparison to the marginalized women of the other poems in the *Lyrical Ballads*, many of them (the mad mother, the forsaken Indian woman, Martha Ray) driven to the brink by their distress and suffering, Dorothy Wordsworth is given a privileged place as she stands with the poet sur-

veying the Wye Valley. In acknowledging her importance in his myth of
redemption, Wordsworth may unconsciously be trying to redeem the
abandoned women who fill the pages of the volume—and perhaps even
the abandoned woman in the narrative of his own life. Wordsworth idealizes his sister, but he stands with her above the Wye Valley in "Tintern Abbey" and never in fact abandons her.

I disagree with Diane Long Hoeveler's conclusion that "William is
speaking, after all, from the growing realization that his imagination is
failing and . . . he is, as any poet would be, bitter. He chooses, probably
unconsciously, to displace his bitterness onto Dorothy, for if she is for
him the emblem of the feminine within, then she is the cause of his imaginative decay."[31] There is no doubt that Wordsworth feared the decay of
his "genial spirits" (113), but, I believe, in 1798 that fear is motivated
by his sense of mortality rather than by a crisis of confidence in his poetic powers. Wordsworth also feared that he would not find a larger audience for his poetry than the ever-responsive sister to whom his meditation is addressed. But this is still different from blaming her for his
anticipated failure of imagination.

THE PATRIMONIAL FIELDS OF "MICHAEL"

At the time that Wordsworth was contemplating the Preface, he was also
writing "Michael," a poem implicitly concerned with the poet's vocation.
Late in the planning of the second edition of the *Lyrical Ballads*,
"Michael" was added to the volume in lieu of Coleridge's "Christabel."[32]
Many have speculated on why Wordsworth insisted on substituting his
own poem; clearly he saw the importance of "Michael" to his poetic program and to his sense of himself as a poet in 1800. In fact, there is a strong
link between the role and responsibility of the poet in "Michael" and
Wordsworth's self-dramatization as a publishing poet in the Preface.

In both "Michael" and the Preface, Wordsworth works out what it
means to be a poet in an age of cultural crisis—more specifically, what
it means to be a male poet in a patriarchal society. In "Michael"
Wordsworth's focus is on the bond established between father and son.
The poet-narrator writes for the delight of "the few natural hearts" who
will be his "second self" when he is gone, thus casting himself as a
father-figure for succeeding generations of poets. But the poet is also a
second Luke who fulfills the promise in poetry that Luke could not fulfill in his action. By privileging the male bond in "Michael," Wordsworth
also privileges the heroic ideals associated with the bond, in this case a

heroism linked with the biblical law and biblical language, with a covenant that binds father irrevocably to son, even if the son does not fulfill the promise. In "Michael" the father-son relationship is rooted in Michael's love of his land, "the patrimonial fields" he wishes so desperately to preserve.

Wordsworth also wants to preserve the model of the family and domestic relationships linked to these patrimonial fields, as his letters of the period demonstrate. For instance, he laments to Charles James Fox in the now much-quoted letter that "the wife no longer prepares with her own hand a meal for her husband, the produce of his labour; there is little doing in his house in which his affections can be interested, and but little left in it which he can love."[33] Wordsworth sees the wife's role in terms of the husband's happiness; she serves him with acts of devotion that make the home the center of affection and love, work and productivity. In "Michael," the narrator describes Isabel as "a woman of stirring life, / Whose heart was in her house" (81–82). But both Michael and the narrator seem to value an abstract principle, individual ownership of landed property, to such an extent that the actual family and domestic affections are sacrificed.[34]

Michael's feelings toward his son, however, are not conventionally masculine, even though his patrimonial concern seems to determine his decisions. Interestingly, Michael establishes a bond with his infant son by sharing in his care:

> Old Michael, while he was a babe in arms,
> Had done him female service, not alone
> For pastime and delight, as is the use
> Of fathers, but with patient mind enforced
> To acts of tenderness; and he had rocked
> His cradle, as with a woman's gentle hand.
>   (153–58)

Wordsworth indicates that this father-son bond was unusually profound by describing Michael as wanting to perform maternal "acts of tenderness." Even within the context of a poem that emphasizes the legacy from father to son, Wordsworth dramatizes a character who values and reinforces the feminine. Wordsworth thus subverts a definition of roles for women and men based on biology. Instead, he redefines the role of fatherhood for his shepherd Michael; he reminds us that the shepherd is after all a nurturing (and therefore conventionally feminine) figure to his flock, in an implicit allusion to the conventional religious symbolism of the pastoral.

But despite these impulses toward nurturing and the feminine in the
early descriptions of Michael and Luke, in the course of "Michael" the
voice that might have expressed a more compromising view regarding
the property—the voice of Isabel—does not prevail. Wordsworth contrasts her silent thoughts (255–73) with Michael's word and his law.
When Isabel first hears of Michael's plans, she is worried but does not
speak. Instead, the narrator gives us insight into her hopeful thoughts
that Luke may follow in the path of another parish boy and return to
his native village a rich and bountiful man. After the letter comes from
the kinsman, Michael simply says:

> "He shall depart to-morrow." To this word
> The Housewife answered, talking much of things
> Which, if at such short notice he should go,
> Would surely be forgotten. But at length
> She gave consent, and Michael was at ease.
>   (317–21)

Michael's "word," with its commanding authority, is contrasted with
Isabel's "talking" and, later, her bustling activity. Wordsworth controls
the influence of Isabel's voice on Michael's word. Michael's values
prevail and Michael's courage is celebrated, but Isabel's silent tragedy
reminds us of what might have been. The father-son bond, however,
remains central to the story, in which the narrator had already explained that

> The Shepherd, if he loved himself, must needs
> Have loved his Helpmate; but to Michael's heart
> This son of his old age was yet more dear—
>   (141–43)

From the outset Wordsworth reinforces his relationship to this bond and
to the story of lost inheritance. As many readers have noted,[35] he substitutes himself and his poem for the broken covenant between Michael
and Luke, relating Michael's tale

> For the delight of a few natural hearts;
> And, with yet fonder feeling, for the sake
> Of youthful Poets, who among these hills
> Will be my second self when I am gone.
>   (36–39)

Wordsworth seemed particularly attached to this story about property
and ownership and patrimonial inheritance in the fall of 1800, when he
was revising the Preface and preparing for the second edition of the *Lyri-*

cal Ballads. In place of the questionable form and subject matter of the feminized gothic tale "Christabel," he substituted the biblical and patriarchal "Michael." Wordsworth's placement of "Michael" thus fulfills the anti-gothic promise of the Preface with a sober narrative that raises low and rustic life to the level of tragedy.

HOME AT DOVE COTTAGE

When, in 1800, Wordsworth settled in what would later be known as Dove Cottage, he was as close as he had come to owning property and working his own plot of ground (Heinzelman, *R&F*, 53 and passim). But he had more to do in carving out his literary place as he worked toward claiming both figurative and literal ownership of his poems. In contrast to the anonymous publication of the 1798 volume of the *Lyrical Ballads*, the 1800 edition bore the name "W. Wordsworth," with Coleridge receiving no credit. Furthermore, Wordsworth actually became the owner of the copyright to the *Lyrical Ballads* in that year. And, as we have seen, Wordsworth was concerned about his readership not in the Preface alone but also in the letters he wrote to such public figures as Charles James Fox after the second edition was published.

Wordsworth's many gestures toward a larger audience during this time all point to his desire not only to be read but to be read in a certain way—by readers who would recognize the social and political implications of his poetry, by readers who had an "accurate taste" for the poetry they consumed. His authority derives, not from personal status, but from poetic tradition: "the common inheritance of Poets." But as he cultivates this wider audience, writing letters and sending volumes to readers, Wordsworth also depends on the moral and emotional support of a very small audience: Dorothy Wordsworth, Coleridge, and then Mary Wordsworth and Sara Hutchinson; later he will rely on Dora Wordsworth and Isabella Fenwick. The "man speaking to men" depends on the sympathetic reading of (mostly) women. Marlon Ross goes so far as to claim that Coleridge, in fact, becomes feminized in Wordsworth's representation of him as a reader both willing to sympathize and in need of instruction.[36]

Women not only *could* be readers, but they were the *first* readers and recorders of much of Wordsworth's poetry. Wordsworth's poetic vocation was nurtured and supported at home as his reputation made its way into the public sphere. The story of his composition of "Resolution and Independence," a poem concerned with the fate of poets, reveals the extent to which Wordsworth required sympathetic readers. In May 1802, after he finished his painstaking composition of "The Leech-Gatherer" (later "Resolution and Independence"), Wordsworth sent a copy to his future wife, Mary Hutchinson, and her sister Sara. The poet got more of a response than he had bargained for. We know from his return letter to them (their letter is lost) that the women complained of tedium in the presentation of the leech-gatherer's family history. Wordsworth responds to their criticism by arguing that "everything is tedious when one does not read with the feelings of the Author."[37] Dorothy Wordsworth seconds her brother's comments with a lecture of her own on how to read William's work:

> When you happen to be displeased with what you suppose to be the tendency or moral of any poem which William writes, ask yourself whether you have hit upon the real tendency and true moral, and above all never think that he writes for no reason merely because a thing happened—and when you feel any poem of his to be tedious, ask yourself in what spirit it was written— whether merely to tell the tale and be through with it, or to illustrate a particular character or truth etc. etc.
>
> (*Early Years*, 367)

According to both Dorothy and William, the reader must be in sympathy with the feelings of the author. Dorothy Wordsworth established a pattern that was followed by the other devoted women of the household. The Wordsworth women learned not only to read William's poetry but also to read the poet and respond to his needs. Dorothy's little lecture on "The Leech-Gatherer" can be seen as a lesson for his future wife and sister-in-law on how to live with William. But while both William and Dorothy were quick to correct the sisters, William went on to alter the poem according to their suggestions, revealing that he not only needed their emotional support but also trusted their ability as readers. They were able to make suggestions because, like Dorothy and unlike the world of contemporary reviews, they cultivated an atmosphere of trust and sympathy. Perhaps it was these sympathetic first readers who became the models for Wordsworth's picture of "the People" who would one day appreciate his poetry.

The Wordsworth women would essentially replace Coleridge in the role of nurturer and supporter of William's genius, for by the early years of the century the old intimacy between the friends was lost. When Wordsworth addressed and patronized a heartsick and lonely Coleridge in *The Prelude*, their roles had already begun to change. In the autumn of 1803 Coleridge complained that Wordsworth was self-centered and "hypercondriacal" from "living wholly among *Devotees*—having every the [*sic*] minutest Thing, almost his Eating and Drinking done for him by his Sister, or his Wife."[38] Coleridge envies the domestic support that made Wordsworth's poetry possible. Later, Coleridge became a very different kind of reader of Wordsworth in the *Biographia Literaria* (1817), enumerating Wordsworth's weaknesses with a (for Wordsworth) painfully incisive intelligence. But the Wordsworth women never relinquished their intellectual and emotional support of Wordsworth's poetic career. As we shall see, they nurtured him through the difficult early years of the century and later shared in his success with readers—many of them women—in the 1820s and 1830s.

Wordsworth's French Revolution

The Sonnets of 1802

Milton is his great idol, and he sometimes dares to compare himself with him. His Sonnets, indeed, have something of the same high-raised tone and prophetic spirit.

Hazlitt, The Spirit of the Age, *1825*

The sense of massive passion, concentrated, and repressing the utterance it permits itself, is that which moves us in his political verse.

A. C. Bradley, Oxford Lectures on Poetry, *1909*

As we have seen in previous chapters, in the two-part *Prelude* Wordsworth was attracted to those qualities conventionally associated with the feminine, whereas in the Preface of 1800 he distanced himself from the feminine and from the women writers who may have influenced him. In the sonnets of 1802, Wordsworth's attitude toward women and his relationships with them are central. In these poems, in fact, Wordsworth's reconstruction of his private relationships of the 1790s is entangled in his reconstruction of his political past; boundaries between public and private history, political and sexual transgression, are blurred. In the sonnets Wordsworth employs two related strategies to contain these interrelated problems: a public stance and an idealization or distancing of the female subject. Like all such strategies, Wordsworth's methods reveal to us much of what they were meant to conceal. His process of revision, as seen in one sonnet originally entitled "The Banished Negroes," also demonstrates that Wordsworth continued to reimagine the events of revolutionary Europe well into old age. David Erdman reminds us in "Wordsworth as Heartsworth" that "Wordsworth hints at the intimate and inseparable connection between his French love and his French politics" in *The Borderers*, in the "Vaudracour and Julia" episode of *The Prelude*, and in the Solitary's story in *The Excursion*.[1] I would add the sonnets of 1802 and many of the later poems to that list.

The sonnet has traditionally been used as a vehicle for both personal and political expression, as in the Petrarchan love tradition of the sixteenth century and in Milton's politicizing of the sonnet in the seventeenth century. We recall that Wordsworth's first published poem at age seventeen was a sentimental sonnet entitled "Sonnet on Seeing Miss Helen Maria Williams Weep at a Tale of Distress." For a time after this Wordsworth scorned the sonnet, but he later returned to it, perhaps after hearing Dorothy recite Milton's sonnets in May 1802: "Wm wrote two sonnets on Buonaparte after I read Milton's sonnets to him."[2] Before this Wordsworth may have associated the genre with the many women writers who wrote sonnets in the late eighteenth century—the very writers from whom he disassociates himself in the Preface. Whatever the reason for his rejection, he seems to have turned toward the sonnet in Calais because it served, as I shall argue, both his political agenda and his personal need to shape his experience. The fact that he published many of the sonnets in the months following his journey emphasizes Wordsworth's polemical intentions. For Wordsworth, the sonnet was the perfect meeting ground for private and public thoughts.

CALAIS, 1802

In August 1802, when Wordsworth was about to marry Mary Hutchinson, he went to France with his sister to settle affairs with Annette Vallon and their daughter Caroline. While in Calais during this uneasy pause in the wars between England and France, Wordsworth composed a small group of sonnets.[3] Except for a brief but powerful entry in Dorothy Wordsworth's journal, these sonnets form the only account we have of the trip. Although the sonnets have not until recently been seriously and critically considered as records of Wordsworth's month in Calais, they tell us much about his thoughts on marriage, paternity, and England, both in their explicit assertions and in their silences on the very issues we would expect to be given voice. Commentators have traditionally drawn a distinction between the political sonnets, inspired by the Miltonic model, and the one "personal" sonnet composed in Calais, "It is a Beauteous Evening." Mary Moorman concludes that Wordsworth "was, as a poet, capable of remarkable detachment from his immediate circumstances" (*Moorman* 1:565). Moorman implies that there is no connection between the political and the personal impulses of the sonnets. But Wordsworth's "remarkable detachment" is complicated by conflicts that united his public and private concerns in Calais in 1802. Wordsworth's public thoughts are shaped by his presence in Calais with Annette Vallon and Caroline, and by his absence from England and Mary Hutchinson.

It is not hard to imagine why this trip to Calais could have been difficult for Wordsworth. Wordsworth's intention was to clear the way for his marriage to his lifelong friend Mary Hutchinson by "divorcing" Annette Vallon. His month in Calais followed a tense period in which he was working on the third edition of the *Lyrical Ballads*, revising the Preface, adding the Appendix on poetic diction, and also struggling with the composition of "Resolution and Independence," a poem (as we saw in the last chapter) concerned with the fate of poets. At the same time William had begun again to receive letters from Annette, which clouded his thoughts of marriage to Mary.[4]

The Peace of Amiens gave Wordsworth his first opportunity to go to France in nearly a decade, but such a trip would be likely to have given rise to painful political and personal memories. Calais was a kind of neutral ground, not associated with Annette Vallon's family (who presumably would feel betrayed by Wordsworth's actions) and not as dangerous for Annette, with her royalist views, as other cities might be. Calais, of course, was the part of France closest to England, with only twenty-five miles separating its harbor from the cliffs of Dover. But the very setting of Calais, the site of centuries of contention and violence between England and France, could have caused Wordsworth uneasiness. The siege of Calais by the English under Edward III, followed by a two-hundred-year occupation (1347–1558), ignited the imaginations of such contemporaries as Blake. In early drawings and paintings, such as *The Keys of Calais*, Blake associates the English tyranny during and after the ten-month siege apocalyptically with the tyranny and pestilence of his own time.[5] From within Calais, the Peace of Amiens must have seemed very fragile indeed. The fort at the entrance of the harbor (described in Dorothy's journal) and Wordsworth's consciousness of distant and recent history taught him that Calais was no ordinary resort town. Dorothy records that the full month they spent in Calais was long, hot, and uncomfortable: "We lodged opposite two Ladies in tolerably decent-sized rooms but badly furnished, with large stores of bad smells and dirt in the yard, and all about."[6] Walking by the shore and looking out to sea became the main occupations of the month; looking beyond the confinements of Calais, across the water, seems to have been consoling for both Dorothy and William. In Dorothy's words, "The town of Calais seemed deserted of the light of heaven, but there was always light, and life, and joy upon the Sea" (153).

THE WEIGHT OF TOO MUCH LIBERTY

In the Calais sonnets, Wordsworth recognizes the naiveté and confusion of the early days of the Revolution in the context of Napoleon's developing power. Finding himself in France for urgent personal reasons, Wordsworth is disgusted by the parade of his countrymen who have come to France to gawk at the spoils of Napoleon:

> Men known, and men unknown, Sick, Lame, and Blind,
> Post forward all, like Creatures of one kind,
> With first-fruit offerings crowd to bend the knee
> In France, before the new-born Majesty.[7]

Wordsworth is dismayed by the apparent willingness of English men and women to worship the "new-born Majesty" of Napoleon, in betrayal of their own legacy of freedom. The language here suggests that these people—"Sick, Lame, and Blind"—foolishly look to Napoleon as if he would reward their obeisance with a miracle. In "To a Friend, Composed near Calais," Wordsworth also contrasts past and present, remembering when a "homeless sound of joy was in the sky" in the early days of the Revolution. How could he fail to connect this youthful joy and hope for the Revolution with his own youthful indulgences, which brought forth an illegitimate child and connected him with a young woman who had lingering hopes that they might one day be reunited? In returning to Calais, Wordsworth experiences nostalgia for the innocent days of youth and revolutionary hopes as well as guilt for the excesses he remembers and the ruin he now sees. In 1802 he is faced with a changed world: the birth of an illegitimate tyranny and the presence of an illegitimate daughter. In these sonnets Wordsworth emphasizes lasting and permanent values over transient attachments:

> A seemly reverence may be paid to power;
> But that's a loyal virtue, never sown
> In haste, nor springing with a transient shower.

Although explicitly deploring the worship of Napoleon here in "Calais, August, 1802," Wordsworth seems to reflect on his own relationship with Annette Vallon and Caroline, especially if we consider the sexual implications of sowing in haste.

The sonnets written during the time in Calais share common themes and responses, but Wordsworth did not write a sonnet sequence, a group of poems to be read in a certain order having narrative coherence. Instead, he limited the focus of each composition within the bounds of the sonnet's fourteen lines, attempting to create integrity and unity within this confinement. As he expresses in his sonnet on the sonnet:

> Nuns fret not at their Convent's narrow room;
> And Hermits are contented with their Cells;
> And Students with their pensive Citadels:
> Maids at the Wheel, the Weaver at his Loom,
> Sit blithe and happy; Bees that soar for bloom
> High as the highest Peak of Furness Fells,
> Will murmur by the hour in Foxglove bells:
> In truth, the prison unto which we doom
> Ourselves, no prison is: and hence to me,
> In sundry moods, 'twas pastime to be bound
> Within the Sonnet's scanty plot of ground:
> Pleased if some Souls (for such there needs must be)
> Who have felt the weight of too much liberty,
> Should find short solace there, as I have found.

In this sonnet, written in 1802 after Calais, Wordsworth could be reflecting on the Calais experience and the psychological discipline he found in writing sonnets during that month. Also, after a spring of poetic experimentation in various lyric forms, Wordsworth may have found the conventional restrictions of the sonnet comforting. A poet's formal and metrical accomplishment under such restrictions carries with it the "sense of difficulty overcome," to echo Wordsworth's own comment in the Preface to *Lyrical Ballads* (*PrW* 1:150). Wordsworth learned from Milton's sonnets that potentially explosive material could be contained and controlled within such a limited form. Like Milton, he finds strength "in sundry moods" by bounding his thoughts within a small plot.[8] Focusing on the individual sonnet, he also adopts a form that, with its frequent addresses and apostrophes, is suitable for working through his present experiences and immediate thoughts.[9]

The dialectic of liberty and restraint raises both personal and political questions. It is likely that Wordsworth felt "the weight of too much liberty" in Calais as he thought back on the liberties of his youth: his romance with Annette Vallon and with the Revolution, both of which produced troublesome consequences for him in 1802. In marriage William would bind himself in a legitimate way to Mary Hutchinson and at the same time disassociate himself from Annette and Caroline. By observing and criticizing Calais under Napoleon's rule, Wordsworth distances himself from past and current events in France. Both of these personal and political maneuvers liberate Wordsworth for his future. Wordsworth attains his freedom to marry Mary Hutchinson after enduring a month in the "prison" of Calais. As we read these sonnets we feel the pull of the sea and of England as the speaker tries to move away from Calais proper, expanding his thoughts and images beyond his confinement. Writing sonnets modeled on the Miltonic structure and having native English associations carries Wordsworth beyond France even while he was immured in Calais.

In the sonnet entitled "Composed by the Sea-Side, near Calais, August, 1802," Wordsworth meditates on the landscape and the vista across the water, explicitly turning what he sees into an emblem of his public thoughts about England:

> Fair Star of Evening, Splendor of the West,
> Star of my Country! on the horizon's brink
> Thou hangest, stooping, as might seem, to sink
> On England's bosom; yet well pleased to rest,
> Meanwhile, and be to her a glorious crest
> Conspicuous to the Nations. Thou, I think,
> Should'st be my Country's emblem; and should'st wink,
> Bright Star! with laughter on her banners, drest
> In thy fresh beauty. There! that dusky spot
> Beneath thee, it is England; there it lies.
> Blessings be on you both! one hope, one lot,
> One life, one glory! I, with many a fear
> For my dear Country, many heartfelt sighs,
> Among Men who do not love her linger here.

In his study of Wordsworth's sonnets, Lee M. Johnson points out that "Wordsworth describes the union of the evening star with England in nuptial terms" and refers us to Spenser's "Epithalamion" as a probable source for Wordsworth's language.[10] We might also note that Wordsworth's language resembles Dorothy's journal description of "the west Coast of England like a cloud crested with Dover Castle . . . The Evening star and glory of the sky" (152). But Johnson does not say that unlike the nuptial images in Spenser, which lead to union and fulfillment, Wordsworth's treatment remains tentative and uncertain. Even the punctuation and choppy phrases in line 3 awkwardly slow down any possibility of contact: "Thou hangest, stooping, as might seem, to sink . . ." The image of the star, associated in "London, 1802" with the soul of Milton, does not sink on "England's bosom," but, rather, remains "on the horizon's brink." Perhaps Wordsworth expresses here, as he does in sonnets written upon his return to England, that England needs heroes of the stature of Milton now to "give us manners, virtue, freedom, power" ("London, 1802"). If the star represents the possibilities for England— based on its heroic past—as a light unto the nations, those prophecies are unfulfilled in 1802. Wordsworth also ironically undercuts the power of England by casting "her" in a conventionally feminine role. The poet ends the sonnet with an emphasis on his fears for his country and his feelings of alienation while lingering in France.

In several of the sonnets written before and after the Calais journey, Wordsworth takes up this question of potential and leadership for England. He perceives in contemporary England a lack of great men like those of the past, and he emphasizes (in the phallic associations at the beginning of the following sonnet, which was composed between May and December 1802) the need for great *men* to revitalize the nation:

> Great Men have been among us; hands that penned
> And tongues that uttered wisdom, better none:
> The later Sydney, Marvel, Harrington
> Young Vane, and others who called Milton Friend.
> These Moralists could act and comprehend:
> They knew how genuine glory was put on;
> Taught us how rightfully a nation shone
> In splendor: what strength was, that would not bend
> But in magnanimous meekness. France, 'tis strange,
> Hath brought forth no such souls as we had then.
> Perpetual emptiness! unceasing change!
> No single Volume paramount, no code,
> No master spirit, no determined road;
> But equally a want of Books and Men!

On the surface this sonnet disparages everything French in favor of everything English. But the sonnet does not divide neatly into two parts—one on England and one on France. Instead, line 10 brings into focus what has been implicit: great men have been among the English in the past. Without explicitly deploring the lack of books and men in contemporary England, Wordsworth directs the reader's thoughts more to the tensions between England past and England in 1802 than to his overt contrast between France and England. In naming such Republicans as Vane, Wordsworth had already alluded to the moral strength for which Milton praised these very men in his own sonnets. The tension between past and present is increased by the metrical pun in line 8, with the word *strength* foregrounded by its placement in a weak metrical position and surrounded by two unstressed words in strong metrical positions: "In splendor: *what strength was* that would not bend." The awkwardness of this focus on *strength* further emphasizes the lack of moral strength in contemporary England. It also serves as a kind of sexual pun on the virility of the men of Milton's age, on the connection between moral virtue and manliness. Not only does France pose a threat to England, but England poses a threat to itself. Wordsworth implies that England now needs a bright star to shine on the nation.

It is both fitting and ironic that in this sonnet Wordsworth envisions the star of hope in the form of Milton, the great literary and political patriarch whose reputation as a father and a husband was at least open to question. In his poem *Milton,* for instance, Blake appropriately has Milton come to terms with his sixfold Emanation (three daughters and three wives) when he begins to unsave himself from the boredom of heaven. Wordsworth identifies in many ways with Milton—as defender of the English people, advocate of legitimate divorce, and author of *Paradise Lost* (England's "single Volume paramount"). To Wordsworth's English imagination, Milton is both book and man. By viewing Milton as a great mythic figure, Wordsworth (unlike Blake) can overlook any personal failings. Milton's "soul was like a Star and dwelt apart" ("London, 1802"). Where now will England find such a bright star to shine on the nation?

The nuptial imagery of the "Bright Star" sonnet takes on greater significance if we remember the purpose of Wordsworth's journey to Calais. Wordsworth's impending marriage and his desire to be a bright poetic star hover over this sonnet, much as the star itself hovers over "England's bosom." The speaker's "heartfelt sighs" seem more appropriate to a love sonnet and Petrarchan conventions than to a manifestly public work. The poem, in fact, presents the love relationship in conventional terms, with the male contemplating the female who lies waiting for her lover. England as motherland becomes a passive female body—a "dusky spot"—awaiting the illumination of the male star. In a later revision of the poem, Wordsworth emphasizes the personification of England as a woman by substituting "she" for "it" in line 10: "there she lies." The orthography of the sonnet, in which both "Star" and "Country" are capitalized throughout, also enriches the personification. Keats, I think, read this sonnet as sexual, too, for in his "Bright star, would I were steadfast as thou art" the speaker wishes to be

Wordsworth's bright star "Not in lone splendor hung aloft the night" (2) but "Pillow'd upon my fair love's ripening breast" (10). Keats imagines the erotic fulfillment inherent in the images Wordsworth introduces. Keats's fantasy, like Wordsworth's description of anticipated fulfillment, takes as its vantage point male desire and male perceptions of the female.

In Wordsworth's sonnet the star remains aloft, leaving the reader with what J. Hillis Miller finds characteristic of Wordsworth's shorter poems, "the blankness of an irresolution."[11] But perhaps *blankness* is not exactly the right word here, for the "irresolution" of this sonnet tells us much about the poet's ambivalence in contemplating, from the beaches of Calais, his country and his marriage to Mary Hutchinson. The poem's particular unity, which Wordsworth so valued in the sonnet form, typically derives from this irresolution: the sonnet is framed by the image of the hanging, resting star at the beginning and the lingering poet at the end. The poet addresses the star repeatedly, intensifying his desire to become the star over the horizon. The repetition of "should'st" in line 7 emphasizes the poet's hope that the star will provide the same harmony as the star that Spenser praises in "Epithalamion":

> How chearefully thou lookest from aboue,
> And seemst to laugh atweene thy twinkling light
> As ioying in the sight
> Of these glad many which for ioy doe sing,
> That all the woods them answer and their echo ring.[12]

But there is no joyful resolution in Wordsworth's poem, no echoing harmony. Faithful Mary lies waiting, but William is not yet ready to join in "one hope, one lot, / One life, one glory."

Through the nuptial metaphor, however, Wordsworth links his personal ambivalence with his public hopes and fears, articulating both in the same breath. Wordsworth's preoccupation with marriage becomes the underlying metaphor of his thoughts about England. Or, in seeming to write about the fate of England, Wordsworth implicitly tells us much more about himself and his attitude toward both his future wife and the French woman who has temporarily impeded his marriage and whose unacknowledged presence haunts the poem.

ABRAHAM'S BOSOM

Wordsworth's impending marriage was also, of course, complicated by his responsibility to Caroline. Although he did make a financial settlement on Caroline in 1816 when she married, he would never provide a

home for her or be a father to her. The poet who knew the pain of growing into adolescence without a father was now abandoning his child and
her mother. We know from his treatment of the "Vaudracour and
Julia" episode in *The Prelude*, a veiled and distorted narrative of his
relationship with Annette, that Wordsworth had difficulty confronting these events in his autobiographical poem. As one reader has stated,
"In 'Vaudracour and Julia' the woman is in a convent, the child dead
in infancy, and the man insane."[13] Only in recent criticism such as
this, though, have readers looked closely at Wordsworth's dealings
with Caroline and Annette from their point of view rather than either
simply dismissing the relationships as insignificant for Wordsworth's
mental development or sentimentalizing his attitude toward Annette
and Caroline.[14]

The one poem in which Wordsworth addresses Caroline as a "dear
Girl" ("It is a Beauteous Evening") is traditionally viewed as a beautiful
utterance of love and generosity on the part of the speaker and an affir-
mation of the child's unconscious participation in the spiritual life. According to Moorman, the poem vindicates Wordsworth as a father to
Caroline:

> The sonnet indeed shows that he was by no means indifferent to his lively lit-
> tle French daughter. He had evidently hoped to find in her some repetition of
> his own and Dorothy's mystical ecstasies when brought into communion with
> Nature. He found it not, but his disappointment was tender and fatherly, as
> he listened to her screams of delight.

> (*Moorman* 1:564)

Moorman implies that Wordsworth uses imagery of natural tranquillity
and religious veneration to convey this harmonious vision:

> It is a beauteous Evening, calm and free;
> The holy time is quiet as a Nun
> Breathless with adoration; the broad sun
> Is sinking down in its tranquillity;
> The gentleness of heaven is on the Sea:
> Listen! the mighty Being is awake
> And doth with his eternal motion make
> A sound like thunder—everlastingly.
> Dear Child! dear Girl! that walkest with me here,
> If thou appear'st untouched by solemn thought,
> Thy nature is not therefore less divine:
> Thou liest in Abraham's bosom all the year;
> And worshipp'st at the Temple's inner shrine,
> God being with thee when we know it not.

It seems odd that in the sonnet identified as the only "personal" sonnet of the Calais group Wordsworth creates a sense of distance. Caroline is not referred to as a daughter but as the more general "Child" and "Girl." In other poems in which a particular woman is addressed, such as "Tintern Abbey," Wordsworth articulates the relationship clearly: "My dear, dear Sister" (122). Also, whereas in the other Calais sonnets the setting is identified either in the title or in the sonnet proper as Calais, in this poem the location is generalized as a seashore at sunset.

What do the vagueness and distancing accomplish here? Contrary to the traditional view, represented in this case by Moorman, I find that Wordsworth generalizes because he is evading his responsibilities to his illegitimate daughter Caroline. He uses conventional religious language to sanction his actions, and he finally places Caroline in the hands of God—a substitute for the father Wordsworth knows he will never be.

Stylistic details support this reading. The sonnet contains an unusually frequent recurrence of the verb *is* rather than active verbs with strong metrical stresses. This recurrence contributes to the mood of tranquillity, which in turn is punctuated by excited commands and apostrophes, the speaker's voice asserting itself in the scene and by its presence placing the auditor there also. The poem is composed of three main divisions: the first five lines describe the scene without reference to an auditor; the next three lines command the auditor to "Listen"; and the last six lines directly address the "Dear Child!" If we view the divisions from the perspective of sonnet form, we see the strongest break between lines 8 and 9, dividing octave and sestet. Line 8 is the only internal line ending in a period. This strong break is uncharacteristic of (although not unique in) Wordsworth's sonnet-writing practice, in which lines 8 and 9 are usually enjambed (as they are in the "Fair Star" sonnet) to give "a pervading sense of intense Unity" (*LY* 2:652–53) and to defeat the traditional expectation of a break. But the strong break here divides the child from the divinity of the scene created in the octave. The child is presumably untouched by the "solemn thought" of either the speaker or the "mighty Being" presiding over the world.

From this sonnet we know very little of the child addressed in line 9 other than that she appears to be untouched by the spiritual beauty of nature. Although we do not learn much more about Caroline from Dorothy's journal, we picture her as a lively child, responding to the vivid beauty of the sea: "It was also beautiful on the calm hot night to see the little Boats row out of harbour with wings of fire and the sail boats with the fiery track which they cut as they went along and which closed up after them with a hundred thousand sparkles balls shootings, and streams of glowworm light. Caroline was delighted" (153). Dorothy significantly uses a key Wordsworthian word, *delighted*, to suggest Caroline's vitality and responsiveness. In the sonnet, however, the girl is not delighted. Nor is she given any voice in the poem. Appropriating the authority of voice to himself, the speaker tells the girl who she is, where she lives, and what her limitations are.

Although the generic expectations of the sonnet per se would not prevent voice being granted to an addressed person, Wordsworth gives "It is a Beauteous Evening" some qualities of a dramatic monologue, in which the auditor, of course, is allowed no response. Arnold imagines a similar scene in "Dover Beach," a poem whose "Listen!" echoes the voice of Wordsworth's poem and whose speaker contemplates France from the English side of the Channel. Arnold, who seems to have taken his instruction from Wordsworth, is much more intrigued by the meditations of his own mind than by the inner life of the female auditor.

The main assertion Wordsworth's speaker makes about the addressed child occurs in the last three lines:

> Thou liest in Abraham's bosom all the year;
> And worshipp'st at the Temple's inner shrine,
> God being with thee when we know it not.

Now although Wordsworth, in numerous contexts, praises the language of the King James Bible as being a truly philosophical and universal paradigm for the English language, he never advocates the use of special terminology from the Bible or any other source.[15] An expression like "Abraham's bosom" is uncharacteristic of Wordsworth; it is the kind of prefabricated poetic diction that Wordsworth had condemned in the Appendix of the previous spring. Moreover, the phrase is ambiguous here at best. Although it occurs several times in the New Testament, the appearance and interpretation most commonly referred to is Luke 16:22, where the beggar Lazarus dies and is "carried by angels into Abraham's bosom," while the rich man is consigned to the torments of hell. In this context the beggar's fate is, of course, preferred, since he will enjoy the blessings of comfort and rest. But the beggar is dead. According to the *Interpreter's Dictionary*, "Abraham's bosom" is the "place where the good go at the moment of death," and Abraham himself is an eschatological figure.[16] Wordsworth, it seems, imagines the girl not just in God's or the patriarch's protection, but dead. Like his celebrated Lucy, she has no motion or force while she is lying in Abraham's bosom. Wordsworth not only disavows his paternity in this sonnet, but he also symbolically kills the child. In this sense the allusion to Abraham involves another ironic twist: Abraham was a father willing to sacrifice his child—from different motives, however.

In this symbolic sacrifice and in the very form of addressing the child, Wordsworth turns the historical Caroline into an abstraction. No longer existing for her own delight, she becomes enshrined in the poem that addresses her. She is not even given the power of thought, because in the last line where we might expect a repetition of the second person pronoun, the speaker proclaims, "God being with thee when *we* know it not." Although the "we" is ambiguous here, it does not seem to suggest a community of knowledge in which the girl shares. Rather, the "we" speaks for the authority of those who know, those who can be touched by thought.

The phrase "Abraham's bosom" introduces another interesting problem, since "bosom" suggests the nourishment and protection offered by the female. Phyllis Trible, in a study of Hebrew in the Jewish Bible, reveals that God is referred to as having both masculine and feminine qualities. Although God as male is sanctioned by the rhetoric of patriarchy, in the Bible "God is a woman, whose bosom (*hēq*) gives care and nourishment to Israel," as well as a stern God the father.[17] The phrase "Abraham's bosom" may be a remnant of the gender-mixing that Trible finds throughout the Bible.

Perhaps Wordsworth was attracted to such a phrase because the androgynous image suggests a comfort he could never give the child. The image he substitutes in place of a father combines both mother and father, a kind of millennial or heavenly image. Caroline's natural mother finds no place in this poem. In the sonnet, the girl's protector is not an earthly parent, and the girl's hopes are placed far away from the England to which Wordsworth longs to return. I do not mean to imply that Wordsworth was consciously trying to evade his paternal responsibility, but, rather, that his very strong sense of his responsibility led to a genuine internal struggle over Caroline. Furthermore, as we shall see in the following pages, Wordsworth maintained correspondence with Annette and Caroline, visited them in Paris, and gave them at least limited financial support. But in this sonnet he distances himself from his daughter's claims. In contrast, in Wordsworth's elegiac sonnet for his daughter Catharine (1808–12), "Surprized by Joy," there are no evasions: he acknowledges that she is "deep buried in a silent tomb" (3), but exclaims "how could I forget thee?" (6).

The easy religious resolution of this sonnet falters when we uncover the association of the religious phrases with death and confinement. Even the devout image of the nun (perhaps under a vow of silence, the "quiet time") suggests confinement and limitation, as Wordsworth himself recognized in "Nuns Fret Not." Although the restriction of nuns and hermits translates into a positive metaphor for sonnet-writing, in the context of Wordsworth's thoughts about Caroline the image of the breathless nun is chilling. It is at Caroline's expense that Wordsworth attains his freedom and tranquillity in "It is a Beauteous Evening." She has no choice. Wordsworth envisions, not a girl on the verge of discovering her sexuality, but a chaste, nun-like figure, a disembodied spirit placed by her father in an imaginary convent. Perhaps Charlotte Brontë was thinking of Wordsworth when, in *Shirley*, she had Caroline Helstone meditate on the circumscribed life of the "old maid" Miss Ainley: "'She allowed there was, and ever had been, little enjoyment in this world for her; and she looks, I suppose, to the bliss of the world to come. So do nuns—with their close cell, their iron lamp, their robe strait as a shroud, their bed narrow as a coffin.'"[18] As we shall see in later chapters, Wordsworth continues to be attracted to such images of spiritual confinement in relation to women.

When faced with his illegitimate child, Wordsworth falls back on conventional wisdom and language that releases him from responsibility. He imagines a future for Caroline and omits Annette Vallon. Any alternative solutions to the problem of his daughter would have been too complicated and too disruptive for him. Within the restrictions of the sonnet form, Wordsworth resolves his problem. Like the conventional lover-speaker of a Petrarchan sonnet, he objectifies his subject *in* the sonnet but also *out* of existence.[19] He thus finds solace in both convention and form.

Wordsworth wrote sonnets in Calais as a way of legitimizing his personal experiences while seeming to comment primarily on historical circumstances or general human relationships. The sonnets written in Calais reveal, not "remarkable detachment," but preoccupation with the personal circumstances he was trying to control. Although Wordsworth may have tried to submerge or disguise this private self, his sonnets are more revealing and powerful because he failed to do so.

THE WHITE-ROBED NEGRO

"On Sunday the 29th of August we left Calais at 12 o'clock in the morning, and landed at Dover at 1 on Monday the 30th. I was sick all the way. It was very pleasant to me when we were in harbour at Dover to breathe the fresh air, and to look up and see the stars among the Ropes of the vessel."[20] This is Dorothy Wordsworth's description of the return voyage she and William took after the month in Calais. Dorothy's journal, as we have seen, hints at the Wordsworths' personal anxieties of 1802 but does not prepare the reader for the range of topics in the sonnets. In particular, her description of the return crossing includes no mention of what is central in William's poetic record: their encounter with a black woman on the vessel, a woman, according to Wordsworth, who was expelled from France along with all others of her race. This poem was perhaps completed by 1 September 1802, a few days after the crossing.[21] In its earliest form, as published in the *Morning Post* on 11 February 1803, the sonnet is a protest against this latest outrage of the French government.[22]

If the poems written in Calais reveal the interrelationship of Wordsworth's personal and political anxieties, the sonnet describing his return voyage (revised repeatedly throughout his career) reveals that these anxieties remained with the poet for many years. In the return-voyage sonnet Wordsworth continues to focus on what he sees as the mystery of the woman, even when the political questions have come to seem more certain to him, following the abolition of slavery and the slave trade in Britain.

As far as I know, this sonnet is Wordsworth's most explicit treatment of a racial subject. Besides its specific reference to the plight of blacks in France, the poem is interesting because, as the polemical immediacy of 1802 passed, Wordsworth revised the image of the woman. Rather than reconstruct an image of a historical woman, Wordsworth relies more and more on conventions of race and gender, none of which explains what he sees as her mysterious otherness. The sonnet of 1802, entitled "The Banished Negroes," reads as follows:

> We had a fellow-Passenger that came
> From Calais with us, gaudy in array,
> A negro woman, like a Lady gay,
> Yet silent as a woman fearing blame;
> Dejected, downcast, meek, and more than tame:
> She sate, from notice turning not away,
> But on our proffer'd kindness still did lay
> A weight of languid speech, or at the same
> Was silent, motionless in eyes and face.
> She was a Negro Woman driv'n from France
> Rejected like all others of that race,
> Not one of whom may now find footing there;

> What is the meaning of this ordinance?
> Dishonour'd Despots, tell us if you dare.[23]

The sonnet falls into two sections, emphasizing stages in the speaker's thoughts. In the first nine lines, the speaker briefly describes the woman. Although he and, presumably, others on board try to elicit a response from her, she remains an enigma to the speaker, with her gaudy dress contrasting with her dejected demeanor. The repetition in line 10—"She was a Negro Woman"—marks the end of the speaker's attempt to know or understand her and the beginning of his mention of her political circumstances as a refugee.

The ordinance that Wordsworth refers to was a French statute of 2 July 1802 regarding the status of "aucun noir, mulâtre, ou autres gens de couleur, de l'un et de l'autre sexe" (any black, mulatto, or other persons of color, of either sex). The ordinance effectively forbade all people of color from entering the continental territories of France, and stated that any people of color currently residing there who did not have government approval would be expelled. A note refers specifically to sending these people to San Domingo, where Napoleon had reinstituted slavery in the summer of 1802, reversing the Convention's abolition of slavery in 1794. As if making explicit the racial fears behind the decree, there is also a clause forbidding intermarriage between whites and people of color.[24] The ordinance, however, does not call for the expulsion of all people of color from France, as Wordsworth suggests, although it certainly makes it difficult for them to remain. It is not clear whether Wordsworth misunderstood the ordinance or whether he deliberately exaggerated or dramatized its effect. For Wordsworth, these racist decrees, along with press reports of the events in San Domingo, particularly regarding Napoleon's betrayal of Toussaint L'Ouverture, were further expressions of despotic rule.[25] Also, considering the faith he had once placed in France, these assaults on human dignity would have been particularly appalling to Wordsworth and would perhaps have served as a reminder of the gulf between 1792 and 1802.

Wordsworth's polemical impulse in this sonnet, I believe, allowed him to focus his thoughts outward on the plight of the blacks and away from the immediate pressures of his own situation on the return from Calais and from his French family. Perhaps this is why he misinterprets the decree: to make his own separation more final, to make the passage back across the Channel signify a passage in his own life. Public indignation, in that case, might serve to contain his still unresolved conflicts. In fact, in a brief reference, Alan Liu suggests that the African woman "is a shadow version . . . of *Veuve*-Annette. Aeneas-like in 1802, the poet drives dead east over Westminster Bridge to meet the shadow of his own Dido. Only after burying her in mind can he then return to Mary, his fated Bride, and to London, his Rome."[26] With Caroline in the bosom of Abraham and the shadow version of Annette buried, perhaps the poet could make the transition to a new life. In order to move in that direction, Wordsworth places blame squarely on the "Despots" who have caused the woman's suffering, finding some solace, perhaps, in a situation that seems so much more clear-cut than his own circumstances. The communal "We" of the opening line may simply include Dorothy Wordsworth, but it could stand for the majority of English people on the vessel, as opposed to the French endorsers of tyranny. As if to heighten the contrast between England and France at all costs, Wordsworth ignores England's ignominious treatment of blacks, including the fact that by the 1790s his country was responsible for over half of the African slave trade.[27]

The title, "The Banished Negroes," deflects attention from the woman who originally inspired the piece and focuses on the larger political context of exile and dispossession. According to Mary Moorman, on 29 January 1803, an anonymous editorial paragraph (perhaps written by Coleridge) appeared in the *Morning Post*, proclaiming that a "dozen Sonnets of a Political nature, which are not only written by one of the first Poets of the age, but are among his best productions," would be published. "Each forms a little Political Essay, on some recent proceeding" (quoted in *Moorman* 1:571). In "The Banished Negroes," the presence of the Negro woman on the boat from Calais seems outwardly to be the occasion for Wordsworth's protest against the ordinance. As such, the poem fits well into the sonnet series, with an emphasis on general protest and the plight of people of color in France. Wordsworth also published the poem in the context of the British debate over abolition of the slave trade and in the context of the capture and imprisonment of Toussaint L'Ouverture.[28]

But Wordsworth could not rest with this public stance or with this polemical intention. When the more immediate polemical impulse had subsided, it seems, Wordsworth returned to what he had abandoned in 1802: his questions about the woman's identity and meaning. To me, this further suggests that she is identified with Annette Vallon and with Wordsworth's continuing attempts to come to terms with his past. Wordsworth revised the poem in 1820, 1827, 1836, 1838, 1840, 1843, and then finally in 1845, when he made substantial changes. No longer entitled "The Banished Negroes," the sonnet now commemorates the day on which it was perhaps completed:

SEPTEMBER 1, 1802

Among the capricious acts of tyranny that disgraced those times, was the chasing of all Negroes from France by decree of the government: we had a Fellow-passenger who was one of the expelled.

> We had a female Passenger who came
> From Calais with us, spotless in array,—
> A white-robed Negro, like a lady gay,
> Yet downcast as a woman fearing blame;
> Meek, destitute, as seemed, of hope or aim
> She sate, from notice turning not away,
> But on all proffered intercourse did lay
> A weight of languid speech, or to the same
> No sign of answer made by word or face:
> Yet still her eyes retained their tropic fire,
> That burning independent of the mind,
> Joined with the lustre of her rich attire
> To mock the Outcast—O ye Heavens, be kind!
> And feel, thou Earth, for this afflicted Race!

(*PW* 3:113–14)

The introduction of the headnote in the 1827 revision paradoxically both displaces the historical immediacy of the original and makes it more of an official history of "those times," now seen from the perspective of years gone by. The preface acts as a frame for the story that follows, setting the context but also allowing for the meditation on the woman. Perhaps the "scanty plot" of the sonnet's ground could not contain a focus both on the ordinance and on the woman.

In the revised scene, the Negro woman becomes the center of attention for the speaker. Wordsworth wants to interpret and possess what he sees as the woman's mystery, suggested by a series of unresolved oppositions: silence and speech, dark skin against white robes and fiery eyes, destitution and rich attire. Because he sees her as a symbol of what he does not understand, the poet sets the woman apart from the travelers and invests her with mystery. When the speaker cannot interpret her lustrous clothes and burning eyes, he ends the poem abruptly with a general and generic prayer: "O ye Heavens, be kind! / And feel, thou Earth, for this afflicted Race!" The prayer takes the place of the political protest and the outrage of the earlier version. Although, as we have seen in "It is a Beauteous Evening," Wordsworth sometimes relies on formulaic religious expressions when he can resolve a human problem in no other way, in this case the religious tone may be connected to the abolitionist tradition in which questions of race and religion were mixed.[29]

In 1827 and in the final revision, Wordsworth's presentation of both race and gender seems more general and formulaic. The "fellow" passenger becomes a "female" passenger, simultaneously highlighting her sex and distancing her from the other passengers. Preconceptions about gender determine explicit comments (such as "downcast as a woman fearing blame"), yet the woman seems to frustrate any attempt to categorize her or even to sympathize with her. This woman is neither the "lady gay" of poetic traditions (including sonnet traditions) nor the archetypal abandoned woman, who laments her state or who is pathetic in her passivity. Wordsworth's "white-robed Negro" does not turn away in shyness or shame, but returns the gaze of the other travelers. She refuses to be either the receptacle for the speaker's mystery and darkness or merely the object of his gaze.

The fellow-passenger of the earlier versions is curtly described as "gaudy," but this woman seems regal in her spotless white robes. Wordsworth implies that although she has been cast out of France as a refugee, she maintains a true nobility. In fact, she may have been someone who had attained a comfortable status in France, as many people of color had at the end of the eighteenth century (which makes her expulsion a dispossession of property as well).[30]

Wordsworth's presentation of the woman to some extent reflects the colonialist mentality shared by much abolitionist writing, including poems by Hannah More, Anne Yearsley, and James Montgomery.[31] His dramatization of the woman as a regal figure with fiery eyes evokes the European stereotype of the noble savage, whose innocence and emotionalism contrast with Western sophistication and rationality. This view is made more plausible by Wordsworth's description of the fire in her eyes burning "independent of the mind." The use of "fiery" also suggests the sexual dimension of the stereotype,[32] implicit in Wordsworth's substitution of "proffered intercourse" for "proffer'd kindness."[33]

Yet Wordsworth's "white-robed Negro" resists being exploited by conventional categories and patronizing attitudes. She is not a mere childlike victim: she does not play the role of the oppressed figure grateful for any show of kindness. Instead, she answers all queries with "A weight of languid speech" or "No sign of answer made by word or face." Her silence seems to be a sign of strength rather than weakness: she re-

fuses to enter into a discourse that does not fully recognize her humanity. Unlike Wordsworth's Lucy, who is deprived of all motion and force,
or his Emily Norton, who, as we shall see, is silenced by the narrator as
well as by her father and her brother in *The White Doe of Rylstone*,
Wordsworth's "white-robed Negro" *chooses* silence as her form of expression. Nor does the black woman become a vehicle for the poet's or
the reader's consolation, as is often the case with Wordsworth's silently
suffering women. We can see that Wordsworth's response to the woman
is deeply ambiguous and ambivalent, for in the representation of the
"white-robed Negro" we find the conventional image in conflict with a
more transforming vision of the Negro woman. Wordsworth has created a figure who will not be shaped or contained by the poet's desire,
who will not become a screen on which the poet projects his identity.

Significantly, Wordsworth's tribute to Toussaint L'Ouverture (which
in all versions from the *Morning Post* on was published directly before
the sonnet about the black woman) does not reveal such a conflict or
such fascination with *his* mystery; rather, he is compared with the forces
of nature and the spirit of liberty. The sonnet to Toussaint follows in the
tradition of Milton's political sonnets, in which the poet pays tribute to
(male) heroism and public achievement through a portrait of a known
figure. But the unknown Negro woman embodies mysteries of both race
and sex for the poet, perhaps because for Wordsworth, sexuality and
gender are even more volatile categories than race or class.

It is possible that Wordsworth's conception of the "white-robed Negro" was influenced by Marie-Guillemine Benoist's *Portrait of a Negress*
(fig. 3). The painting was completed in 1800, purchased by the Crown
for the museum of contemporary French art at the Luxembourg (adjacent to the Louvre) in 1818, and transferred to the Louvre proper in
1826. It was made into a widely distributed engraving in 1829, which
Wordsworth could have seen.[34] Benoist's woman is spotlessly dressed in
a white gown and turban.

Wordsworth did not add the expression "white-robed" until 1845, so
it is possible that if he did see the painting, it was not until his trip to Paris
in 1837. I think it more likely, however, that he may have seen it in 1820.
In fact, Mary Wordsworth recorded in her unpublished journal that on
30 September 1820, the Wordsworths' large traveling party ended their
European tour with a month in Paris. Two days after their arrival in Paris,
"Mary met Annette for the first time 'in the Louvre at one o'clock.'"[35]
The significance of the meeting with Annette Vallon could have led
Wordsworth to link the painting to his 1802 poem, written on the

Figure 3.   *Portrait of a Negress*. Painting by Marie-Guillemine Benoist. 1800.
By permission of the Musée du Louvre, Paris.

occasion of his earlier visit to his former lover. Wordsworth's additions
to the poem in 1827 could have been influenced by this painting: the emphasis on the woman's sad (not fiery) eyes and her silent dignity, as well
as the startlingly beautiful contrast between her darkness and the white-
ness of her robes. Even if there was no direct influence, the intertextual
relationship between the poem and the painting is fascinating.

Wordsworth's later poetry seems generally to be more pictorial than the work of his best-known decade (1797–1807), and the revisions of this sonnet perhaps reveal his thinking in visual images. Hugh Honour points out that by the 1820s the educated public was quite accustomed to seeing both portraits of black historical figures and, more commonly, *études* or studies of anonymous blacks. Wordsworth would have had access to private artworks in this tradition, including Sir Joshua Reynolds's sympathetic *Study of a Black Man* (1770), which had been acquired by his friend and patron Sir George Beaumont in 1796.[36] But Benoist's portrait seems more relevant than any other print or painting to Wordsworth's re-vision of this sonnet. Wordsworth, I think, would have been moved by Benoist's interest in the individual subject, and perhaps would have been sensitive to the political implications of a portrait of a black woman first displayed in Paris in 1800.[37]

When Benoist first exhibited her painting at the Salon in 1800, it was compared in design to the style of her teacher Jacques-Louis David; it was also criticized by a racist reviewer as a beautifully executed painting of an ugly subject. This position may reveal sexist disgust at a woman's participation in "the act of painting [which, according to Honour] necessitated a kind of intimacy that was, perhaps, felt unseemly by male dominated white society." But, as Honour points out, the painting not only reveals the beauty of the subject but also the great affinity and responsiveness of the artist for her subject's humanity and dignity. Honour suggests that the subject may have been a servant brought to France from the Antilles, noting that the white turban reveals that the woman was not a slave.[38] Conceived during the years between 1794 and 1802, years in which slavery had been abolished and then reinstated, the painting opens itself to several possibilities of interpretation. Benoist's own affinity with this woman as a woman can be seen in the context of feminist discourse at the time, which compared the restrictions on European women to the oppression of African slaves.[39] Benoist does not resist the identification with her subject, but uses the political iconography (of the one bare breast as a symbol of liberty) to create a deeply intimate portrait.

Whereas the viewer of Benoist's painting feels an intimacy with the subject, the reader of Wordsworth's sonnet remains at a distance. Relying on conventional language and imagery, Wordsworth creates this distance, perhaps intentionally, to make what he regards as a universal statement about the plight of Africans. Wordsworth wants to understand the "white-robed Negro" he has created, but he cannot reconcile his conflicting visions of her, perhaps intensified by her connection to the

mysteries of his own past. In no version of the sonnet is the burden of the
mystery lifted: the poet and his readers are left with the weight of silence.

What is most paradoxical about the sonnet is that Wordsworth does
in fact identify with the woman. He questions her the way he questions
the leech-gatherer, as if to say, "Explain yourself. Tell me how you live
with your loss, with your sadness." Wordsworth creates more than a fiction of his own sense of mystery: he looks into the woman's eyes and on
some level sees a part of himself as well as the shadow of Annette. In
1802 and continuing his efforts over the years, he tries to transcend
France, wanting, like Dorothy, to see "the stars among the Ropes of the
vessel," but he is pulled back to the deck of the boat. Mary Jacobus
argues that in *The Prelude* Wordsworth's "ideology of transcendence"
requires silence on material conditions of society such as the blights of
slavery and colonialism.[40] The various incarnations of "The Banished
Negroes" reveal just how weighty that silence could be.

CHAPTER FOUR

Impassioned Wives and Consecrated Maids

"Laodamia," The White Doe of Rylstone, *and* The Excursion

I have but a little space on this private side of the sheet to
sigh for thee and tell thee, that I am giddy at the thought of
seeing thee once more, to tell thee also that those parts of my
day are in my thoughts a thanksgiving to God for having
blessed an unworthy Creature as I am with such a treasure,
as thy gentle, thy loving, thy faithful[,] thy pure spirit; for
having bound us by the sacred bond of husband and wife,
and for having bound us still more closely together by those
sweet darlings whose images pass and repass across my mind
all day long like the clouds in the firmament.

William to Mary, 19 August 1810

In Wordsworth's revisions of "The Banished Negroes" we have seen the
poet's continued fascination with the Negro woman. Wordsworth's letters throughout his middle and later years demonstrate that, contrary to
the more accepted notion that in his conservative turn Wordsworth for-
got or resolved the questions raised by his experiences in the 1790s, in
fact they troubled him throughout his life. In a letter from 30 March
1835, for instance, Wordsworth tells his correspondent that "the scenes
that I witnessed during the earlier years of the French Revolution when
I was resident in France, come back on me with appalling violence" (*LY*
3:39). Another correspondent, Thomas Colley Grattan, reports in 1828:
"I remarked Wordsworth's very imperfect knowledge of French, and it
was then that he accounted first by telling me that five and twenty years
previously he understood and spoke it well, but that his abhorrence of
the Revolutionary excesses made him resolve if possible to forget the language altogether; and that for a long time he had not read or spoken a

word of it" (ed. note, *LY* 1:616). This reported comment is particularly interesting if we recall that in the ninth book of *The Prelude* Wordsworth claims that he originally went to France, "Led thither chiefly by a personal wish / To speak the language more familiarly" (1805 version, 36–37). In this chapter I shall demonstrate that in having once learned the language and lived through the revolutionary years, Wordsworth could not completely forget his French experiences, no matter how hard he tried. His poetry of the second decade of the century reveals that his fear of rebellion against authority of any kind (political, religious, familial) was shaped by the memory of revolutionary excesses.

It might seem strange to argue that in his middle and later years Wordsworth was still reliving this dimension of his past. By now, according to one myth, Wordsworth was already the stodgy and smug conservative of Rydal Mount, the Distributor of Stamps for Westmorland and part of Cumberland, soon to be lamented as an apostate by Shelley and other young radicals. But Wordsworth's essential conservatism, to which he returned in the 1790s before the composition of the *Lyrical Ballads*, led him to think about the meaning of instability and rebellion in both the political and the private sphere.[1] Although Wordsworth's distrust of revolutionary violence and uncontrolled passion was well established by 1814, the poet was still troubled by conflicts of passion and rebellion entangling his public and private lives.

As David Erdman indicates in "Wordsworth as Heartsworth," the story of the Solitary in *The Excursion* provides another example of the inseparability of Wordsworth's "French love and French politics."[2] We recall that the Solitary is disillusioned both by the loss of his family and by the loss of his ideals in the Revolution. He is held up as a negative example in that poem—as someone who can neither forget the language of the past nor reconcile himself to that of the present. In *The Excursion* Wordsworth wants to distance himself from the attitudes of the Solitary, in much the same way that he rejects the speculative revolutionary Rivers in *The Borderers*, the play he wrote in the 1790s as he worked through the events in France.

Wordsworth's presentation of the female characters in poems of his middle period perhaps reveals even more of his preoccupation with the consequences of rebellion. In both "Laodamia" and *The White Doe* Wordsworth focuses on two female characters and their very different responses to tragic loss. What is interesting about both poems is that Wordsworth centers the tension between rebellion and submission on these women characters because he finds them and their circumstances not only interesting but close to his own life and to his experience of loss. He does not create these female characters simply to objectify them; he feels their dilemmas deeply. I shall conclude this chapter by suggesting that Wordsworth resolves the tensions inherent in these poems with a more accommodating and pious vision of consolation in *The Excursion*.

"LAODAMIA"

WORDSWORTH IN 1814

According to most readings of "Laodamia," Wordsworth condemns the excessive passion and frustrated mourning of the eponymous Laodamia, who cannot accept the death of her husband Protesilaus, the first Greek killed on the shores of Troy. Recently scholars have placed the poem in the context of William and Mary Wordsworth's protracted grief over the loss in 1812 of two of their children, Catharine and Thomas, within six months of each other. In "The Poetry of Familiarity," Donald H. Reiman suggests that Wordsworth may identify with Protesilaus and may be expressing "resentment toward his wife for his own feelings of sexual and creative inadequacy" in the face of devastating loss.[3] Reiman's suggestion is provocative but not entirely convincing, primarily because it neglects evidence of Wordsworth's strong, if uncomfortable, identification with Laodamia, the passionate, rebellious woman who cannot or will not subdue her will. Although Wordsworth overtly favors the heroic and stoical position of Protesilaus, who returns to earth for three hours to exhort his wife to look toward eternity, he has trouble condemning Laodamia. In an early version of the ending, the narrator urges the reader to "judge her gently who so deeply loved." Only after years of tinkering with the ending does Wordsworth have the narrator reach the conclusion in 1845 that Laodamia perished "as for a wilful crime, / By the just Gods whom no weak pity moved" (159–60).[4] Textual and biographical history, as well as Wordsworth's interpretation of classical sources—the sixth book of the *Aeneid*, Ovid's *Heroides*, and Euripides' *Iphigenia in Aulis*[5]—reveal a poet much more uncertain over the problems of gender, passion, and rebellion. Not surprisingly, in dictating notes on his poetry to Isabella Fenwick in 1843, Wordsworth claimed that "Laodamia" gave him "more trouble" than anything of similar length he ever wrote (*PW* 2:518–19).

The Cornell edition reveals that this "trouble" extended well beyond the composition of "Laodamia" in 1814 and its first publication in the 1815 volume. As we have seen with "The Banished Negroes,"

Wordsworth was an inveterate reviser of his poetry; the changes in "Laodamia" reveal his ambivalence toward Laodamia and her rebelliousness and concerning the moral stance he should take as judge of her actions. He revised the poem in 1820, 1827, 1832, 1836, 1840, 1843, 1845, and finally in 1849, the year before his death. Although many of the changes are incidental, the most significant ones focus on the question of judgment.

The year 1814 brought to the fore many intersecting conflicts involving Wordsworth's private and political concerns. Wordsworth's plans to marry Mary Hutchinson in 1802 had been complicated by his obligations to Annette Vallon and Caroline; now, in the summer of 1814, his life was once again ruffled by letters from France. Wordsworth makes no explicit mention of these letters. As was often the case, Dorothy assumed responsibility as family correspondent and mediator. From Annette's letter to Dorothy the Wordsworths learned that Caroline was engaged to be married. French law required the father's consent to the marriage. That was no problem. But Caroline apparently felt a strong attachment to her father's family and requested that her aunt Dorothy attend the ceremony. This would have been possible, since political changes had once again opened up travel between France and England. In the spring of 1814 an agreement had been signed between the allies and the French, and Napoleon was sent to Elba. But even though the political coast was clear, Dorothy's letters reveal continued uncertainty about such a trip to France after twelve years. Dorothy procrastinated long enough for the wedding to be put off from October 1814 to April 1815; meanwhile, Napoleon escaped from Elba and returned to France in March 1815. Following Waterloo, the wedding was rescheduled for August 1815, in the hope that Dorothy could be present. But Dorothy could not bring herself to decide, and Caroline was finally married in February 1816 with no members of her father's family present.[6]

This chronology illustrates how interwoven were the Wordsworths' lives with historical events. It also reveals a continued anxiety over William's French family. Anything that was so upsetting to Dorothy and to other members of the household must have affected William, who after all had a larger part to play in the little drama than his silence would indicate. While his choice of a universalizing classical subject in "Laodamia" might at first glance seem to indicate that Wordsworth had distanced himself from the immediate conflict, I see his choice of subject as directly related to the issues of passion and rebellion that the letters from France once again brought up. I am not saying that Wordsworth felt his apparently fleeting passion for Annette Vallon reawakened after more than twenty years; certainly the recently discovered letters between William and Mary Wordsworth attest to the poet's unembarrassed passion for his wife.[7]

But once again the human consequences of Wordsworth's earlier, illicit passion arise in the figure of Caroline, the child whom he had probably seen only once since her birth in 1792, when he wrote the sonnet ("It is a Beauteous Evening") consigning her to the protection of her heavenly Father. Now, in the face of another crisis involving his French daughter, Wordsworth turns not to the sonnet form but to another source of stability and delight: Greek and Latin literature. Wordsworth had returned to the classics (many of which he had first studied at Hawkshead Grammar School) in the early years of the nineteenth century, but it was not until around 1814 that he began to write explicitly on classical subjects. Geoffrey Hartman has argued that Wordsworth's return to the classics parallels his return to earlier scenes in his own life in the familiar works of the Great Decade, such as *The Prelude* and "Tintern Abbey," to reflect on his present life and circumstances.[8]

Wordsworth had been attracted to the republican themes of Milton's sonnets, but he had used the Miltonic sonnet in 1802 primarily to contain and structure his own experience. His imagination of the classics in 1814, however, seems to involve a passionate feeling for classical themes and characters rather than a desire to appropriate formal structures. In writing "Laodamia," Wordsworth was interested in the characters of Laodamia and Protesilaus, in their points of view and motivations, in the implications of their tragedy of unfulfillment, and in the various myths of their lives. In a sense, these concerns brought the classical story closer to his own life, rather than distancing it.

In the plight of Laodamia, I think, Wordsworth recognized his own dilemma as a man who had known rebellion and had struggled to submit to various personal and political losses and been forced to face the consequences of his actions.[9] And at the very time Wordsworth wrote the poem, his household was disrupted by the oddly intertwined fates of Napoleon and Caroline, illegitimate ruler and illegitimate daughter. Laodamia's "rebellious passion" (74) was not foreign to the man who was at war with himself and his country in the 1790s, or who struggled to accept with resignation the deaths of his brother in 1805 and his children in 1812. In 1930 Herbert Read suggested that Wordsworth's "memory of his own immoderate passion still preyed on his mind" and that "the story of Laodamia was not felt objectively enough, for it was

confused with his own mental history." But whereas Read implied that
an author should (or could) be "objective" and saw Wordsworth's "confusion" as an indication of "the gradual decay of Wordsworth's poetic
powers," I see the tensions between past and present, public and private,
as revelatory and enriching.[10]

JUDGE HER GENTLY

To argue for Wordsworth's identification with Laodamia opposes the
view of Wordsworth as a sublimely egotistical poet who could not empathize with a female character. Certainly Wordsworth's poetry is filled
with women who become abstractions or emblems of someone else's
consolation: Caroline in "It is a Beauteous Evening," Margaret in "The
Ruined Cottage," or the silent but apparently obedient sister in several
scenes of instruction. But, once again, the characterization of Wordsworth as a poet who appropriates the feminine for his own poetic im-
perialism simply does not do justice to the complexity of a character like
Laodamia or to Wordsworth's own passionate and empathic response
to her fate. Such a picture of Wordsworth, in fact, does not accurately
represent the poet beyond the Great Decade, if it is even accurate for that
period. "Laodamia," a central poem of Wordsworth's middle period, is
a dramatic example of Wordsworth's ability to empathize across gender
lines. Even the choice of a dialogue, in which the female character
emerges from the silence of women in other poems, reveals a new attempt to enter into Laodamia's thoughts and feel her passion:

> "Supreme of Heroes—bravest, noblest, best!
> Thy matchless courage I bewail no more,
> That then, when tens of thousands were deprest
> By doubt, propelled thee to the fatal shore:
> Thou found'st—and I forgive thee—here thou art—
> A nobler counselor than my poor heart.
>
> But thou, though capable of sternest deed,
> Wert kind as resolute, and good as brave;
> And he, whose power restores thee, hath decreed
> That thou shouldst cheat the malice of the grave;
> Redundant are thy locks, thy lips as fair
> As when their breath enriched Thessalian air.["]
>   (49–60)

As is evident in this passage, Wordsworth skillfully achieves an intimate
yet formal tone in "Laodamia," combining such lines as "I forgive thee—
here thou art" and the Miltonic image of redundant locks.

Why does Wordsworth feel so strongly for this character? Laodamia's tragic resistance to the consolations of religion and the afterlife at-
tracts Wordsworth more than the un-Wordsworthian heroism of Protesilaus because he himself has known the power of the passions that have
driven Laodamia to despair—both the passions associated with his experiences in France and those of his mourning for his brother and children. Of the two characters, it is the woman who feels and expresses her
love and her loss most intensely and humanly. Protesilaus, a happy spirit
in Wordsworth's poem, speaks with a formality and smugness that is
broken only when he directly explains his choice and laments his loss:

> ["]The wish'd-for wind was given:—I then revolved
> Our future course, upon the silent sea;
> And, if no worthier led the way, resolved
> That, of a thousand vessels, mine should be
> The foremost prow in pressing to the strand,—
> Mine the first blood that tinged the Trojan sand.
>
> Yet bitter, oft-times bitter, was the pang
> When of thy loss I thought, beloved Wife;
> On thee too fondly did my memory hang,
> And on the joys we shared in mortal life,—
> The paths which we had trod—these fountains—flowers;
> My new-planned Cities, and unfinished Towers.
>
> . . . .
>
> And thou, though strong in love, art all too weak
> In reason, in self-government too slow;
> I counsel thee by fortitude to seek
> Our blest re-union in the shades below.
> The invisible world with thee hath sympathized;
> Be thy affections raised and solemnized.["]
>   (121–32, 139–44)

When Protesilaus remembers his life and speaks directly of his love,
Wordsworth has him repeat phrases to reveal his emotion ("Yet bitter,
oft-times bitter"), but in the later stanza he falls into his characteristic
preachy and abstract mode. Laodamia, however, typically speaks what
Wordsworth at an earlier time would have called "the genuine language of passion" (*PrW* 1:160), animated not by abstractions but by
bold figures:

> ["]The Gods to us are merciful—and they
> Yet further may relent: for mightier far
> Than strength of nerve and sinew, or the sway
> Of magic potent over sun and star

Is love, though oft to agony distrest,
And though his favourite seat be feeble Woman's breast.["]
                                                                (85–90)

Laodamia's self-denigrating allusion to "feeble Woman's breast" does
not cancel the way she embodies her passion in language, from the nerves
and sinews of the body to the sun and stars of the universe. The Appendix on poetic diction (1802) could be a gloss on this passage, for like
Wordsworth's primitive poet, Laodamia uses "daring, and figurative"
(PrW 1:159) language.

It seems much more difficult for Wordsworth to distance himself from
this passionate woman than it is for him to praise the self-sacrificing character of Emily in The White Doe of Rylstone or Dorothy in The Prelude,
because he does not idealize Laodamia. In creating Emily as a consolatory figure Wordsworth eases the tension that might have arisen in the
narrative from the struggle between rebellion and obedience. The passive and obedient Emily, as we shall see, is preemptively silenced and denied any desire. But Laodamia is much more like her creator than
Wordsworth's angelic, self-sacrificing woman, and in her fate Wordsworth recognizes and laments his own. Because of this close identification, "Laodamia" is much more difficult for the poet to bring to closure
than The White Doe, a poem about a distanced saint. In condemning
Laodamia in later editions of the poem, Wordsworth is condemning a
part of himself.

The Miltonic rhetoric of rebellion and submission helps to clarify
these dynamics. As David Simpson has argued, Wordsworth's engagement with Milton goes well beyond Harold Bloom's Freudian model of
the struggle with a powerful father-figure. Simpson sees Wordsworth as
repeatedly reworking the drama of damnation and redemption, with
Adam caught between the figures of Satan and the Messiah in his struggles between passion and obedience.[11] Although both Milton and
Wordsworth overtly accept higher authority, neither of them comes to
that acceptance in an uncomplicated way. As Samuel Johnson noted with
characteristic disapproval, Milton had the "political notions" of "an ac-
rimonious and surly republican" at war with authority.[12] Wordsworth,
like Milton, feels the power of rebellion, yet he also knows he must submit to a higher order. In locating the rebellion within a female character in "Laodamia," Wordsworth aligns his presentation with Milton's
depiction of female rebellion in Eve. Both Milton and Wordsworth reveal ambivalence about these female characters: both poets give their

characters dignity, but they also undermine the legitimacy of their characters' rebellious positions. Eve, however, repents and is redeemed in Milton's Christian scheme, whereas Laodamia remains unrepentant and unredeemed. But when Laodamia is finally condemned, it is at great emotional cost to her creator, as Isabella Fenwick's note indicates (*PW* 2:518–19). In fact, in 1843 "Laodamia"—or, more specifically, the female character Laodamia—was still troubling the poet.

Unlike most of the women in Wordsworth's poetry, Laodamia is given a voice, even though the debate format gives Protesilaus the last word and more. Many of Wordsworth's women characters are turned into a memory or an idea that can finally be controlled by the mediation of the poet (Dorothy in "Tintern Abbey," Lucy in "Three Years She Grew," Margaret in "The Ruined Cottage"), but Laodamia remains an agent, not an object. As Protesilaus urges her to control her passion, Laodamia thinks of the various heroes who have defied death:

> ["]—Did not Hercules by force
> Wrest from the guardian Monster of the tomb
> Alcestis, a reanimated Corse,
> Given back to dwell on earth in beauty's bloom?
> Medea's spells dispersed the weight of years,
> And Aeson stood a Youth mid youthful peers.["]
>   (79–84)

Here Laodamia's questioning speech signals both yearning and rebellion. In the more typical Wordsworthian scene of instruction, such as "Tintern Abbey," the woman remains silent and the poet imagines her future fate. In "Laodamia" the woman refuses to submit to the lesson and suffers the consequences of that refusal: death. But, unlike other female characters, *she* has made the choice.

As late as the 1830s, the fate of Laodamia sparked lively debate in the Wordsworth family. In a letter to his brother Christopher Wordsworth and his nephews written in mid to late March 1830, Wordsworth says, "As first written the Heroine is dismissed to happiness in Elysium. To what purpose then the mission of Protesilaus. . . . at present she is placed among the unhappy Ghosts for disregard of the exhortation. Virgil also places her there—but compare the two passages and give *me* your opinion" (*LY* 2:215–16). In his note to the Cornell edition, Carl Ketcham mentions Benjamin Robert Haydon's claim that Mary Wordsworth urged her husband to alter the poem: "'Laodamia,' one of Wordsworth's finest things, his wife persuaded him had *too lenient a fate* for loving her husband so *absurdly*—at her petition he corrected the conclusion as it was first published, and made it as above" (530). Interestingly, Haydon saw the Wordsworths in London after their European tour of 1820, the occasion on which Mary Wordsworth met Annette Vallon for the first time. Was Laodamia, like the banished African woman, a shadow of Annette, the archetypal abandoned woman in Wordsworth's life? If so, the fate of Laodamia is all the more complicated.

Wordsworth, however, did not invent the punishment of death for Laodamia. In a note to the poem, he claims to have derived his inspiration from book 6 of the *Aeneid*, in which Virgil places Laodamia in the Fields of Mourning with other eternally unhappy lovers. Virgil's treatment of Laodamia and Wordsworth's allusion to it (*PW* 2:272n) have led several commentators to defend Wordsworth's revisions of the original plea to "judge her gently." But the Virgilian tone did not come naturally to Wordsworth, as his original plea makes clear. In his discontent, he anxiously searched other sources after finishing an early version of "Laodamia" in 1814. Mary Wordsworth describes William as writing a first draft very quickly and easily, but immediately (and uncharacteristically) returning to his books: "I doubt that he has done this so readily that he will not be contented till he has made himself ill with doing more, for he is reading and hunting among his books—for no *good purpose*, but do not name this."[13] The Cornell text shows in part the results of this hunting and of Wordsworth's struggle with recalcitrant material.

The poem opens with Laodamia praying to the "infernal Gods" (4) to bring back Protesilaus. Laodamia knows that her husband is dead, but, as we have seen, she also knows that others have been brought back from the dead, "Given back to dwell on earth in beauty's bloom" (82). In a manuscript version of the opening lines (found in Dove Cottage MS 3[r] Cornell edition, 363), Wordsworth presents Laodamia as desperate when her prayers do not immediately succeed:

> That rapture failing, the distracted Queen
> . . . .
> Knelt—and embraced the Statue of the God.

This manuscript version is even more explicit about the passion Laodamia feels for Protesilaus than later revisions are. I think this shows that one of the primary problems Wordsworth was dealing with at the time of the original composition involved Laodamia's frustrated eroticism. In later versions, Wordsworth emphasizes both her embodiment ("Her bosom heaves and spreads, her stature grows," 11)

and her attachment to Protesilaus's body ("Again that consumma-
tion she essayed," 26). But the manuscript opening is even more insistent, especially in the replacement of "impassioned" by the more drastic "distracted."

Wordsworth's original conception of Laodamia's frenzy seems to derive from Ovid's portrait of her in "Laodamia to Protesilaus" from the
Heroides, for here Laodamia's sexual passion for Protesilaus is most evident. In Ovid's text, Laodamia does not yet know that her husband is
dead; she writes anxiously to him, reminding him of various prophecies
and dangers. So attached is she to the physical presence of Protesilaus
that in his absence she gazes at a waxen image of him and "hold[s] it to
[her] heart in place of [her] real lord, and complain[s] to it, as if it could
speak."[14] Wordsworth's Laodamia displays a similar tense eroticism in
embracing the statue of the god. Wordsworth also reveals a dangerous
imbalance in this Ovidian Laodamia, but he does not seem to distinguish
between Ovid's comic portrayal of Laodamia embracing the waxen image and Virgil's more heroic stance.

When Laodamia's prayers are granted and Protesilaus returns, Laodamia makes the mistake of thinking that she looks on his "vital presence," his "corporeal mold" (16):

> Forth sprang the impassion'd Queen her Lord to clasp;
> Again that consummation she essayed;
> But unsubstantial Form eludes her grasp
> As often as that eager grasp was made.
> The Phantom parts—but parts to re-unite,
> And re-assume his place before her sight.
>
> (25–30)

When the spirit's form eludes her, Laodamia asks Protesilaus to "Confirm . . . the Vision with thy voice" (32), fearing that she has been tricked
by the gods. But Protesilaus lectures her on Jove's generosity and perfection, telling her that her "fidelity" and his "virtue" have been re-
warded. Protesilaus's words set up not only the assured tone of his speech
but also the gendered standards of behavior. Laodamia has been faithful; he has been strong. Protesilaus then recounts the Delphic oracle that
had "foretold / That the first Greek who touch'd the Trojan strand /
Should die" (43–45). Protesilaus sacrificed himself because "A generous
cause a Victim did demand" (46).

Laodamia can accept his heroism, but she constantly turns her
thoughts back to Protesilaus's physical presence, as Wordsworth emphasizes her sexuality:

> ["]Come, blooming Hero, place thee by my side!
> Give, on this well-known couch, one nuptial kiss
> To me, this day, a second time thy bride!"
>   (62–64)

Both the gods and Protesilaus chastise Laodamia for her excessive passion. The gods withdraw the illusion of life from Protesilaus's image, as if to remind Laodamia that she is speaking to a ghost. As a counterpoint to Laodamia's physical desire, Protesilaus urges her to control

> ["]Rebellious passion: for the Gods approve
> The depth, and not the tumult of the soul;
> The fervor—not the impotence of love.
> Thy transports moderate; and meekly mourn
> When I depart, for brief is my sojourn—"
>   (74–78)

Wordsworth's other poetry of this period, including *The White Doe* and *The Excursion*, echoes these sentiments: Emily Norton, as the positive example, banishes all rebellion from her mind and submits to her loss of home and family, whereas the Solitary and other rebellious figures peopling the landscape of *The Excursion* fail to submit and remain unhappy and alienated. But once again Wordsworth gives Laodamia a choice he denies to other female characters. Laodamia responds to Protesilaus's exhortations by arguing for the transforming strength of physical love, until finally Protesilaus silences her with the injunction "'Peace'" (91), and she speaks no more.

After Laodamia has been silenced, Protesilaus recounts the advantages of the Elysian Fields, but he also speaks to her more from his own masculine experience. At this point (beginning with line 109) Wordsworth's reading of Euripides' *Iphigenia in Aulis* becomes most evident. Protesilaus paraphrases lines from that play describing the Greek troops playing at "ignoble games and revelry" (112) while "the Fleet at Aulis lay enchained" (120).[15] Following the sacrifice of Iphigenia and the releasing of favorable winds, Protesilaus resolves that his will be "the first blood that tinged the Trojan sand" (126). Wordsworth has his Protesilaus follow in the spirit of Iphigenia, who does an about-face and decides in the course of Euripides' play to accept the sacrifice of herself for the sake of her people. Protesilaus remembers most strongly at this point what he has lost and is allowed, we recall, one very human, elegiac lament:

["]Yet bitter, oft-times bitter, was the pang
When of thy loss I thought, beloved Wife;
On thee too fondly did my memory hang,
And on the joys we shared in mortal life,—
The paths which we had trod—these fountains—flowers;
My new-planned Cities, and unfinished Towers.["]
                                                    (127–32)

But Protesilaus describes his choice in terms of heroic action; he was not willing to be accused of cowardice, so "'lofty thought, / In act embodied, my deliverance wrought'" (137–38).

This concept seems alien to Wordsworth's repeated claims in his theory and in his letters that he is interested in thought, not external action or bold gestures. Furthermore, this lofty activity is not a possibility for Laodamia as a woman: Protesilaus's realm is public, Laodamia's is private. Protesilaus can embody his thoughts in action, but Laodamia is called upon to embrace only the passive virtues of resignation and acceptance. Protesilaus, then, advocates for her a position that he himself has not had to endure.

Furthermore, when Protesilaus first described his action he referred to himself as "A self-devoted Chief—by Hector slain" (48). In sacrificing himself he fulfills himself. But when he exhorts Laodamia, he says,

["]Learn by a mortal yearning, to ascend
Towards a higher object:—Love was given,
Encouraged, sanctioned, chiefly for this end;
For this passion to excess was driven—
That self might be annulled . . . ["]
                                                    (145–49)

Laodamia must rid herself of all selfishness, even the remnants that have led Protesilaus to "a higher object." Unable to do that, she dies, not explicitly a suicide, but obviously as a result of her excessive passion. Not allowed to express herself through that passion, Laodamia, like many nineteenth-century fictional heroines, pays the ultimate price of lost selfhood: death. Nor does Laodamia face the prospect of redemption in the religious scheme of the poem.

In this loss of selfhood caused by the silencing and stifling of passion, Laodamia is a predecessor of such characters as George Eliot's Maggie Tulliver in *The Mill on the Floss* (1860), who is torn between duty and passion. Although Maggie, unlike Laodamia, chooses duty and all the

religious and social commitments called up by that word, in the eyes of
her society she has chosen too late. The morality of St. Ogg's cannot accept a woman who has acted on passion, and Maggie is finally subdued
by death. The narrator of *The Mill on the Floss* claims that

> The great problem of the shifting relation between passion and duty is
> clear to no man who is capable of apprehending it: the question whether the
> moment has come in which a man has fallen below the possibility of a re-
> nunciation that will carry any efficacy, and must accept the sway of a passion
> against which he had struggled as a trespass, is one for which we have no
> master-key that will fit all cases. . . . moral judgments must remain false and
> hollow, unless they are checked and enlightened by a perpetual reference to
> the special circumstances that mark the individual lot.[16]

Although Eliot withholds judgment, she resolves the novel with Maggie's death in the arms of her brother Tom—with her transcendence of
her earthly struggle. Their epitaph reads: "In their death they were not
divided." But in her life Maggie was hopelessly divided from Tom, and
she was also self-divided by the struggle between passion and duty. Although Eliot's narrator provides a large and compassionate context for
understanding Maggie, Eliot does not resolve Maggie's fate any more
hopefully than Wordsworth presents Laodamia's. Neither the male poet
nor the female novelist gets beyond the problem of representing female
desire as selfish and self-destructive.

As Carol Gilligan notes in *In A Different Voice*, Eliot's novel reveals
the difficulty inherent in a morality that gives a choice only between passion and duty and does not include the integrity of the self in questions
of duty.[17] Given a morality based on this opposition, the choice for Maggie, as for Laodamia, is between self and absolute self-sacrifice. Like Eliot
in *The Mill on the Floss*, Wordsworth—to his credit—in "Laodamia" is
reluctant to exercise moral judgment on a character bound by such a
constricted choice between passion and duty.

Although Wordsworth's first impulse was to mitigate Laodamia's
guilt, he later reached a more harsh conclusion. But his repeated changes
of the ending reveal his discomfort with the harsh condemnation that he
felt his sources and his moral stance called for. At first Wordsworth
claims that Laodamia died "without crime." In the 1827 version, she
died "not without the crime / Of lovers that in Reason's spite have
loved," and then in the 1840 version she died "from passion desperate
to a crime"; finally, in 1845, she was said to die "as for a [*alt* even as by
a] wilful crime."[18] Wordsworth's final version actually hedges the question, since the meaning of "as" is indeterminate. Wordsworth suggests

the possibility that Laodamia's action may have actually been outside her control, although her punishment is unchanged. In trying to disassociate himself from her rebellion, Wordsworth has a difficult time finding an acceptable stance.

FROM JUDGMENT TO ELEGY

The last eleven lines focus on the elegiac qualities of the story of Laodamia and Protesilaus ("mortal hopes defeated and o'erthrown," 165) and not on the condemnation of passion. This seems to be a way for Wordsworth to move from a judgmental stance toward reconciliation and consolation. In fact, Wordsworth told Isabella Fenwick that the original impulse for "Laodamia" came, not from the heroic image of Protesilaus as a Greek warrior, but from Pliny's description in his *Natural History* of the legendary trees growing out of Protesilaus's tomb, which wither when they grow high enough to see Troy, the scene of Protesilaus's destruction. Described as "A constant interchange of growth and blight!" the trees provide Wordsworth with a final elegiac image as well as with the germ of the poem.

"Laodamia" is not an elegy like "Lycidas," which traces the speaker's movement through the processes of grief, but a poem that dramatizes the failure to accept death and to come to terms with grief. In "Laodamia," Wordsworth focuses on one phase of the elegiac convention, the refusal to submit to the fact of death or the inability to accept the consolation of a spiritual realm. This is the phase represented by Urania, the mother and lover in Shelley's "Adonais," who begs her son to "Stay yet a while! speak to me once again; / Kiss me, so long but as a kiss may live" (stanza 26). As in "Laodamia," the refusal to accept death is linked to an erotic attachment. In both "Laodamia" and "Adonais" that refusal prevents what Freud would call "the work of mourning."[19] The relationship between frustrated eroticism and grieving, in fact, pervades the elegy form and related nineteenth-century portraits of abandoned and frustrated women, such as Tennyson's "Mariana."

Wordsworth does not confront Laodamia's frustrated eroticism per se but instead shifts the emphasis from her failure to a more universal elegy on lost desires, figured in the "knot of spiry trees" (169) in which individuals are intertwined with the history of "Ilium's walls" (172). But by ending on this elegiac note that had appeared at various points in the poem, Wordsworth actually intensifies the more vexing problems of sexuality and rebellious passion—the very problems that the renewed requests of his French family could have called to his mind during the composition of "Laodamia." Although he yearns for a consolation denied Laodamia, Wordsworth seems haunted by her ghost, who arises in the text as a disruptive and unwelcome presence, neither subdued nor consoled.

The restlessness of Laodamia in Wordsworth's text, I think, derives from Wordsworth's continued ambivalence about the consequences of his own passion and his difficulty in working through the processes of mourning, both for lost children and for lost ideals. Wordsworth's language at the end of "Laodamia" sounds familiar to readers of *The Prelude*, in which the poet laments the hopes lost in the aftermath of the French Revolution. In "Laodamia" the poet concludes:

> —Yet tears to human suffering are due;
> And mortal hopes defeated and o'erthrown
> Are mourned by man, and not by man alone,
> As fondly he believes.
>
> (164–67)

Wordsworth refers to the "knot of spiry trees" as an emblem not just of the fates of Laodamia and Protesilaus but also of his own fate in the Ilium of his memory: France. The intertwining branches of his emotional and political lives are also "A constant interchange of growth and blight," hope and disappointment.

Like the poet he considered his great predecessor, Wordsworth found it difficult to exorcise his own rebellious passions and their consequences. By choosing the debate format in "Laodamia," Wordsworth captures the kind of dialectical struggle that also animated Milton's imagination. As Hazlitt recognized in another work of Wordsworth's middle period and perhaps his most Miltonic ever, *The Excursion*, the dialogues "are soliloquies of the same character": Wordsworth's dramas are psychodramas of a mind that "preys upon itself."[20] In this view, the Wanderer's failure to console the Solitary and Protesilaus's failure to persuade Laodamia represent both the power of rebellion in Wordsworth's own mind and his need to subdue that rebellion and to believe in his own fictions.

But Hazlitt's view of the characters in *The Excursion* as reflections of Wordsworth's egotism does not adequately explain his engagement with Laodamia and her fate. In contrast to Wordsworth's other depictions of women, in Laodamia he creates a character who not only has desires but acts on them, as he himself has done. Because Laodamia's desire is seen as powerfully expressive and as a transgression against the religious and social order, Wordsworth is caught between the absolutes of judgment and sympathy, duty and passion, with no clear way to mediate between extremes. Whereas Protesilaus has no trouble exhorting his wife, the poet stages a more uncertain scene of instruction. Consolation came more easily for Wordsworth when he projected his hopes onto his silent sister in "Tintern Abbey." But when he is compelled to imagine a woman as more than a silent auditor without a history or a future of her own, she need not—and Laodamia does not—comply with his vision of her.

THE WHITE DOE OF RYLSTONE

If, in "Laodamia," Wordsworth has difficulty deciding the fate of his rebellious character, in *The White Doe of Rylstone* he creates a female character who submits to every injunction. Wordsworth implies that, because her final submission is to the will of God, Emily Norton is a martyr to a spiritual cause.[21] In fact Wordsworth encases the tale in a vague spirituality, described as "mystical wordiness" in Jeffrey's unrelenting review in October 1815.[22] Although I do not share Jeffrey's scathing assessment of *The White Doe* as "the very worst poem . . . imprinted in a quarto volume" (454), I find the poem troubling because its spirituality obscures a whole range of problems, including Wordsworth's ambivalent attitude toward rebellion and its consequences. Wordsworth presents the story of female self-sacrifice to resolve both political and familial discord, without seeing this kind of sacrifice as itself a problem. Wordsworth sympathizes with all of the qualities conventionally associated with the feminine in *The White Doe*—nonviolence, nurturing, beauty, spirituality; but these perspectives lead to renunciation and death. In earlier and later works the aesthetic of the beautiful is linked to community and acts of piety, but here it brings only isolation.

In retelling the story of the disastrous Norton uprising of 1569 against Queen Elizabeth, Wordsworth selects material from several sources and legends. In her recent introduction to the Cornell edition, Kristine Dugas recounts the compositional history of Wordsworth's poem from its beginnings in 1807 to its publication in 1815. Peter Manning demonstrates that Wordsworth's reluctance to publish the work has more to do with his ambivalence about the tale of revolution than with his worries about the poem's lack of action (a charge made by early readers).[23] But neither of these informative and compelling narratives considers the

implications of Wordsworth's feminization of the material, his creation
not only of the character of Emily Norton (found in neither the traditional ballad material from Percy's *Reliques* nor in the historical records)
but also of her connection to the legendary white doe who makes a
weekly pilgrimage to Bolton Priory after the failed rebellion.

Perhaps the most important source for this feminization was Thomas
Whitaker's *History and Antiquities of the Deanery of Craven*.[24] Whitaker
catalogues various versions of the Norton uprising and is especially intrigued by the legend of the doe: "This incident awakens the fancy. Shall
we say that the soul of one of the Nortons had taken up its abode in that
animal, and was condemned to do penance, for his transgressions against
'the lords' deere,' among their ashes? But for such a spirit the wild stag
would have been a fitter vehicle. Was it not, then, some fair and injured
female, whose name and history are forgotten?" (525). Wordsworth's
imagination seems to be stirred by this surmise: he gives a name and a
history to this fair female and has her sacrifice herself for the transgressions of the Norton men. Wordsworth's emphasis on this female character and on other questions related to gender lie at the heart of this work
which he considered so important to his image as a poet.

AN UNRECONSTRUCTED READING

How might a resisting reader of Wordsworth approach such a poem that
glorifies female martyrdom? She might argue that *The White Doe* is yet
another version of the patriarchal story in which a silenced daughter submits to the tyrannical law of the father, finally renouncing everything but
spiritual aspiration. According to this reading, *The White Doe* is an early
version of the familiar Victorian narrative of female self-sacrifice.

Much evidence supports this reading. Not only Emily but all of the
Norton sons are intimidated by their father, Richard Norton. When
Richard Norton agrees to join Percy and the other Catholic rebels against
the queen, his firstborn son, Francis (a Protestant like Emily), knows that
he cannot bear arms against the Protestant troops. But he dares not defy
his father. He says to himself, "'Might ever son *command* a sire, / The
act were justified to-day'" (455–56), but he does not act upon this
thought. He recognizes what he calls the "natural" bond between "Sire
and Sons" (475), but hints that more than a bond of sympathy holds the
sons to the father:

> ["]I to my Father knelt and prayed;
> And one, the pensive Marmaduke,

> Methought, was yielding inwardly,
> And would have laid his purpose by,
> But for a glance of his Father's eye,
> Which I myself could scarcely brook.["]
> (493–98)

Although Francis does refuse to fight, he will lose his life in honoring the final request of his father.

Exercising his authority, Norton orders Emily to embroider a banner for his battle against the Loyalists. Embroidering would have been regarded as a typical and an appropriate feminine activity, but the banner suggests more than an expression of Emily's femininity. In *The Subversive Stitch*, Rozsika Parker argues that through their embroidery women could express themselves—often subversively, in the design—even though they might silently comply with all expectations placed on them.[25] But because the design, the content of the banner, is forced on Emily, she is denied the use of needlework as a form of self-expression or subversion: there is no analogue to Adrienne Rich's Aunt Jennifer and her tigers here. Although a Protestant herself (she and her brother Francis having been taught this faith by their mother), Emily submits to the will of her father and as a dutiful daughter she embroiders images of a cross and the five wounds of Christ, symbols of Catholicism. The banner represents not only the father's religion, but also his symbol-making power, from which Emily is excluded. Her needlework—forced labor—marks her bondage to the father and his law. The banner, then, represents a religion in which she does not believe and a language she does not speak.

In his one instance of introspection, Richard Norton refuses to blame himself for Emily's suffering or for his family's destruction. Norton assuages his guilt by creating two scapegoats:

> ["]Her Brother was it who assailed
> Her tender spirit and prevailed.
> Her other Parent, too, whose head
> In the cold grave hath long been laid,
> From reason's earliest dawn beguiled
> The docile, unsuspecting Child:
> Far back—far back my mind must go
> To reach the well-spring of this woe![""]
> (885–92)

Confused in the face of doom, Norton blames the disobedient Francis and his late wife for corrupting Emily. To preserve his authority, Norton promotes an inflexible vision of the world in which everyone who does not comply with his ideology is an enemy. For Richard Norton, no negotiation, no compromise is possible.

Emily Norton silently complies with her father's law from the beginning, sewing the banner that represents her father's rule and his religion. Even Francis enforces her silence when he forbids her to plead with her father to give up his doomed cause: Francis's "injunction" (1064) "interdicted all debate" (1066). Wordsworth echoes Milton's "On his Blindness" here with the line, "*Her duty is to stand and wait*" (1070), but the allusion is unsettling. In his blindness Milton justifies the contemplative life as sanctioned by God. Emily, however, is browbeaten into resignation, since, as Francis says, she is "a woman, and thence weak" (535). Wordsworth modifies Milton's last line, "They also serve who only stand and wait," so that the emphasis is on female duty defined from a male perspective. Milton uses the plural pronoun "They" to identify *with* others who serve God; Wordsworth's narrator speaks *for* Emily in her isolation.

As a woman defined by male culture in terms of weakness, Emily has no voice in the world of power, the public arena of religious and political conflict that causes her loss and isolation. She gains spiritual power only when she accepts the complete loss of everything that would have been hers as a dependent of patriarchy. For Emily, there is no alternative between this dependency and renunciation.

But Emily's self-sacrificing spirituality might not be necessary in a world where she had a voice. Such perfect feminine spirituality leads inevitably to death. Emily's "passive stillness" (1090) is not the same as the celebrated "wise passiveness" of the poet, which eventually leads back to life and humanity.[26] The objection to this "passive stillness," in other words, is that in *The White Doe* and in other works Wordsworth associates a mute and numbing passivity primarily with women. Emily's fate is like that of Lucy, reduced to a "thing" in "A Slumber Did My Spirit Seal," or of Margaret in "The Ruined Cottage," whose suffering is redeemed only by the auditor's response to her tale, or of Caroline in "It is a Beauteous Evening," who is buried alive in the bosom of Abraham.

A RECONSTRUCTED READING

Although I find such a reading of *The White Doe* attractive, I think it does not tell the whole story. First of all, it does not account for Wordsworth's emphasis on consolation. While I do not endorse the pre-

vailing modern critical view of the poem's spirituality, as exemplified by
one reader's claim that "Emily subdues her own will to that of her father, and thus begins to imitate the act of transcendent *patientia* that was
the crucifixion of Christ,"[27] I want to understand Wordsworth's conception of feminine spirituality. Is there a way to share in Wordsworth's
spiritual reading of his own poem (amply provided in letters and commentaries) without overt Christian allegorizing and its emphasis on
complete renunciation?

The prefatory stanzas added in 1815 set *The White Doe* in the context of the Wordsworths' loss of their two children as well as the earlier
loss of William's brother John Wordsworth in a shipwreck.[28] The poet
suggests here and in his letters that the original impulse for the poem in
1807 was to write a spiritual tale of consolation, focusing on the peace
that Emily Norton found in accepting her loss as the will of God.
Wordsworth records in several sources—letters, references to attempted
poems, "Peele Castle"—the extent to which he felt the loss of his
brother.[29] Certainly the pattern of loss and consolation is a familiar
Wordsworthian story. But in earlier poems such as "Tintern Abbey" and
the "Intimations" ode the loss is figured in terms of the transition from
innocence to consciousness and sympathy with human suffering. In *The
White Doe* Wordsworth writes of a loss so great that only a complete
renunciation of earthly desires will heal the wound.

But whereas the body of the poem (the seven cantos) sanctions austere renunciation, the prefatory stanzas—written, it seems, in response
to the later loss of Catharine and Thomas—are more complicated. In
these stanzas Wordsworth emphasizes the domestic and familial context
of grieving, with allusions to his married life with Mary Wordsworth:

> In trellis'd shed with clustering roses gay,
> And, Mary! oft beside our blazing fire
> When years of wedded life were as a day
> Whose current answers to the heart's desire,
> Did we together read in Spenser's Lay
> How Una, sad of soul—in sad attire,
> The gentle Una, born of heavenly birth,
> To seek her Knight went wandering o'er the earth.
>
> Ah, then, Beloved! pleasing was the smart,
> And the tear precious in compassion shed
> For Her, who, pierced by sorrow's thrilling dart,
> Did meekly bear the pang unmerited;
> Meek as that emblem of her lowly heart

> The milk-white Lamb which in a line she led,—
> And faithful, loyal in her innocence,
> Like the brave Lion slain in her defence.

William and Mary, as depicted in this little domestic scene, a rather prim bower of bliss, share their "heart's desire" as well as their love of *The Faerie Queene*. Wordsworth focuses on their admiration for Una—her meekness, her innocence, her faith. Most important, Wordsworth admits that his reading of Una's suffering resulted in a pleasant pain and "tear precious." From the safe vantage of their domestic bower and as yet untouched by devastating grief, the couple can enjoy the fiction.

But when faced with devastating loss, "For us the stream of fiction ceased to flow, / For us the voice of melody was mute" (24–25). Only after some time does the poet describe being able to return to Spenser and to *The White Doe*, which had been completed seven years earlier. Once again, he and Mary can appreciate "griefs whose aery motion comes not near / The pangs that tempt the Spirit to rebel" (35–36). As in "Laodamia," Wordsworth rejects the temptation of "the Spirit to rebel," but also admits to its force. In *The White Doe* Wordsworth prevents this spiritual rebellion before it takes shape by modeling his female character upon the obedient Una.

But a problem arises in drawing a parallel between Una and Emily Norton. While it is true that Una suffers "the pang unmerited," she will finally be reconciled with her knight. Although Wordsworth interprets his own narrative in a positive way, Francis Norton forbids Emily to hope and will not let her try to change the course of events. She is not only silenced in terms of speech: she is even denied her own story. Speaking of *The White Doe*, the poet claims that

> This tragic Story cheared us; for it speaks
> Of female patience winning firm repose;
> And of the recompense which conscience seeks
> A bright, encouraging example shows;
> Needful when o'er wide realms the tempest breaks,
> Needful amid life's ordinary woes;—
> Hence, not for them unfitted who would bless
> A happy hour with holier happiness.

How can the narrator accept the isolation of Emily, befriended by the mysterious white doe but set apart from all human community? The very image of the devoted married couple struggling together with their grief subverts any easy faith in such a consolation and presents a more human version of loss and consolation than the poem itself does.

Furthermore, Wordsworth's bright ending resolves none of the political or familial issues raised in the story of the rebellion. Several commentators have noted the connection between the Norton rebellion of 1569 and the events of the early 1790s, as well as a connection between *The Borderers* and *The White Doe* as stories of rebellion.[30] The consequences of the rebellion were still very much with Wordsworth, who, as we recall, claimed as late as 1835 that he was still haunted by the violence of those events. In presenting the Norton rebellion, Wordsworth faced several difficulties. He does not endorse the rebellion of the Catholics against Queen Elizabeth, but he cannot imagine in 1807 that Francis and Emily would rebel against their father, even though they would be justified politically. The only alternative he can present to rebellion is passive resistance, which Wordsworth presents as a feminized (but highly admirable) virtue in both Francis and Emily.

Although there is almost no action in *The White Doe*, there *is* much allusion to violence and death. In keeping with the early Elizabethan setting, religion and spiritual values are embedded in political conflict. In book 7 of *The Excursion* (in lines probably written between January 1813 and May 1814),[31] the Vicar comments that a knight, who "in Eliza's golden days" (924) was buried in the churchyard,

> Lived in an age conspicuous as our own
> For strife and ferment in the minds of men;
> Whence alteration in the forms of things,
> Various and vast.
>
> (1009–12)

Like his Vicar, Wordsworth looks back on decades of instability brought on by revolution and war, fearing the disruption of continued strife and ferment. These fears, evident in the political sonnets of 1802, become intensified in the years leading up to Waterloo.[32]

Even though the prefatory poems added in 1815—"Weak is the will of man" and "In trellis'd shade," as well as the epigraph from Bacon—enforce the spiritual and consolatory reading, the poem comes back to images of violence and decay, such as one found in the opening canto. The poem opens with various parishioners observing the doe in its wanderings about Bolton Priory, each character seeing something different in its weekly pilgrimage:

> Pass, pass who will, yon chantry door;
> And, through the chink in the fractured floor
> Look down, and see a griesly [sic] sight;
> A vault where the bodies are buried upright!

> There face by face, and hand by hand,
> The Claphams and Mauleverers stand;
> And, in his place, among son and sire,
> Is John de Clapham, that fierce Esquire,—
> A valiant man, and a name of dread,
> In the ruthless wars of the White and the Red;—
> Who dragged Earl Pembroke from Banbury church,
> And smote off his head on the stones of the porch!
>   (1:245–56)

This is the view of a female ancestor of Pembroke, who wonders why the doe loiters around this scene. Although presented through the mind of a superstitious "Dame," these images underscore the violent struggles that form the history of the region and foreshadow the fate of the Nortons. Wordsworth implies that if violence can neither be understood nor justified, at least it can be transcended in a spiritual realm.

While the poem ends affirming a feminine spirituality and contains very little action (in comparison to quarto works by Byron or Scott), it does present a different alternative—albeit one unrealized—in Francis. Francis opposes the violence and militarism of his father, but he cannot manage to rebel against his father's law. Instead, Francis urges his father to reconsider, appealing to his familial responsibilities. Rather than launch this suicidal rebellion, Francis urges, he should "live at home in blissful ease" (2:396) for the sake of his family. In contrast to his father and nine brothers who dress themselves in the costumes of war, Francis joins them with "breast unmailed, unweaponed hand" (3:771). Francis's ethic of nonviolence prevents him from joining his father in the rebellion, but his family loyalty also prevents him from rebelling in any active way against his father. Wordsworth has great sympathy for Francis's dilemma, but there is no resolution. Francis's loyalty to his father ultimately causes his death, after he has forbidden Emily to try to intervene.

To a certain extent Francis represents a positive ethic that counters the Norton violence and fanaticism. This ethic is also associated with the Norton mother, who has died many years earlier. In his anxious thoughts about his daughter, Richard Norton blames his late wife for teaching Emily her Protestant faith; but he also seems to resent the maternal influence, the bond formed in infancy. Emily thinks of her mother and

> —Yes, she is soothed:—an Image faint—
> And yet not faint—a presence bright
> Returns to her;—'tis that bless'd Saint
> Who with mild looks and language mild

> Instructed here her darling Child,
> While yet a prattler on the knee,
> To worship in simplicity
> The invisible God, and take for guide
> The faith reformed and purified.
>   (4:1136–44)

Wordsworth creates a classic pre-oedipal scene of instruction: "a prattler" on her mother's knee. Emily remembers the gentleness of the mother, contrasting her "mild looks" with the fierce paternal glance and her "language mild" with the insistent symbol-making of the father. But although the memory of her mother's teaching inspires Emily to try to influence her father, ultimately her mother's memory is only a consolation to her and not an influence on the Norton heritage. As the only daughter in the family and a motherless child, Emily has no community of women with whom to identify.

Wordsworth sees value in the ethical perspective of maternal thinking, to borrow Sara Ruddick's term,[33] but in *The White Doe* he does not envision it as having power against the inflexible position of the Norton patriarchy. Images of caring and nurturing that are at first associated with the relationship between mother and child are transformed into spiritual metaphors for Emily and the doe. In this transference, I believe, Wordsworth veers away from the positive values he has introduced and instead embraces a more restrictive notion of woman's silent suffering, of spirituality and renunciation as the only alternatives to despair.

Spiritualized nature takes the place of the historical facts about the Norton uprising that Wordsworth rejects from Sir Walter Scott (*MY* 1:237). After the destruction of the Nortons, Emily inhabits a feminized world of nature and silence. Even before the downfall, Emily and the doe are presented with a lyrical softness that associates them with nature, innocence, and the beautiful, but also with the mysterious and secretive:

> But where at this still hour is she,
> The consecrated Emily?
> Even while I speak, behold the Maid
> Emerging from the cedar shade
> To open moonshine, where the Doe
> Beneath the cypress-spire is laid;
> Like a patch of April snow—
> Upon a bed of herbage green,
> Lingering in a woody glade
> Or behind a rocky screen—
>   (4:997–1006)

The narrator describes Emily and the doe in terms that connect them with images or scenes rather than with speech or language. They become part of the pictorial landscape they inhabit. Like images of Lucy ("A violet by a mossy stone / Half hidden from the eye") in the cycle of poems written several years earlier, images of Emily and the doe conjure what Wordsworth cannot express about their mysterious communion and substitute for what he does not confront in the narrative of the rebellion.

Wordsworth's decision to invent Emily Norton and focus on her spirituality meant that women actually associated with the story were barely mentioned or suppressed altogether. But at the end of his volume Wordsworth does include the ballad "The Rising in the North." Whitaker had simply hinted at women's role in the story of the doe, but the ballad includes both Lady Percy and the queen. Lady Percy urges her lord (in what will prove sound though unheeded advice) to go to the court and make peace with the queen. Even more aggressive than Lady Percy, the queen responds to the news of rebellion:

> Her grace she turned her round about,
>   And like a royall queene shee swore,
> I will ordayne them such a breakfast,
>   As never was in the North before.
>   (125–28)

Lady Percy does not appear in Wordsworth's poem, and the narrator merely alludes to Elizabeth and her power. Wordsworth is not interested in the paradoxes of Queen Elizabeth's rule, in the meaning of a queen who addressed her troops with the assertion that she had "the body but of a weak and feeble woman" but "the heart and stomach of a King."[34]

NAMBY-PAMBY VERSE

In *The White Doe* Wordsworth focuses on a view of femininity associated with suffering and consolation, not with the power of a queen. He thus opens himself to the charge made by Jeffrey in the review of his 1807 volume: that he should spend his time on more "manly" subjects such as "The Character of the Happy Warrior." Perhaps Wordsworth's sensitivity to these charges, as well as his ambivalence about the rebellion, contributes to his reluctance to publish *The White Doe*. Jeffrey, we recall, had condemned both the subject matter and the style of the 1807 volumes, arguing that Wordsworth wasted his time on such trivial subjects as daisies and daffodils and that his "namby-pamby" expressions, "prettyisms," and "babyish" verse set him apart from the great male

poets with whom Wordsworth himself identified. And as if responding on cue, Jeffrey criticizes what he sees as the "mystical wordiness"
and soft imprecision of *The White Doe*. He singles out the expression
"consecrated maid" for ridicule. The vague spirituality and the mysterious connection of the doe with Emily particularly bother Jeffrey and
other reviewers.[35]

We can place this accusation and Wordsworth's response to such criticism in the context of other Romantic writers. Several recent critics have
revealed similar anxieties in Keats and Byron, and the reputations of Romantic writers in the nineteenth century reveal that the feminization of
the poet was a shared concern.[36] In this view, an overly delicate Keats
dies of negative criticism, Arnold dubs Shelley a beautiful and ineffectual angel, and, following them both, Tennyson contributes to and fears
the feminization of the poet.

Perhaps in response to the tone of the reviews of 1807, highlighted
by Jeffrey's charge of what I will call namby-pambyism and by his own
perception of the direction of his poetry, Wordsworth adopts an even
more militant tone in his "Essay, Supplementary to the Preface" (1815)
than he took in the Preface to *Lyrical Ballads*. In this essay Wordsworth
constructs a self-serving view of literary history in which he argues that
great poets are never popular in their time. In the course of this argument Wordsworth conceptualizes the poet as an original genius, a "Hannibal among the Alps". Building on the view presented in the 1800 and
1802 Prefaces, Wordsworth creates an image of the poet as powerful,
even dictatorial. A series of rhetorical questions leads the reader to consider "where lies the real difficulty of creating that taste by which a truly
original poet is to be relished?" concluding, "Finally, does it lie in es-
tablishing that dominion over the spirits of readers by which they are to
be humbled and humanised, in order that they may be purified and ex-
alted?" (*PrW* 3:80–81).

But to take the essay and other claims at face value raises problems.
First of all, the persona that Wordsworth presents here conflicts with that
of much of his poetry of the period. Second, Wordsworth's grand claims
in the 1815 "Essay" overcompensate for his unease about his audience
and his lack of popularity. Third, the militant tone of the "Essay" is con-
tradicted by letters of the period, where Wordsworth presents himself as
anything but Hannibal. In fact, in the drama surrounding Wordsworth's
unwillingness to publish *The White Doe* in the years between 1808
and 1815, he seems absolutely unsure of his dominion over readers. In
one letter (31 March 1808) Dorothy Wordsworth plays the militant one,

urging her brother, in a Lady Macbethish way, "Do, dearest William!
do pluck up your Courage—overcome your disgust to publishing—It is
but a *little trouble*, and all will be over, and we shall be wealthy, and at
our ease for one year, at least" (*MY* 1:207). So uncertain is Wordsworth
about *The White Doe* and his readership that he can respond positively
neither to this entreaty nor to many others. Perhaps his brooding uncertainty recalls Hamlet more than Macbeth.

Wordsworth's ostensible reason for not publishing *The White Doe* is
that it is a poem without conventional action and as such can appeal
only to a small group of intelligent readers. Coleridge warns Wordsworth that *The White Doe*, "which does not employ the common
excitements of lively interest, namely curiosity, and the terror or pity
from unusual external events and Scenes—convents, dungeons, *etc.*"
(*PW* 3:546), is not likely to capture the majority of readers—especially
those, we might add, whose taste had not been purified by the *Lyrical
Ballads*. In the *Eclectic Review* (January 1816), Josiah Conder makes a
parallel observation: "The story is, however, so much more like history,
than romance, so destitute of plot, and so purely tragical, that it forms
a much better subject for a ballad, than for a poem of seven cantos, in
which the reader is led to expect more of incident and detail."[37]
Wordsworth responds indirectly to these strictures by claiming that his
poem is not for ordinary readers—or readers of gothic romances who
thrive on incident and "outrageous stimulation," to borrow the language
of the 1800 Preface (1:130). He claims in a letter to Coleridge (19 April
1808), bristling from Charles Lamb's criticism of *The White Doe*:

> When it is considered what has already been executed in Poetry, strange
> that a man cannot perceive, particularly when the present tendencies of soci-
> ety good and bad, are observed, that this is the time when a man of genius
> may honorably take a station upon different ground. If he is to be a Drama-
> tist, let him crowd his scene with gross and visible action; but if a narrative
> Poet, if the Poet is to be predominant over the Dramatist,—then let him see
> if there are no victories in the world of spirit, no changes, no commotions,
> no revolutions there, no fluxes and refluxes of the thoughts which may
> be made interesting by modest combination with the stiller actions of the
> bodily frame, or with the gentler movements and milder appearances of
> society and social intercourse, or the still more mild and gentle solicitations
> of irrational and inanimate nature.

> (*MY* 1:222–23)

If we substitute "Novelist" for "Dramatist," we have the same opposition as in the Preface. Once again, Wordsworth objects to "gross and

visible action" (echoing the "gross and violent stimulants" of the 1800 Preface [1:128]), and he presents his argument in a defensive tone. But Wordsworth is also thinking of male rivals.

Perhaps Wordsworth's rejection of the role of the male poet as a writer of swashbuckling and dramatic tales, as in the popular quarto works of Byron and Scott, influenced both his years of reluctance and his final decision to publish the poem. In writing *The White Doe* in loose octosyllabic verse, structuring the poem in cantos, and publishing it in an expensive quarto form, Wordsworth placed his work squarely in the context of these two popular contemporary poets.[38] But he knew that his poem lacked the action and appeal of Byron and Scott. Perhaps Wordsworth's decision finally to publish *The White Doe* was inspired by Byron's comments in his dedication to *The Corsair* (January 1814) that "Scott alone of the present generation, has hitherto completely triumphed over the fatal facility of octosyllabic verse."[39] Wordsworth may have seen this as a challenge to his skill as a metrical poet—his ability to overcome this difficulty while paradoxically working with such understated and unsensational material.

In contrasting the poet and the dramatist, Wordsworth privileges not power and dominion but the still and gentle movements of the spirit. He repeats forms of the words "still" and "gentle," giving their meanings priority over the commotions and revolutions of the material world. Wordsworth's rhetoric suggests that the poet is the writer of the beautiful, the conventionally feminine, while the dramatist is associated with the sublime. Wordsworth apparently sees no contradiction in the "man of genius" espousing such conventional feminine virtues and qualities, but mildness and gentleness are not the qualities with which he associates the poet in his public proclamations.

Theresa Kelley argues in *Wordsworth's Revisionary Aesthetics* that in *The White Doe* the mildness of the beautiful subdues the revolutions of the sublime. Kelley points out that Wordsworth introduces a passage from *The Borderers* (written 1797) into *The White Doe* in 1836, but subdues it by framing it with a consoling vision of the beautiful.[40] To build on Kelley's argument by posing the question of gender, another way that *The White Doe* revises *The Borderers* is that Wordsworth rewrites the story of the daughter. Neither in *The Borderers* nor in the roughly contemporaneous "The Ruined Cottage" does the woman character herself find consolation for her distress. In "The Ruined Cottage," Margaret dies unconsoled; in *The Borderers*, Matilda, after devoting herself to the care of a father who explicitly reminds her of her duty, is

finally abandoned by her distraught lover. Her last words in the play—
her plea that "It is a strong disease—O, save him, save him" (5:257, early
version 1797–99)—remain unanswered, and the play ends with her
lover's sublime insistence on his own solitary suffering:

> No prayers, no tears, but hear my doom in silence!
> I will go forth a wanderer on the earth,
> A shadowy thing, and as I wander on
> No human ear shall ever hear my voice,
> No human dwelling ever give me food
> Or sleep or rest, and all the uncertain way
> Shall be as darkness to me, as a waste
> Unnamed by man! and I will wander on
> Living by mere intensity of thought,
> A thing by pain and thought compelled to live,
> Yet loathing life, til heaven in mercy strike me
> With blank forgetfulness—that I may die.
>
> (264–75)

Having caused the death of Matilda's father after Rivers falsely con-
vinced him of the father's treachery, Mortimer focuses on himself and
his own pain. Matilda becomes the victim both of her father's ideals and
of her lover's despair. She is left to suffer in silence.[41]

Wordsworth rewrites the fate of Matilda in *The White Doe* by having Emily Norton find consolation in renouncing the things of this world.
In putting so much value on Emily's spiritual triumph over suffering and
over the conditions leading to suffering, Wordsworth sublimates his own
strong passions and disappointments. He also rewrites the ever-present
story of the abandoned woman, who here does not go mad or kill herself but instead becomes a nun-like figure trapped in a narrative of renunciation. From the purely spiritual perspective of Emily Norton and
considering the gentle stillness of the doe, the narrative of revolution and
rebellion means nothing.

BOOK 6 OF *THE EXCURSION*: THE CONSOLATIONS OF PIETY

The White Doe is a transitional work in Wordsworth's career, poised
between the sublime poetry of the Great Decade and the works of the
later years. But it is also a poem that in its final form qualifies its own
otherworldly spirituality. While Wordsworth associates spiritual renunciation with Emily Norton in *The White Doe*, he also connects spirituality with home and hearth, as we have seen, by focusing on images of

domestic bliss in the prefatory stanzas of 1815. Rather than endorse the austere renunciation of earlier cantos, these stanzas foster piety, a religious perspective based not on transcendence but on devotion to the intertwined values of God, home, and family.

This pattern is evident in the sixth book of *The Excursion* (the first of two books entitled "The Churchyard Among the Mountains"), which culminates in a vision of domesticity, love, and piety, but only after painful stories of their absence have been told. According to Reed, all the lines I refer to were "Probably written between 3 Jan 1813 and c late May 1814,"[42] roughly the same period I have discussed in reference to "Laodamia" and *The White Doe*. In all three narratives female characters and conventional gender expectations are central.

The first story, centered on a local woman who had intelligence and learning beyond her class and sex but was deficient in ordinary human affection and piety, begins on line 675. In his note to Isabella Fenwick, Wordsworth comments on this woman:

> This person lived at Town End, and was almost our next neighbour. I have little to notice concerning her beyond what is said in the Poem. She was a most striking instance how far a woman may surpass in talent, in knowledge, and culture of mind, those with and among whom she lives, and yet fall below them in Christian virtues of the heart and spirit. It seemed almost, and I say it with grief, that in proportion as she excelled in the one, she failed in the other. How frequently has one to observe in both sexes the same thing, and how mortifying is the reflection!
>
> (*PW* 5:459–60)

In 1843, when Wordsworth dictated these comments to his friend, he speaks of "Christian virtues," which also appear more prominently in revisions of the text in 1845. The Vicar describes the woman as finding no contentment from her learning; in fact he describes her as a slave to her passion for knowledge, as if this desire were a kind of sexual transgression. Her hunger for knowledge leads her to other passions, "avaricious thrift" (709) and a twisted, possessive "maternal love" (710) for her only son. When (presumably) her husband died early in their marriage, the woman was indignant about her "dire dependence" (717) and "the weakness of her sex" (719).

I suppose it would be too much to expect for this country Vicar to have read Mary Wollstonecraft on female weakness and dependency, but Wordsworth seems to be able to exercise no imagination concerning Aggy Fisher (so identified by de Selincourt) and her life. Her story, however, is rich in lost possibilities. Obviously frustrated in her talents

within the narrow confines of the village, the historical Aggy comes to
life in Dorothy Wordsworth's *Journals*, where she talks a great deal, analyzes her neighbors and their relationships, and complains about the
beggars whom Dorothy and William welcome. But in *The Excursion*, all
of the woman's energy is constricted by conventional morality and social expectations. Like Mrs. Joe in *Great Expectations*, another woman
frustrated in her talents, the woman lashes out against this imposed
weakness. And like Mrs. Joe, she finally makes peace with the world
through the author's pious, Christian resolution; all her conflicts are reduced to this:

> ["] . . . With a sigh
> She spake, yet, I believe, not unsustained
> By faith in glory that shall far transcend
> Aught by these perishable heavens disclosed
> To sight or mind. Nor less than care divine
> Is divine mercy. She, who had rebelled,
> Was into meekness softened and subdued;
> Did, after trials not in vain prolonged,
> With resignation sink into the grave;
> And her uncharitable acts, I trust,
> And harsh unkindnesses are all forgiven,
> Tho', in this Vale, remembered with deep awe."
>   (766–77)

In this passage Aggy Fisher is reduced to an emblem of resignation and
submission, a vehicle for communal feelings of charity and forgiveness.
Wordsworth acknowledges no basis for her frustrations other than
meanness.

The next story is a narrative more generally familiar to readers of
Wordsworth: a story of a young woman seduced and abandoned by her
lover (a "rash betrayer," 1006) and left with a child to care for on her
own. Her grave and that of her infant inspire the Vicar's narrative:

> ["]There, by her innocent Baby's precious grave,
> And on the very turf that roofs her own,
> The Mother oft was seen to stand, or kneel
> In the broad day, a weeping Magdalene.
> Now she is not; the swelling turf reports
> Of the fresh shower, but of poor Ellen's tears
> Is silent; nor is any vestige left
> Of the path worn by mournful tread of her
> Who, at her heart's light bidding, once had moved
> In virgin fearlessness, with step that seemed
> Caught from the pressure of elastic turf

Upon the mountains gemmed with morning dew,
In the prime hour of sweetest scents and airs.
—Serious and thoughtful was her mind; and yet,
By reconcilement exquisite and rare,
The form, port, motions, of this Cottage-girl
Were such as might have quickened and inspired
A Titian's hand, addrest to picture forth
Oread or Dryad glancing through the shade
What time the hunter's earliest horn is heard
Startling the golden hills.["]

(811–31)

The Vicar's description suggests that the young man promised marriage but broke his vow. After she was abandoned Ellen gave birth to a child, and her spirit was renewed by feelings of maternal love. But when the baby died from illness after Ellen had gone off to work and left it in her mother's care, Ellen could not recover. Although Ellen had faith and was accepted by her mother and the Vicar, she reproached herself for her situation. The Vicar repeats the Magdalene image:

["] . . . a rueful Magdalene!
So call her; for not only she bewailed
A mother's loss, but mourned in bitterness
Her own transgression . . .["]

(987–90)

The Magdalene allusion once again contrasts with Ellen's earlier, innocent beauty, made universal by the comparison to a mythological figure painted by Titian. At the same time that the Vicar preaches forgiveness and charity, he reminds the reader that Ellen had committed a "transgression" that led to her unhappiness. She deserves, the Vicar implies, the sympathy that Jesus bestowed on Mary Magdalene (commonly interpreted as a repentant prostitute), but, we might add, only in a constrictive morality would Ellen be thus compared. Perhaps Wordsworth was thinking not just of Luke 7:38 but of his own earlier reference to Mary Magdalene in the ninth book of *The Prelude*, a painting of a weeping Mary Magdalene by Charles le Brun (in the 1805 version, 72–80) that had affected him in revolutionary France. Once again he rewrites the story of transgression and abandonment to achieve a happier resolution. The Vicar's narrative ends with Ellen's pious acceptance of her fate, and she becomes an emblem of spiritual hope.

In each of these narratives from *The Excursion* Wordsworth shows a form of transgression against custom that prevents a life of domestic happiness. In the last narrative that is included in later editions of the sixth book of *The Excursion*, the Vicar tells the story of a widower and his six daughters, a "sisterhood" (1182) who make a home for their bereft father and devote themselves to his contentment. The book originally ended with another story about a man who lost his first wife and almost lost his land but was happily saved from the loneliness of widowerhood by a formidable-sounding "virtuous Woman, of grave years / And of prudential habits" (1241–42) and from economic ruin and loss of his "paternal fields" (1220) by the "liberal hand" (1238) of his creditor.[43] Perhaps Wordsworth wanted to end this book on a more idyllic note, so the Vicar provides a long description of the garden, the emblem of the family's self-sufficiency and happiness:

> "Brought from the woods the honeysuckle twines
> Round the porch, and seems, in that trim place,
> A plant no longer wild; the cultured rose
> There blossoms, strong in health, and will be soon
> Roof-high; the wild pink crowns the garden wall,
> And with the flowers are intermingled stones
> Sparry and bright, rough scatterings of the hills.
> These ornaments, that fade not with the year,
> A hardy Girl continues to provide;
> Who, mounting fearlessly the rocky heights,
> Her Father's prompt attendant, does for him
> All that a boy could do, but with delight
> More keen and prouder daring; yet hath she,
> Within the garden, like the rest, a bed
> For her own flowers and favourite herbs, a space,
> By sacred charter, holden for her use.["]
>   (1149–64)

The cultivated garden in which wild plants are tamed and trained to grow according to plan seems to represent the possibility of hope and happiness. The Vicar sees the garden as the girls' responsibility and their birthright ("By sacred charter"). Perhaps there is no trouble yet in this garden because none of the daughters is yet herself "a full-blown flower" (1130). And the poverty, doubt, and desire that motivated the other tales are banished from this idyllic space. Whatever the other narratives have led us to expect, Wordsworth ends this one with the Vicar's approving glance inside their home, where he sees the eldest daughter at her spinning wheel, teaching "some Novice of the sisterhood" (1182) the skill she knows so well. Although emphasis is on the redemptive power of this sisterhood, we should note that the father has taught his motherless daughter to spin and that the energetic younger girl does "all that a boy could do." This flexibility reminds us of the world of "Michael," where domestic labor is shared by all. But there are no patrimonial fields to lose here—only the modest plot of cultivated ground.

It is not such a big step from this idyllic setting to the domestic ideology of Victorian England. The image of six daughters ministering to their widowed father is a variant of a familiar Victorian narrative, especially the picture of the oldest daughter "teaching some Novice of the sisterhood" (1182), taking on a motherly role. As we shall see in the next chapter, Wordsworth had an abiding interest in the education of daughters.

These images of domestic bliss, from the prefatory stanzas of *The White Doe* to *The Excursion*, depend on the family functioning in unison. There can be no discordant voices, no major rebellions, and no disruptive passions. Wordsworth's vision of domestic happiness does not include dangerously passionate or unruly women like Ellen or Aggy Fisher. Even blameless female figures who threaten this domestic world, like Caroline in "It is a Beauteous Evening," must be banished. Wordsworth's vision depends on women who sacrifice their individual desires to find happiness in home life or in the world beyond. As we shall see, in his own life Wordsworth expected no less from the women he loved.

CHAPTER FIVE

Wordsworth as Paterfamilias

The Later Poetry and Life

Wordsworth wants the cheering society of women.
The Diary of Henry Crabb Robinson, *22 May 1837*

It was sympathy he wanted, to be assured of his genius, first
of all, and then to be taken within the circle of life, warmed
and soothed, to have his senses restored to him, his barren-
ness made fertile, and all the rooms of his house made full
of life.
Virginia Woolf, To the Lighthouse, *1927*

Isabella Fenwick was no blind worshipper. . . . She found no
obsequiousness at Rydal Mount. Coming from Greta Hall,
where Kate and Bertha Southey ministered silently to their
dazed father, she considered 'the storms that sometimes visited the Mount . . . more healthful and invigorating than such
calms.'
Frederika Beatty, William Wordsworth of
Rydal Mount, *1939*

In his late writings Wordsworth endorses an ideology of womanhood
that limits women's achievement by emphasizing "womanly virtues" associated with home and hearth. Even more than the contemporary
women poets he often disparaged, Wordsworth was by this time a poet
of domesticity, whose identity was linked both to the Lakes in general
and to his home, Rydal Mount, in particular (see figures 4 and 5). The
image of Wordsworth and his friends picnicking at Coniston in the two-
part *Prelude* strangely presages the world of Rydal Mount, a cultivated
and well situated "manor house." By the late 1820s and 1830s, the time

Figure 4. *Rydal Mount.* Watercolor by William Westall from Dora Words-worth's Book. 1831. By permission of the Wordsworth Trust, Dove Cottage, Grasmere, England.

of Wordsworth's greatest popularity, he had become associated with the house, where he received the hundreds of visitors who came to pay homage. In this chapter I will consider what it means for Wordsworth to be a poet of domesticity and what roles his daughter Dora and other women play in the world of Rydal Mount. We should also bear in mind that Wordsworth was writing for a proto-Victorian audience, not for some remote posterity.

The prevailing modern critical view of Wordsworth as a visionary and sublime poet has excluded most of his poetry after the Great Decade from serious discussion. In his conclusion to "Wordsworth at St. Bees: Scandals, Sisterhoods, and Wordsworth's Later Poetry," first published in 1985, Peter Manning eloquently calls for new readings of the later Wordsworth that consider the poetry for what it is rather than what it is not.[1] Manning refers to Hartley Coleridge's assessment of Words-worth, which I have also taken as a starting point. Responding to the well-received *Yarrow Revisited* (1835), Hartley Coleridge remarks:

Figure 5. *Wordsworth on Helvellyn*. Painting by Benjamin Robert Haydon. 1842. By permission of the National Portrait Gallery, London.

I think I perceive in Wordsworth's last volume a decided inclination to the playful, the elegant, and the beautiful; with an almost studied exclusion of the profound feeling and severe thought which characterised the offspring of his middle age. . . . they are perfect, perhaps more perfect, in their kind than any of their predecessors: but the kind is less intense, and therefore, incapable of that unique excellence which the disciples adore. . . . I am delighted . . . to see such freshness and loveliness of imagination, in a man upon whom old age has descended not without its attendant trials and sorrows.[2]

Hartley Coleridge does not see only the playfulness and beauty of Wordsworth's later poetry: his picture of the man refutes the myth of Wordsworthian decline, although it confirms that changes have occurred. *Playful* and *fresh* are words rarely used to describe Wordsworth's later poetry, but I have found much to corroborate Hartley Coleridge's judgment.

While Peter Manning has written about the later poetry, several other recent commentators have written about Wordsworth as poet in his later years or in relation to other poets of the 1830s. But they do so without reading the poetry in detail. Marlon Ross, for instance, contrasts Wordsworth as a poet of domesticity with Felicia Hemans, proposing in *The Contours of Masculine Desire* that a passage from *An Evening Walk* (1793) describing a rooster captures "every element of Wordsworthian domesticity with uncanny inclusiveness": "This domestic scene is not a community of shared desire, but a hierarchy of emotion with all attention focused on the 'monarch.' The 'sister-wives' may be seen as equal not only in their sharing of a common space, but also in their equal adoration of the male monarch" (310). While there are no doubt some elements of truth in this description, Wordsworthian domesticity contains more complexities than this portrait indicates—and Wordsworth's attitudes certainly changed and developed. Furthermore, the women of the household admired William, but they did not all approach him with a reverent tone: Sara Hutchinson's wry sense of humor extended to her brother-in-law; Dora lovingly teased her father as "trumpery old Daddy brisk & fat & well & busy verse making as possible";[3] Mary Wordsworth sometimes refused to take dictation if her husband got too gloomy. Perhaps Sara Hutchinson's early note to De Quincey about *The Convention of Cintra* gives a sense of what I mean. On 5 May 1809 she takes a lightly satirical attitude toward Wordsworth's fears of publishing politically controversial material. Following William's serious worry about "Prosecution in any of the courts of law" (*MY* 1:329), Sara adds: "We females shall be sorry to find that the pamphlet is not published for we have not the least fear of Newgate—if there was but a garden to walk in we think we should do very nicely—and Gaol in the country would be quite pleasant" (*MY* 1:330). Sara's letter suggests a sense of female solidarity: she speaks collectively for the women in the family, assuming their unity and identity.[4] There is also sly humor in her portrayal of women's home life as consistent with prison.

Furthermore, although Wordsworth's literary work occupied the center of the household, Wordsworth did not take for granted the help he received. In a letter home from a tour with Crabb Robinson (5 July 1837), Wordsworth writes:

> Dearest Mary, when I have felt how harshly I often demeaned myself to you, my inestimable fellow-labourer, while correcting the last Edition of my poems, I often pray to God that He would grant us both life, that I may make some amends to you for that, and all my unworthiness. But you know into what an irritable state this timed and overstrained labour often puts my nerves. My impatience was ungovernable as I thought then, but I now feel that it ought to have been governed. You have forgiven me I know, as you did then, and perhaps that somehow troubles me the more. I say nothing of this to you, dear Dora, though you also have some reason to complain.
>
> (*LY*: 3:423–24)

As we know, Wordsworth was a relentless reviser who depended on members of his household to help him carry out the work. This letter reveals both what Wordsworth could be like to live and work with, as well as his ability to criticize his behavior as household tyrant. When Crabb Robinson reported to the poet that De Quincey had said that Wordsworth had a better wife than he deserved, Wordsworth, reportedly, fully agreed.[5]

Wordsworth poignantly—and typically—feels the need of home and family most strongly when he is away from Rydal Mount. In a much more petulantly humorous mood, he complains in his next letter that the bachelor Robinson "has no home to go to but chambers, and wishes to stay abroad, at least to linger abroad, which I, having the blessing of a home, do not. Again, he takes delight in loitering about towns, gossiping, and attending reading-rooms, and going to coffee houses; and at table d'hôtes, etc., gabbling German, or any other tongue, all which places and practices are my abomination" (*LY* 3:426, 17 July 1837). For his part, Robinson tells other friends that he could not play the proper feminine role to keep Wordsworth happy on the tour, although he tried.[6]

Kurt Heinzelman adopts the term "cult of domesticity" in his discussion of the Wordsworths' transition from the Grasmere years, when commodity production was attached to the home, to a "cultic valorizing of the household" after production has been separated from the home (*R&F*, 53). Heinzelman locates this shift in the Wordsworths during the Rydal Mount years, but he focuses on "the Wordsworth household before it became codified and acquired its Victorian interiors—before that is, the radical Wordsworthian mythos . . . became enmeshed in what historically may be called a 'cult of domesticity.'"[7]

To build on Heinzelman's analysis, I will consider the ethos of Rydal Mount. Although Wordsworth never owned the property,[8] Rydal Mount was both a home and a symbol of home for the Wordsworths from 1813 until the end of their lives. We can to a certain extent reconstruct this home by reading the poetry and letters of the period and by reading what friends such as Crabb Robinson, Isabella Fenwick, and Hartley Coleridge say about the Wordsworths' lives. While the world that developed at Rydal Mount may be called a cult of domesticity and while Wordsworth certainly saw "womanly virtues" as closely associated with home and family, the division of the domestic sphere from the public sphere was not absolute. The home was the vantage point from which the Wordsworths made sense of the larger world. And during these years, Wordsworth worked at home and took an active part in the education both of his own children and of the children of the village. A later tradition developed in which the local children visited Rydal Mount each year on Wordsworth's birthday for a party—a gesture that suggests feudal noblesse oblige rather than bourgeois interiority.[9] It seems, then, that the world of Rydal Mount brought together an odd mix of attitudes and traditions, some reflecting and some diverging from the larger culture.

I would argue that the Wordsworths' household at Rydal Mount has more in common with the middle-class homes that Davidoff and Hall describe in *Family Fortunes* as typical *before* middle-class men began to establish the family away from their place of work.[10] As long as the business is attached to the home, the spheres intersect. Also, M. Jeanne Peterson argues that although there was no ideology of equality of men and women in upper-middle-class Victorian marriages, women and men were nonetheless coworkers and cocontributors to a single career. They shared work and affection, and the middle-class wife had tremendous influence on the development of her husband's career.[11] When William refers to Mary as his "inestimable fellow-labourer" he means it, despite the tradition that sees Wordsworth as more akin to Woolf's egotistical Mr. Ramsay.

DORA: "FOR SHE WAS ONE I LOVED EXCEEDINGLY"

The Wordsworths' only surviving daughter, Dora, who was born in 1804 at Dove Cottage and died in 1847 at Rydal Mount, plays a central role in Wordsworth's life and poetry after the Grasmere years. Wordsworth wrote several poems about Dora, and in his later years he was influenced by her in his representation of women in poems such as "The Triad" and "The Egyptian Maid." Eventually Dora tried to compensate for the loss of two of Wordsworth's closest female supporters: Dorothy Wordsworth, whose mental and physical decline began in 1829, and Sara Hutchinson, who died in 1835. Perhaps, too, Dora's burden and her sense of her own duty were greater because she was the only daughter: Catharine had died at the age of four, and Caroline was never a part of the family circle—indeed, there is no indication in family letters or journals that Wordsworth's English children even knew of their French sister.

Family letters refer to the personalities of all of William and Mary's children. Dora (christened Dorothy after her aunt) is regarded as the wild and wayward one in her early years. She is the subject of much discussion, as well as an attempt by her elders to "subdue" her behavior. The elder Dorothy refers to her niece in several letters, in revealing ways:

> Dorothy improves in mildness and her countenance becomes more engaging, but she is not so richly endowed with a gracious nature as her Brother—perhaps it is that she is more lively, and we see indeed that her waywardness is greatly subdued. She is at times very beautiful, and *elegance* and *wildness* are mingled in her appearance more than I ever saw in any child.
>
> (*MY* 1:377, to Jane Marshall, 19 November 1809)

> Dorothy is a delightful girl—clever, entertaining, and lively—indeed so very lively that it is impossible for her to satisfy the activity of her spirit without a little naughtiness at times—a waywardness of fancy rather than of temper.
>
> (*MY* 1:389, to Lady Beaumont, 28 February 1810)

> Dorothy's temper is very obstinate by fits, and at such times nothing but rigourous confinement can subdue her. She is not to be moved by feelings, and the misfortune is that the more indulgence or pleasure she has, the more unmanageable she is.
>
> (*MY* 2:246, to Catherine Clarkson, 15 August 1815)

In each of these letters to female friends Dorothy Wordsworth reveals an attitude shared by other members of the family regarding feminine behavior: Dora's spirit must be tamed, an ironic conclusion from the wild-eyed sister of "Tintern Abbey." Dorothy Wordsworth seems confident that her female friends will concur with her assessment of Dora and her attempts to shape her niece into a more appropriate form for a girl. Dora was finally sent away to school in order to mold her character.

The Wordsworths want a subdued Dora, not an idle or frivolous girl. Dorothy comments to the writer Maria Jane Jewsbury that Dora's "poor head has been submitted to a French Hairdresser!—This *does* vex me—I cannot condone the notion of seeing her decked (nay not decked—depressed) by big curls—and Bows and Giraffe Wires" (*LY* 1:608, 21 May 1828). Despite the French hairdresser, the Wordsworths' program was apparently successful up to a point, for Dora's contemporaries paint a picture of daughterly devotion to the exclusion of personal desires. In praising the literary talent evident in the travel journal describing Spain and Portugal which Dora published just before her death in 1847, Dora's contemporary Sara Coleridge observed that "The Rydal Mount career frustrated a real talent."[12] And in 1830 Hartley wrote to Derwent Coleridge that "Dora, as sweet a creature as ever breath'd, suffers sadly from debility. I have my suspicions that she would be a healthier matron than she is a Virgin, but strong indeed must be the love that could induce her to leave her father, whom she almost adores and who quite doats upon her."[13] Without much real regret, Mary Wordsworth also writes to Edward Quillinan (25 November 1828) that Dora "has threatened to be a German student, but Colds and Poetry—for she is now her Father's amanuensis—if they go on at their present pace, will leave no time for aught else" (*LY* 1:666). Instead of considering her own talent or life apart, Dora channeled her intelligence and good humor into Rydal Mount, until her marriage in 1841 at the age of thirty-seven. Sara Coleridge's term "the Rydal Mount career" is quite revealing, for the role of daughter of the Mount *was* a demanding job. But "career" must be ironic.

According to all accounts, Dora Wordsworth fulfilled the role of the poet's daughter to perfection until the late 1830s, when she herself was in her thirties. The crisis occurred when Dora (whose health had been fragile since her early twenties) made known her desire to marry Edward Quillinan, a long-time family friend, a widower, and a Catholic. Until this tension arose, it seems that there had never been a major conflict between Dora and her parents—or any conflict at all since her early days of temper tantrums. Indeed, the reason this conflict was so painful to all involved was that there was great love and devotion on both sides, as observers such as Hartley Coleridge recognized. But Dora wanted her own life, and, as we shall see in the next chapter, underwent much grief in order to get it.

Although Wordsworth wrote several poems about Dora, beginning with the beautiful tribute "Address to My Infant Daughter," he wrote very little new poetry specifically about her in much later years. But Dora remained a presence in her father's life to the end and influenced his revisions. Wordsworth wrote the "Address to My Infant Daughter" when the child was a month old in 1804 and published it in 1815, but he did not add the name "Dora" to the end of the title until 1849, in a poignant memorial to Dora two years after her death.

In this poem Wordsworth sets up the comparison between baby Dora, "Frail, feeble, Monthling!" (16), and the moon:

> Even now—to solemnise thy helpless state,
> And to enliven in the mind's regard
> Thy passive beauty—parallels have risen,
> Resemblances, or contrasts, that connect,
> Within the region of a father's thoughts,
> Thee and thy mate and sister of the sky.
> And first;—thy sinless progress, through a world
> By sorrow darkened and by care disturbed,
> Apt likeness bears to hers, through gathered clouds
> Moving untouched in silver purity,
> And cheering oft-times their reluctant gloom.
> Fair are ye both, and both are free from stain:
> But thou, how leisurely thou fill'st thy horn
> With brightness! leaving her to post along,
> And range about, disquieted in change,
> And still impatient of the shape she wears.
> Once up, once down the hill, one journey, Babe,
> That will suffice thee; and it seems that now
> Thou hast foreknowledge that such task is thine;
> Thou travellest so contentedly, and sleep'st
> In such a heedless peace. Alas! full soon
> Hath this conception, grateful to behold,
> Changed countenance, like an object sullied o'er
> By breathing mist; and thine appears to be
> A mournful labour, while to her is given
> Hope, and renovation without end.
>   (PW 2:40–65)

Dora's life becomes an allegorical journey through clouded skies. The poet thinks of the moon in constant cyclical change, at leisure to fill its horn with brightness. In contrast, the infant babe makes her journey through life once, and the poet's recognition of this difference leads him to despair of human happiness. He develops the metaphor of clouding over to suggest that the happy comparison between child and star is now darkened. Significantly, the female child's life is seen as "mournful labour" (suggesting childbirth) as opposed to eternal hope and rebirth.

The human child seems at best a poor stepsister of her mate in the sky.

But the father's gloomy thoughts are themselves renovated when he looks again upon his smiling infant:

> —That smile forbids the thought; for on thy face
> Smiles are beginning, like the beams of dawn,
> To shoot and circulate; smiles have there been seen;—
> Tranquil assurances that Heaven supports
> The feeble motions of thy life, and cheers
> Thy loneliness: or shall those smiles be called
> Feelers of love, put forth as if to explore
> This untried world, and to prepare thy way
> Through a strait passage intricate and dim?
> Such are they; and the same are tokens, signs,
> Which, when the appointed season hath arrived,
> Joy, as her holiest language, shall adopt;
> And Reason's godlike Power be proud to own.
>
>   (66–end)

The father responds to the child's smiles—he meets the child halfway and revises his gloomy thoughts. The smile, which to the speaker suggests the divine presence, also becomes an emblem of the child's desire to move into the world with the hope of finding love. Perhaps when Keats praised Wordsworth for thinking into the human heart and exploring the dark passages of life (*Letters of John Keats*, 95, 3 May 1818), he was thinking of this poem as well as more celebrated ones such as "Tintern Abbey." Certainly, Wordsworth reveals here, as he does in *The Prelude*, that he is a remarkably astute observer of human psychology and of the bonds established in infancy between the subject and the world.

The child, in other words, has an instinctive desire to love and be loved, just as earlier in the poem the speaker had identified "Mother's love, / Nor less than mother's love in other breasts" (28–29) as "in the main, a joyless tie / Of naked instinct, wound about the heart" (37–38). This is interesting not just because of the recognition of instinctual ties, but also because the speaker wants to extend "Mother's love" to "other breasts," in this case to the father. So close is the bond that he feels with his infant daughter that he must search beyond the region of the father's thoughts and into the mother's heart. Perhaps the poet imagines what his own mother felt for him. Like the shepherd Michael, the father feels the need to nurture, to provide "female service," rocking the infant's "cradle, as with a woman's gentle hand" ("Michael," 54, 58). I do not see this in either case as an attempt to appropriate the feminine in a negative sense, but, rather, as an understanding of bonds that are not customarily recognized in men. Wordsworth represents the father as having an affinity with nurturing and care but often being deprived of it by custom and convention. Maternal images give Wordsworth a way to express the intensity of a father's love.

We could say the same for Coleridge's representation of himself in "Frost at Midnight": he offers a seemingly maternal love and blessing to baby Hartley, gently rocking his cradle. But criticism has been kinder—or at least different—to Coleridge, acknowledging feminine virtues as a part of his personality, whereas Wordsworth emerges as the most masculine of men, the promoter of the egotistical sublime. But in Wordsworth's meditation on the infant Dora we see him searching for ways to imagine the life ahead of her and to express the intensity of his own love.

The allusion to "heaven's eternal year" in line 15 of "To My Infant Daughter, Dora" places Wordsworth's intimate apostrophe to Dora in the context of Dryden's elegy "To the Pious Memory of the Accomplisht Young Lady Mrs. Anne Killigrew," whom Dryden addresses:

> Cease thy Celestial Song a little space;
> (Thou wilt have Time enough for Hymns Divine,
>   Since Heav'ns Eternal Year is thine.)[14]

Wordsworth asks:

> But what is time? What outward glory? Neither
> A measure is of Thee, whose claims extend
> Through "heaven's eternal year."
>   (13–15)

The conscious allusion to Anne Killigrew and her untimely death, marked by quotes in Wordsworth's line, seems to signal Wordsworth's brooding over mortality and his constant fear of loss. Seeing his baby as a frail monthling, Wordsworth has a premonition of death, of the ever-present threat that is realized in his lament for little Catharine, "Surprized by Joy."

In contrast to the involved love and tense imaginings of "Address to My Infant Daughter," we recall the detachment and abstraction of "It is a Beauteous Evening," where the speaker does not attempt to imagine the older child's life but tries instead to find a way to reconcile her to his absence. Instead of a father who thinks of himself as nurturer and protector, the father makes the child's heavenly Father into an androgynous protector. In the sonnet Caroline is addressed as a "Dear Child," but in the later poem the child is clearly identified as his daughter. And, as if to strengthen the bond and express the inexpressible loss, the infant becomes "Dora" in 1849 and for all time. For whatever reason—lingering guilt, weakly formed bonds, sense of impropriety—Caroline enters Wordsworth's poetry obliquely, while Dora's presence in his life is acknowledged and celebrated.

With Dora, Wordsworth shows a possessiveness not evident in his earlier relationships with women or with his other children. Wordsworth both depends on Dora and expects her to depend on him. Wordsworth's perception of this emerges in a poem he wrote in 1816, when Dora was almost twelve. The poem, number 24 in the *Poems of Sentiment and Reflection*, begins with this quote from Milton's *Samson Agonistes*: "*A little onward lend thy guiding hand / To these dark steps, a little further on!*" This poem arises from Wordsworth's fear that blindness would result from an inflammation of the eyes he had long suffered. Family letters are filled with allusions to Wordsworth's condition, which at times prevented him from reading and made strong light painful to him; he wore "green shades" long before it was chic to do so. In quoting from *Samson*, Wordsworth alludes to Samson's blindness and his need for a guiding hand, as well as to Milton's own condition. In dramatizing the father's plea to his daughter while alluding to blindness, Wordsworth also conjures King Lear.

In his poem Wordsworth claims that he is not yet "among those who lean / Upon a living staff, with borrowed sight" (9–10), although he fears such dependency:

> —O my Antigone, beloved child!
> Should that day come—but hark! the birds salute
> The cheerful dawn, brightening for me the east . . .
> (11–13)

Later Wordsworth changed the line to "O my own Dora, my beloved child!" He made this change in the manuscript by 1845 (according to Carl Ketcham, Cornell edition, 223), I believe, not primarily because he had second thoughts about alluding to Antigone leading Oedipus (although that *is* a chilling image), but because he once again felt compelled to reaffirm his closeness to Dora. He revised the poem, which had obliquely alluded to Dora at almost twelve, to confirm his intense love for her and her influence on his poetry and life. In 1816, when the poem was composed, Wordsworth cannot even follow through on the thought that the day might come when he would require complete care: he cuts

off the thought with "but hark!" in much the way he cuts off his de-
spairing thoughts in "Tintern Abbey" with an abrupt syntactic shift.

Once the speaker cuts off the thought, he turns to focus on himself
as Dora's guide through life. He turns literally and metaphorically to
the light:

> For me, thy natural Leader, once again
> Impatient to conduct thee, not as erst
> A tottering Infant, with compliant stoop
> From flower to flower supported; but to curb
> Thy nymph-like step swift-bounding o'er the lawn,
> Along the loose rocks, or the slippery verge
> Of foaming torrents.—From thy orisons
> Come forth; and, while the morning air is yet
> Transparent as the soul of innocent youth,
> Let me, thy happy Guide, now point the way,
> And now precede thee, winding to and fro,
> Till we by perseverance gain the top
> Of some smooth ridge, whose brink precipitous
> Kindles intense desire for powers withheld
> From this corporeal frame; whereon who stands
> Is seized with strong incitement to push forth
> His arms, as swimmers use, and plunge—dread thought!
> For pastime plunge—into the "abrupt abyss,"
> Where Ravens spread their plumy vans, at ease!
>
> (14–32)

Wordsworth displaces his feeling of being endangered from himself to
Dora, on "the slippery verge." He calls Dora forth from her "orisons"
to join him on a dangerous journey. Geoffrey Hartman offers an oedipal reading of these lines, in which the father displaces his incest wish
by imaginatively consigning Dora (Ophelia-like) to a nunnery in the next
stanza.[15] Certainly the language is suggestive—the speaker wants to fly
from the cliff, to push forth, to plunge into the abyss. These images al-
lude to Satan in *Paradise Lost*, who asks:

> . . . whom shall we send
> In search of this new world, whom shall we find
> Sufficient? who shall tempt with wand'ring feet
> The dark unbottom'd infinite Abyss
> And through the palpable obscure find out
> His uncouth way, or spread his aery flight
> Upborne with indefatigable wings
> Over the vast abrupt, ere he arrive
> The happy Isle . . .
>
> (2:402–10)

But in Wordsworth's poem the speaker, of course, consciously rejects this "uncouth" challenge to fly into the abyss. Even in thought this is a rash and sublime gesture, contrary to the paternal guidance the poet praises earlier in the stanza. Paternal love curbs this desire.

Instead, the speaker opts for what he regards as a safer journey "Through woods and spacious forests" (34) to observe the stately work of nature:

> . . . we such schools
> Of reverential awe will chiefly seek
> In the still summer noon, while beams of light;
> Reposing here, and in the aisles beyond
> Traceably gliding through the dusk, recall
> To mind the living presences of nuns;
> A gentle, pensive, white-robed sisterhood,
> Whose saintly radiance mitigates the gloom
> Of those terrestrial fabrics, where they serve,
> To Christ, the Sun of Righteousness, espoused.
>   (39–48)

Not only, as Hartman argues, is the incest wish displaced by the image of the nuns, but the sublime landscape of "dark unbottom'd infinite Abyss" is transformed into an imaginative landscape of stillness and soft, reposing light: a scene of the beautiful. But though the scene is beautiful the associations are troubling, because the nymph-like steps of the daughter are spiritualized, almost out of existence. And as we have seen in other circumstances, Wordsworth associates women with spirituality as a way to resolve difficult tensions in his attitude toward them, as in "It is a Beauteous Evening." Now Wordsworth resolves the tension between Dora as an autonomous person on the verge of discovering her sexuality and a dutiful daughter who will be curbed and conducted by the father who thinks of her (at least by indirect association) as belonging to "A gentle, pensive, white-robed sisterhood." Even the syntax, which places emphasis on the father's desire "To curb" rather than on what his child *is* now that she is no longer a tottering infant, supports the father's wish. Paradoxically, the speaker also seems to curb his own desire in the "saintly radiance" of the imagery, turning his nymph into a nun, to paraphrase Barbara Johnson.[16]

Having spiritualized his Antigone, the speaker imagines a landscape that they might inhabit, inspired by passages of "holy writ" (50):

> Passage lies
> Through you to heights more glorious still, and shades
> More awful, where, this Darling of my care,

Advancing with me hand in hand, may learn
To calm the affections, elevate the soul,
And consecrate our lives to truth and love.
                                        (52–end)

Now the speaker can imagine entering such a landscape without fear, with a daughter who is transformed into an Eve-like soulmate. Through all his revisions, Wordsworth keeps the echo of the penultimate line of *Paradise Lost*, "They hand in hand with wand'ring steps and slow," as if to underscore both the new beginning and the allusion to Eve. Once purified of the nymph-like associations, Dora can become his Eve, his partner, as they face the world "hand in hand." (Interestingly, in the "glad preamble" to *The Prelude*, the speaker had faced the world alone: "The earth is all before me.") Although this transformation of daughter into helpmate is troubling, for Wordsworth it reconciles the problem of guidance, since *both* are taught "To calm the affections." The poem thus closes with an allusion to another Miltonic passage, more subtly placed in the text than the pre-text from *Samson Agonistes* in this scene of daughterly instruction.

In addition to the Miltonic, Shakespearean, and classical allusions, the poem recalls Milton's daughters and the various eighteenth- and nineteenth-century interpretations of their fate, from their representation in Blake's *Milton* to the painting of the Bard and his daughters by Fuseli to Dorothea Brooke in *Middlemarch* fashioning herself as the supremely dutiful daughter that Milton apparently never had. Dora seems to have been a much more willing companion and scribe than Milton's daughters, following a pattern of daughterly service that began early in her life.

Wordsworth's love for Dora had always been strong, as evidenced by his "Address to My Infant Daughter" and by the loving comments of family members. His love for Dora was no doubt intensified in 1812 by the loss of Catharine. In the sonnet written after Catharine's death, Wordsworth expresses his grief and her continuing presence in his mind:

Surprized by joy—impatient as the Wind
I turned to share the transport—Oh! with whom
But Thee, deep buried in the silent tomb,
That spot which no vicissitude can find.
                                        (*PW* 3:1–4)

Wordsworth's anxious love for Dora is best understood in the context of his constant memory of loss and fear of losing once again. The poet reveals this preoccupation in the first sonnet of part 3 of *Ecclesiastical Sketches* (1822):[17]

> I saw the figure of a lovely Maid
> Seated alone beneath a darksome tree,
> Whose fondly-overhanging canopy
> Set off her brightness with a pleasing shade.
> No Spirit was she: *that* my heart betrayed,
> For she was one I loved exceedingly;
> But while I gazed in tender reverie
> (Or was it sleep that with my Fancy played?)
> The bright corporeal presence—form and face—
> Remaining still distinct grew thin and rare,
> Like sunny mist;—at length the golden hair,
> Shape, limbs, and heavenly features, keeping pace
> Each with the other in a lingering race
> Of dissolution, melted into air.

Wordsworth explains in his note to Isabella Fenwick (*PW* 3:568–69) that he composed this sonnet while on the road from Grasmere to Ambleside, in recollection of a dream he had about Dora. In the sonnet Wordsworth expresses both his fear of losing her "bright corporeal presence" and his sense of just how fragile that presence is. Preoccupied with the fearful premonition of loss, this sonnet seems to be a descendant of the earlier Lucy poems, in particular "Strange fits of passion." But Lucy has grown up now; the poet imagines her loss from a father's point of view. And the poet's expression is more direct: while in the latest version of "Strange fits of passion" we are left with the human premonition, "If Lucy should be dead," in the sonnet the "lovely Maid" *does* melt into air.

The opening image of the "lovely Maid" sitting under the canopy of a huge tree suggests the father's protective fears for his daughter. But the image also recalls Blake's pictorial representation of guardianship in the *Songs of Innocence and of Experience*, where the shade of a massive tree can be both protective and stifling. Without making the sinister implications of guardianship apparent, Wordsworth fears that even his great protectiveness and exceeding love will not be enough to preserve Dora. Although his motives are mixed with genuine love, Wordsworth wants to control Dora's life by keeping her with him, even before she begins to show alarming signs of bad health.

Wordsworth's references to nuns from "Nuns Fret Not" through "A Little Onward" are generally positive. But when faced with a real convent in Bruges while traveling with Dora and Coleridge in the summer of 1828, Wordsworth responds differently. Wordsworth and Dora are saddened by the life of confinement; in reminiscing to Isabella Fenwick, Wordsworth commented of "Incident at Bruges" that "Dora and I, while taking a walk along a retired part of the town, heard the voice as here described, and were afterwards informed that it was a Convent in which were many English. We were both much touched, I might say affected, and Dora moved as appears in the verses" (*PW* 3:468). In her travel journal from the 1828 tour Dora confirms her father's recollection. She reveals that "On entering Bruges all my giddy & joyous feelings fled. I was deeply impressed by the solemn grandeur which pervades her streets— deserted, yet not decayed, regular in the beautiful irregularity" (Dove Cottage Manuscript 110, Saturday, 21 June).

In "Incident at Bruges" the speaker describes walking down the street with his companion when they hear the sound of a harp and a beautiful English voice coming from a convent tower. It is dusk and the travelers seem to hear nothing but the sound and to see nothing but the imposing tower against the backdrop of the setting sun. Wordsworth willingly shares this experience with his companion, using the plural "we" rather than the "I" so frequent in earlier poems. The travelers imagine that the nun, probably an Englishwoman, is unaware of the beauty of the evening: "if the glory reached the Nun, / 'Twas through an iron grate" (22–23). The speaker continues to muse:

> Not always is the heart unwise,
>   Nor pity idly born,
> If even a passing Stranger sighs
>   For them who do not mourn.
> Sad is thy doom, self-solaced dove,
>   Captive, whoe'er thou be!
> Oh! what is beauty, what is love,
>   And opening life to thee?
>
> Such feeling pressed upon my soul,
>   A feeling sanctified
> By one soft trickling tear that stole
>   From the Maiden at my side;
> Less tribute could she pay than this,
>   Borne gaily o'er the sea,
> Fresh from the beauty and the bliss
>   Of English liberty?
>   (25–40)

Here the speaker idealizes both the nun and the "Maiden." Wordsworth apparently perceived Dora's chastened spirits on entering and walking through Bruges and contrasted her usual gaiety with her feeling for the nun's confinement. Wordsworth's "self-solaced dove" is like Tennyson's Lady of Shalott before she sees Lancelot. Knowing the difficulties that will arise in Dora's "opening life," I read this poem also as a sad prophecy of Dora's own future when she tries to find a way out of her tower.

Perhaps Wordsworth felt assured of Dora's happiness in 1828, so that there was no uneasiness in his allusions. Dora was twenty-four at the time and may not have yet felt troubled by her relationship with her father. Most of her existing letters—both published and those in manuscript at the Wordsworth Library—date from a few years later than this scene. It seems from Dora's letters of the early 1830s that she did feel pressure from several areas: she felt the need to help even more in the household and in the extended family now that her aunt Dorothy was in decline; her developing relationship with Edward Quillinan was not easy; most of her close women friends were marrying and she felt abandoned. She tells Maria Jane Jewsbury in December 1831 that "When you are gone I have but one *friend* left me, Edith [Southey], & she too only hangs by a thread as her Lover may come for her any day so you must forgive my lamenting over your happiness."[18] But in his poetry and letters Wordsworth focuses, not on this Dora, but on an idealized Dora, the perfect daughter for whom he can be the perfect father.

One story gleaned from Wordsworth's later letters reveals the happiness, dedication, and playfulness of his love for Dora—with no hint of the darker side. This tone is typical of Wordsworth's comments about Dora; her anxieties are not reflected in his letters. In writing to William Rowan Hamilton in 1830, when Dora was twenty-six, Wordsworth describes a trip he made alone on Dora's pony from the Lakes to Cambridge, so that she could have her pony while she was visiting her relatives at Cambridge. Wordsworth dramatizes himself as a knight in shining armor (of sorts) on a sacred quest—perhaps more like Don Quixote than a straightforward knight. I quote at length because the letter is so revealing:

> So late as the 5th of November, I will tell you where I was; a solitary equestrian entering the romantic little town of Ashford-in-the-Waters, on the edge of the wolds of Derbyshire, at the close of day, when guns were beginning to be let off and squibs to be fired on every side, so that I thought it prudent to dismount and lead my horse through the place, and so on to Bakewell, two miles farther. You must know how I happened to be riding through these wild regions. It was my wish that Dora should have the benefit of her pony while at Cambridge, and very valiantly and economically I determined, unused as I am to horsemanship, to ride the creature myself. I . . . reached the end of

my journey safe and sound—not, however, without encountering two days of tempestuous rain. Thirty-seven miles did I ride in one day through the worst of these storms.

(*LY* 2:353)

Wordsworth both embellishes and mocks his own chivalry, but he also reveals the depths of his love and concern for this daughter. Like his romance "The Egyptian Maid," the tone of this letter is at the same time light and serious.

Wordsworth's dependency on and possessiveness of Dora intensified as Dora became a young woman. In 1826, when Dora was twenty-two, Wordsworth received a request from a young man who wanted to marry her. His response is telling:

The opinion, or rather judgment, of my daughter must have been little influenced by what she has been in the habit of hearing from me since her childhood, if she could see the matter in a different light. I therefore beg that the same reserve and delicacy which have done you so much honor may be preserved; and that she may not be called to think upon the subject, and I cannot but express the hope that you will let it pass away from your mind.

(*LY* 1:424)

And, for all we know, pass away it did. Wordsworth assumes that Dora will think in the same way, but he does not wish to test the assumption.

Because Wordsworth looks at Dora in relation to his own desires as a father and not as a young woman with different aspirations, he sees her in conventional and idealized ways. For instance, he writes in 1826, "My Daughter, Dora by name, is now installed in my House in the office of regular tea maker, why cannot you come and swell the chorus of praises she draws forth for her performance of that important part of feminine duty?" (*LY* 1:474). Although the tone is playful and the language happily inflated, the passage introduces what will become a powerful Victorian cliché: the domestic angel stationed before the urn dispensing cups of tea and charm. But this is not to dismiss the image as insignificant: Wordsworth thinks of Dora and other women as providers of the domestic calm upon which his happiness is founded.

WOMANLY VIRTUES: "THE TRIAD"

Wordsworth could and did recognize unconventional qualities in women, but he indicates that a woman's intellectual or artistic talent should be under the control of her feminine, domestic identity. For instance, Jeffrey Robinson analyzes Wordsworth's "strangely proprietary attitude" toward a sixteen-year-old poetic prodigy, Emmie Fisher,[19] and quotes the following letter:

> I have said little or nothing to her about literature, being so much more anxious to impress her with the paramount importance of womanly virtues, and acquiring those Domestic habits which may make [her?] useful in a station however humble. Her mother, I fear, has more worldly ambition than I wish her Daughter to partake; who is, I believe, at present entirely free from it.
>
> (*LY* 4:235, 30 August 1841)

The worldly ambition that fired young William Wordsworth and other bards is off-limits to a woman; for her the possibility of a poetic vocation is out of the question. Women of all classes must be "useful." The women of the Wordsworth household recapitulate this view to an extent. Dorothy Wordsworth comments of Maria Jane Jewsbury: "She has remarkable talents—a quickness of mind that is astonishing, and notwithstanding she has had a sickly infant to nurse and has bestowed this care upon the rest of her Brothers & Sisters, she is an authoress" (*LY* 1:435, 1 April 1826). Like her brother, Dorothy Wordsworth values Maria Jane Jewsbury for her feminine devotion, but she also recognizes her remarkable achievement of authorship in spite of her devotion to her family. Whereas Dorothy appreciates the difficulties Jewsbury has overcome, William's view resembles that of Robert Southey, the Wordsworths' neighbor and Poet Laureate of England, who gave Charlotte Brontë that infamous bit of advice: "Literature cannot be the business of a woman's life, and it ought not to be. The more she is engaged in her proper duties, the less leisure will she have for it, even as an accomplishment and recreation."[20]

Nowhere are Wordsworth's conventional views of "feminine duty"— especially for daughters—more evident than in a poem entitled "The Triad," composed in 1828 and published in *The Keepsake*, a popular gift annual for the Christmas season. Here Wordsworth dramatizes his persona as paterfamilias, not as visionary poet. The speaker imagines a heroic youth from "Olympian clime" (in a kind of latter-day judgment of Paris) who returns to earth to select a wife from among the "Phantasms" of three young women, later identified by Wordsworth as Edith Southey, Dora Wordsworth, and Sara Coleridge, daughters of the three poets. Although there are dramatic possibilities in the idea, Wordsworth does not imagine the material dramatically. Instead, he uses the fiction of the Olympian youth to paint portraits of the three young women as ideals of womanhood presented from a male point of view. We glimpse

no bodies, only modest blushes and feminine ringlets: beauty and delicacy framed by the poet's gaze. These portraits are distinct from each
other, but, as Sara Coleridge herself was to note, "There is no truth in
the poem as a whole, although bits and pieces of truth, glazed and magnified, are embodied in it" (*PW* 2:522).

The speaker presents each of the women to the youth as a potential
wife, addressing the first (Edith Southey) as such:

> "O Lady, worthy of earth's proudest throne!
> Nor less, by excellence of nature, fit
> Beside an unambitious hearth to sit
> Domestic queen, where grandeur is unknown;
> What living man could fear
> The worst of Fortune's malice, wert Thou near,
> Humbling that lily-stem, thy sceptre meek,
> That its fair flowers may from his cheek
> Brush the too happy tear?"
>
> (*PW* 2:52–60)

Edith Southey becomes a domestic queen presiding over her hearth with
a gentleness and sympathy that could comfort any man. She is a lady in
the senses of both the chivalric past and the pre-Victorian present. No
matter what happens, this woman will provide domestic calm and
refuge, happy in that she is as unambitious as her hearth. Idealized Dora
(whom Wordsworth can think of as a potential wife only in poetry)
"bears the stringed lute of old romance, / That cheered the trellised ar-
bour's privacy, / And soothed war-wearied knights in raftered hall"
(101–3). Wordsworth imagines Dora as the servant of man, inhabiting
the world of romance to soothe and comfort. Dora's guiding virtue is
the "self-forgetfulness" (160) appropriate to a devoted wife. Dora as a
young woman who performs her "feminine duty" at Rydal Mount fulfills Wordsworth's belief that a woman's accomplishment is best contained within domestic life. Finally, Sara, the most intellectually accom-
plished of the three, is praised not so much because of as in spite of her
learning. When considering the bookish Sara, the youth is urged not to
"dread the depth of meditative eye" (193), implying that there is a woman's heart there, too. Even Sara's intelligence and learning must fit into
the context of a woman's domestic life.[21]

Wordsworth as a paternal matchmaker not only confirms the domi-
nant gender ideology, but he also adopts the conventional method for
defining and constructing women from a male perspective that objectifies through idealization. As in the portrait of Jemima Quillinan, de-

scribed in "Lines Suggested by a Portrait from the Pencil of F. Stone" (from *Yarrow Revisited*), Wordsworth finds "emblematic purity" (*PW* 4:122, line 12) in these images of women. As Sara Coleridge noted, the portraits are both "glazed" and "magnified." Presumably she means that the poet glosses over many imperfections before he magnifies his images of perfection. "Glazed" may also suggest that the women are made artificial like pottery or painting—given an unnatural lustre for the purposes of display. Sara Coleridge gently resists being turned into a chaste art object: her comments give a voice to the "mute Phantoms" (212) imagined by the poet.

But Wordsworth does not give the women a voice in "The Triad"; he simply places them and their accomplishments in a world where they are defined in terms of their relationships with men who determine their destinies. He recognizes that they have artistic and intellectual abilities, but these abilities must be channeled into home and family—in Southey's words, into "proper . . . business of a woman's life." Most significantly, Wordsworth idealizes his own daughter as a typical early nineteenth-century woman; the narrator curbs and controls any other desires she might have.

GENDER PLAY IN "THE EGYPTIAN MAID"

"The Egyptian Maid; or the Romance of the Water Lily," published in *Yarrow Revisited*, brings into focus Wordsworth's attitude toward women in the later poetry. It also raises related questions of genre and gender, since he terms his only Arthurian poem a romance and places at its center a female character, Nina, the Lady of the Lake. Dora Wordsworth seems to be the presiding genius of this poem. Wordsworth wrote "The Egyptian Maid" quickly and happily in 1828, after several nonproductive months. Family letters reveal that during its composition the poet was unusually free from the ailments that generally plagued his attempts at writing. Mary Wordsworth reports to Edward Quillinan, "Wm . . . has within the last 8 days composed a Poem (for the next Keep-sake) of about 300 lines without let or hindrance from one uneasy feeling either of head or stomach" (*LY* 1:665, 25 November 1828); and in the same letter Wordsworth himself adds that "The Poem Mrs W—mentions is a sort of Romance—with no more solid foundation than the word—water lily but dont mention it—it rose out of my mind like an exhalation" (667). Although the literary source of this "exhalation" is Milton's description of Pandemonium in the first book of *Paradise Lost*

("Out of the earth a Fabric huge / Rose like an Exhalation," 710–11),
Wordsworth does not recall the sublime context of the Miltonic scene.
Rather, Wordsworth associates the genre of romance with ease and playfulness: the genre seems to provide both the space for a fantasy of female
power and a way to contain that power so that it does not become a
threat. Wordsworth embraces the magic of romance that he had rejected
twenty years earlier in *The White Doe of Rylstone*, but he dismisses any
serious implications. Significantly, Wordsworth revises his earlier stance
in terms of both genre and gender.

On the same day that the Wordsworths wrote to Quillinan, William
wrote a letter to George Huntly Gordon, in which he connects his romance directly with Dora:

> Our employments are odd enough here; my Daughter is at this moment, in
> my sight, finishing a picture of a Dragon—and I have just concluded a kind
> of romance with as much magic in it as would serve for half a Dozen—but I
> prefer poems to Dragons for my aerial journey. I hope you will be pleased
> with this poem of 360 verses when you see it—it rose from my brain, with-
> out let or hindrance, like a vapour.
>
> (*LY* 1:663)

Here the "exhalation" becomes "vapour," but Wordsworth continues
to emphasize the lightness and ease of composition. He also identifies his
poem as a romance in a qualified way (the "sort of" becomes "kind of"),
as if not wanting to claim too much for this 360-line poem. He draws a
connection between Dora and his romance: both father and daughter,
metaphorically speaking, are dragon-makers, creators of pictures and
plots in which aerial journeys and magical transformations are possible.
Dora inspires her father, accustomed to making his own life the matter
of his song, to write his first Arthurian romance. Dora, indeed, inspires
both the magic of romance and Wordsworth's wish to contain and do-
mesticate the feminine power and mystery associated with it.

Wordsworth judges "The Egyptian Maid" to be a strange poem, but
he seems to have been liberated by the Arthurian fantasy. As Mary
Wordsworth reveals, this poem was first destined for *The Keepsake*
along with "The Triad," although it was not actually published until
1835. Wordsworth's letters reveal that he became quite absorbed in the
poem, but this does not preclude the possibility that he also shaped it for
the *Keepsake* audience—casual readers of embellished gift books. This
is a far cry from the nervous author of *The White Doe* devising a theory
of reception around his fears of publication. Now Wordsworth resents
that he has to consider publishing in a keepsake simply because he is offered a tempting amount. He writes to a publisher, Samuel Carter Hall

(5 June ?1835): "You are perhaps aware that the Annuals with their or-
naments, have destroyed the Sale of several Poems which—till that Invention of some evil Spirit (a German one I believe) was transplanted to
this Country—brought substantial profit to their Authors, [and] were regarded as Standard works. . . . Competition, the Idol of the Political
economists, in fact ruins every thing"(*LY* 3:55–56). Resentful of his own
contributions to this "Idol," Wordsworth would have much preferred
to control the profits and presentation of his own "Standard works."[22]
Perhaps the crowning irony is that Wordsworth used the money he received from *The Keepsake* to finance his 1828 tour (*LY* 1:64n).

"The Egyptian Maid," nonetheless, is one of Wordsworth's conces-
sions to the popular market. In seeming to write an airy and insubstan-
tial romance, Wordsworth may have felt safely removed from his private life and his conflicted age, and thus the poem would be suitable for
casual drawing-room consumption. But despite its lightness, Wordsworth's poem presents anxious and ineffective fathers. And in this work
written for the most conventional kind of publication, Wordsworth
surprises us with unconventional gender roles: bumbling men and
strong women.

In "The Egyptian Maid" Wordsworth takes his characters' names
from Malory, but he creates his own narrative of the ship, *The Water
Lily*, carrying an Egyptian maid to Arthur's court. Since this poem is not
as well known today as it was in the 1830s, some plot summary may be
necessary. Merlin wrecks the ship because he envies its beauty and independence, but Nina, whose role remains unacknowledged, brings
about a happy resolution of events. The main text of "The Egyptian
Maid" falls into three episodes: Merlin's jealousy of and destruction of
the ship, Nina's instructions to Merlin and the rescue of the Egyptian
maid, and the awakening of the maid by Galahad at Arthur's court. This
main text is followed by the pious angels' song, an orthodox commentary on the main narrative.

"The Egyptian Maid" begins with Merlin "pac[ing] the Cornish
sands" as he spots a ship coming into view. Merlin is pleased with the
sight, even more pleased as the vision becomes clear:

> Upon this winged Shape so fair
> Sage Merlin gazed with admiration:
> Her lineaments, thought he, surpass
> Aught that was ever shown in magic glass;
> Was ever built with patient care;
> Or, at a touch, produced by happiest transformation.
> (*PW* 3:12–17)

While it is conventional to depict ships as feminine, Wordsworth here emphasizes gender. Utterly beautiful in "Shape" and "lineaments," the ship becomes the object of Merlin's insistent gaze. For a while Merlin is satisfied to gaze in admiration, but he eventually becomes jealous of this autonomous creation and wants to control it: "'My art shall tame her pride—'" (28). The pride Merlin attributes to the ship is an affront to his power. A conflict develops in which Merlin calls up a storm. The ship "wantonly [laves] / Her sides, the Wizard's craft confounding" (43–44), but finally Merlin succeeds in destroying her: "The storm has stripped her of her leaves; / The Lily floats no longer!—She hath perished" (53–54). Wordsworth depicts Merlin's action as a kind of sexual transgression, in which the ship is "stripped" and destroyed.

Throughout these stanzas, the narrator describes the ship as a beautiful creature, seemingly unaware of the danger she is in. In the manuscript, the lines "[Merlin] cast / An altered look upon the advancing Stranger" (24–25) had been "Full soon a sullen look he cast / Upon the bright unconscious Stranger." Wordsworth's use of "wantonly" in line 43 could suggest a lascivious or flirtatious quality, but it seems more likely to express the sportiveness of the "for ever fresh and young" (46) ship. In the dynamics of this scene the ship is more a victim of Merlin's "freakish will" (23) than a conscious enticer of his gaze.

Following this description, the narrator turns to the reader in an attempt to control the response to the episode:

> Grieve for her, she deserves no less;
> So like, yet so unlike, a living Creature!
> No heart had she, no busy brain;
> Though loved, she could not love again;
> Though pitied, *feel* her own distress;
> Nor aught that troubles us, the fools of Nature.
>   (55–60)

By reminding us that the ship is not a living creature, the narrator paradoxically reinforces the episode as representing a human drama. Such a fate, the lines imply, *can* befall one who loves and feels.

In this opening episode the female remains powerless, prey to male destruction: both the ship and the maid are victims and no more. But Wordsworth soon subverts any sense of Merlin's invincibility. Merlin flees back into his cave, "repentant all too late" (69), sulking like a naughty boy who has gotten what he wants and still is not happy. Merlin's will dissolves before Nina, who descends upon him to explain the

consequences of his caprice. The scene is comic in its reversal of expectations: the powerful sorcerer remains silent as the Lady of the
Lake chastises, explains, and instructs. Nina explains that the ship with
the emblematic lily flower—"a sign of heathen power" (75)—was
carrying a young princess who would renounce her heathen faith and
marry a Christian from Arthur's court. While Nina goes off to find the
sleeping beauty, Merlin pores over his books in search of a way to
awaken her.

When Merlin brings the princess to Caerleon in a car pulled by
swans, he accepts no responsibility for her fate. He simply explains
to the court that she was the victim of a shipwreck. Indeed, he implicitly takes the credit for the rescue and suggests that it is he who will
be able to wake the princess from her death-like sleep ("I, whose
skill / Wafted her hither," 244–45). In reality, Nina is the power behind
Merlin's posturing.

Nina controls the final moment when Galahad's touch awakens the
princess. Although Galahad seems to be responsible, the narrator reveals
that Nina has manipulated the denouement:

> For late, as near a murmuring stream
> He rested 'mid an arbour green and shady,
> Nina, the good Enchantress, shed
> A light around his mossy bed;
> And, at her call, a waking dream
> Prefigured to his sense the Egyptian Lady.
>
> (301–6)

This passage evokes images of paradise—specifically, two scenes from
Paradise Lost: Adam's dream (8:452–90), which Keats likens to the
imagination (37, letter to Bailey, 22 November 1817), and Satan's disruption of Eve's sleep (5:28–95). Nina's prefigurative vision is all to the
good here and leads directly to Galahad's success. Like the Adam of
Keats's interpretation, Galahad awakens and finds truth; the princess
awakens to a recreated paradise with the swans singing "Like sinless
snakes in Eden's happy land" (323).

Arthur, unaware either of Merlin's guilt or of Nina's role, praises
"God and Heaven's pure Queen" (342) for the happy union of the
princess and Galahad. Arthur's orthodox Christian response foreshad-
ows the eight-stanza angels' song that concludes the poem. But as the
opening stanzas of that conclusion reveal, the angels' song adds a moralistic and judgmental commentary:

> Who shrinks not from alliance
> Of evil with good Powers
> To God proclaims defiance,
> And mocks whom he adores.
>
> A Ship to Christ devoted
> From the Land of Nile did go;
> Alas! the bright Ship floated,
> An Idol at her prow.
>
> By magic domination,
> The Heaven-permitted vent
> Of purblind mortal passion,
> Was wrought her punishment.
>   (355–66)

These lines misread the narrative, placing a narrowly moralistic interpretation on what had been a much more open and generous story. The
stanzas are reminiscent of the glosses added to *The Rime of the Ancient
Mariner*, which function less to clarify than to complicate. The angels see
the ship as a mockery of God, because the "Idol" at her prow marks an
unholy alliance with the Christian mission of the ship. The angels claim
that Merlin was allowed to vent his "purblind mortal passion," by which
means the ship "Was wrought her punishment" for carrying the Idol.

The contradictions of the angels' song, with its ambiguous and con-
torted syntax, bring the unresolved tensions in Wordsworth's suppos-
edly carefree fantasy to the foreground. While it is true that the poem
presents an easy dichotomy between heathen East and Christian West in
the main narrative, the ship and the lotus carved on the prow are in fact
represented in a much more positive way through Nina's eyes as she
searches for the princess in the wrecked ship:

> Soon did the gentle Nina reach
> That Isle without a house or haven;
> Landing, she found not what she sought,
> Nor saw of wreck or ruin aught
> But a carved Lotus cast upon the beach
> By the fierce waves, a flower in marble graven.
>
> Sad relique, but how fair the while!
> For gently each from each retreating
> With backward curve, the leaves revealed
> The bosom half, and half concealed,
> Of a Divinity, that seemed to smile
> On Nina, as she passed, with hopeful greeting.
>   (121–32)

The goddess represented by the lotus is benevolent, certainly not the threatening idol described by the angels. Nina herself had explained that "a Goddess with a Lily flower" (76) was an emblem "Of joy immortal and of pure affection" (78).

Furthermore, in his note preceding the published poem, Wordsworth claims that "the Lotus, with the bust of the Goddess appearing to rise out of the full-blown flower, was suggested by the beautiful work of ancient art, once included among the Townley Marbles, and now in the British Museum" (*PW* 3:232). Wordsworth writes in the spirit of Keats standing before a Grecian urn, and not as a moralistic censor of pagan art. Add to that Wordsworth's love of the lotus or water lily, recorded by Isabella Fenwick: "This plant has been my delight from my boyhood, as I have seen it floating on the lake" (*PW* 3:502), and the angels' condemnation of the image of the lotus becomes even more suspect.

The angels' song is subtly connected to the politics of gender. In "The Egyptian Maid" Wordsworth evokes the kind of female power that Nina Auerbach identifies in *Woman and the Demon*—a "self-transforming power surging beneath apparent victimization"—for while he creates the passive sleeping beauty he sets another woman at the heart of her awakening.[23] But Wordsworth is careful to identify Nina with virtue and benevolence, not with the sexually charged demonism that Auerbach finds in other sources. Nina rescues the sleeping "Damsel" (141) and carries her to Merlin for the journey to Caerleon. Heaven praises her action: "Thou hast achieved, fair Dame! what none / Less pure in spirit could have done" (153–54). But in the third part of the narrative Wordsworth deflects attention from Nina's powers, instead focusing on the awakening princess, who speaks not a word, and concluding with the angels' song.

Nina orchestrates the resolution, while men—particularly fathers and kings—prove ineffective. Arthur laments for the princess and her father, who has surrendered his daughter to Arthur's court as a reward for Arthur's freeing his realm from invaders. The poem centers on Arthur's lament for the maid, "Is this her piety's reward?" (214). Arthur feels responsible because of the vow he has made to her father, and he imagines the father's response:

> "Rich robes are fretted by the moth;
> Towers, temples, fall by stroke of thunder;
> Will that, or deeper thoughts, abate
> A Father's sorrow for her fate?
> He will repent him of his troth;
> His brain will burn, his stout heart split asunder.["]
> (217–22)

Arthur remains as helpless to save the princess as was the ocean to save
the ship: "But Ocean under magic heaves, / And cannot spare the Thing
he cherished" (49–50). Like Tennyson's Arthur, Wordsworth's king is
well-meaning and avuncular, but not in control.

Merlin, however, demonstrates a type of male power that seems
both to fascinate and to repel Wordsworth. Just as Merlin observes
the female ship, so does the poet-persona in Wordsworth's earlier
sonnet "With Ships the sea was sprinkled far and nigh" (1807;
PW 3:18):

> A goodly Vessel did I then espy
> Come like a giant from a haven broad;
> And lustily along the bay she strode,
> Her tackling rich, and of apparel high.
> The Ship was nought to me, nor I to her,
> Yet I pursued her with a Lover's look.

In a letter written to Lady Beaumont about this sonnet, Wordsworth explains the way the mind of the perceiver focuses on this one ship out of
the mass of ships at sea, follows the ship, and then lets it go (*MY*
1:145–51). What Wordsworth and later critics of the sonnet have not
noted is the metaphorical structure in which the poet-persona is a lover
pursuing this impressive feminine object, who strides "lustily along the
bay." On the metapoetic level this is a Petrarchan love sonnet about the
poetic process—the male poet identifies the object of his desire but his
gaze cannot hold her in place: "She will brook / No tarrying." The poet's control is limited, and the object exists in the poem as a fleeing presence. She has not been tamed.[24]

In "The Egyptian Maid," the object's beauty and independence
threaten Merlin's sovereignty, so he exerts his will over her. In attempting to appropriate the ship, he destroys it through his transgression.
While the poet-persona of the sonnet merely records Merlin's failure to
hold the object, in fact Merlin betrays the potentially destructive power
of the artist's gaze, in much the same way that in many of his poems
Browning reveals what Carol T. Christ has called the "transgressive impulse" of the male artist.[25]

From his earliest poems, Wordsworth recognized the dangers of the
desire for appropriation. Ambivalence about the psychic costs of conquest and domination, for instance, appears in "Nutting" (1798), a
poem about transgressive male power often cited in feminist readings of
Wordsworth.[26] We recall that in "Nutting" the "sweet mood" (39)
abruptly ends:

> . . . Then up I rose,
> And dragged to earth both branch and bough, with crash
> And merciless ravage: and the shady nook
> Of hazels, and the green and mossy bower,
> Deformed and sullied, patiently gave up
> Their quiet being . . .
>
> (43–48)

In "Nutting" the boy "sall[ies] forth" (5) as an invader of the bower of romance, a questing hero disturbed by a recognition of his own power into a discovery of otherness. Considering the violence of this action and imagery, it is no wonder that Wordsworth did not include this poem in *The Prelude*, the narrative of his life, even though thematically it fits with the boat-stealing episode as a haunting transgression.

What distinguishes Merlin in "The Egyptian Maid" from other transgressors is that Wordsworth makes him a comic character who creates mischief and then sulks back into his cave. The drama of "Nutting" is transformed in "The Egyptian Maid" by debunking humor, a transformation that resembles the difference between Laodamia as imagined by Virgil, on the one hand, and by Ovid, on the other. Wordsworth also counters Merlin's transgression with Nina's restorations. Although all would be chaos without Nina, her role is concealed to preserve the illusion of male power. Wordsworth, then, writes a poem that upholds the pieties of his time but also reveals how the masculine world is secretly held together by women. What a remarkable poem for the poet of Rydal Mount to imagine: a powerful and competent woman bringing order to the mess caused by sulking magicians and ineffectual kings. Perhaps this is Wordsworth's oblique way of coming to terms with the women who have created his household and made his poetic career possible. And perhaps, too, Wordsworth knew it: the playfulness of the poem allows him to let down his guard as he praises not masculine power but the feminine beauty embodied by the lotus and the princess. And not just beauty and delicacy, but strength. I also see a kind of self-deprecating humor in "The Egyptian Maid" that reminds us of the poet laughing himself to scorn at the end of "Resolution and Independence." The playfulness, however, masks a serious concern with the roles of father and daughter.

But the poem succeeded with readers who saw it as a simple male-centered romance, with no regard for the role of Nina. One reviewer enthusiastically proclaimed that "The lady revives, and the knight is blest," concluding that after reading "The Egyptian Maid" he could say that

"The days of chivalry are *not* yet gone, while such poems are produced." In this review from *Fraser's Magazine* 11 (June 1835), the poem becomes a simple tale of Merlin's ingenuity and Arthur's chivalry: a perfect patriarchal fantasy.

HOUSEHOLD WORDSWORTH

Despite the emphasis of the *Fraser's* reviewer, women, of course, played a major role in Wordsworth's poetry, in its reception, and in his daily life. And Wordsworth helped to cultivate a new attitude toward poetry both in the way he presented himself and in the way he was viewed by others in the 1820s and 1830s. Although Wordsworth did become popular with men at Cambridge in the 1820s, he himself sensed that his real popularity was with women, especially in the 1830s. In a letter of 1836, for instance, Wordsworth claims that "The ladies appear to be my chief admirers, and whatever the creatures may think of me I appear in the absence and default of others to be grown into popularity" (*LY* 3:241). Interestingly, Wordsworth seems to see himself filling the gap that literary history has seen him occupying between the deaths of Byron and Scott and the ascendancy of Tennyson. He also credits his popularity to women readers here and in another letter of 1836, in which he says, "My admirers are greatly increased among the female sex" (244).

Women writers and readers of the period confirm Wordsworth's view. Felicia Hemans, arguably the most popular poet of the 1820s and 1830s, especially in America, saw Wordsworth as a poet of domesticity.[27] In her tribute "To Wordsworth" she situates the poet

> . . . by some hearth where happy faces meet,
>   When night hath hushed the woods, with all their birds,
> There, from some gentle voice, that lay were sweet
>   As antique music, linked with household words;
> While in pleased murmurs woman's lip might move,
>   And the raised eye of childhood shine in love.[28]

Hemans's Wordsworth is not the Romantic conqueror of our mythology, not the solitary poet of the egotistical sublime, but the poet of household affections, of family and hearth. Hemans praises Wordsworth for the very qualities for which she was admired. Although Wordsworth did not award his rival uncritical admiration, he did see himself in the 1830s in the same way Felicia Hemans and Maria Jane Jewsbury saw him: as a poet who celebrated domesticity and sought to find his way into the hearts of his countrymen (and women) through his poetry.

In the 1830s Wordsworth wants to reconfirm an image of himself as having always been the British poet of household affections. He takes indignant exception to Henry F. Chorley's unauthorized biography of himself in *The Authors of England* for claiming that he had written "fierce" poems in his youth that he had been forced to disavow. Wordsworth writes to his publisher Moxon that "Miss Martineau I am told has said that my poems are in the hearts of the American People. That is the place I would fain occupy among the People of these Islands" (*LY* 3:519). Typically, Wordsworth sees himself in terms of Britain and British literature. Hemans could have the Americans, who "in their present state of intellectual culture" would find her more useful than his "more powerful productions" (*LY* 3:139n). Although Wordsworth sees himself in the role of household poet, he will not allow his reputation to become completely feminized, and he still uses the charged language of the Preface to *Lyrical Ballads* and the "Essay, Supplementary" of 1815.

Male writers and readers confirm this view of Wordsworth as a poet of home and hearth. In an interesting anecdote, Tennyson's biographer Robert Martin describes Tennyson and Edward FitzGerald on a visit to the Lake District, home of the poet whom Tennyson called the "dear old fellow" and FitzGerald "the Daddy."[29] Their nicknames for Wordsworth reveal the extent to which he was regarded as a paterfamilias of English poetry by its new practitioners, whether with Tennyson's admiration or FitzGerald's mixed feelings about Wordsworth's alleged solemnity. While visiting the Lakes, Tennyson was rereading much of Wordsworth and reading the new volume *Yarrow Revisited*, which, according to Martin, reached Ambleside while Tennyson was still there (202). Tennyson also wrote his most Wordsworthian poem, "Dora," in 1835, a poem based on Mary Russell Mitford's story "Dora Creswell" from *Our Village* (1828) and overlaid with a good bit of the Wordsworthian pastoral "Michael." The Wordsworth whom Tennyson imitated in "Dora" was a poet of home and hearth—but a home and hearth associated with a rural England that was vanishing even in 1800, as the plot of "Michael" makes clear. To Tennyson, Wordsworth seemed to be the primary example of a male poet who was reinscribing the affections in poetry—and locating woman's place within that domestic sphere.

Putting Tennyson's "Dora" and Wordsworth's "Egyptian Maid" side by side, we can see that "Dora" is much more "Wordsworthian" than Wordsworth's own poem is. Consider, for instance, these lines, so reminiscent of the language and tone of "Michael":

> Then there came a day
> When Allan called his son, and said, 'My son:
> I married late, but I would wish to see
> My grandchild on my knees before I die:
> And I have set my heart upon a match.
> Now therefore look to Dora; she is well
> To look to; thrifty too beyond her age.'
>   (8–14)

Wordsworth is reputed to have told Tennyson that he had been trying all his life to write a pastoral like "Dora." In fact, Wordsworth had succeeded in such poems as "Michael" and "The Brothers," both of which derive their grandeur from a stark biblical style and simple syntax, a style that Tennyson consciously copied in "Dora" and one so unlike that of his better-known lyrics and narratives. Ironically, "The Egyptian Maid," with its Arthurian trappings and musical rhythm, seems closer to Tennyson's early poems, with which Wordsworth was familiar.[30] What links all of these poems is a concern with fathers and their relationships to their children, as well as an attraction to (and a standing back from) women. Both "Dora" and "The Egyptian Maid" describe a world in which women mediate disputes and bring families together, but get very little outward credit for their actions.

Both the older pastoral "Michael" and the new poems in *Yarrow Revisited*, which included "The Egyptian Maid" and "The Triad," reinforced for readers of the 1830s the view of Wordsworth as poet who celebrated the home as uniting the authority of the father (even questionable fathers like Wordsworth's Arthur and his earlier Michael) with the moral strength (and sometimes unacknowledged power) of the mother. "The Egyptian Maid," despite its fantastic setting and events and its chivalric manners, reinscribes these homey values onto romance. Like the ideal Victorian home, it both celebrates and controls a powerful feminine presence—not just passive maidens but powerful women.

From his earliest poetry, as we have seen, Wordsworth had revealed a tendency to the monologic and to male definitions of female experience. In "Tintern Abbey" Wordsworth looks into his sister's "wild eyes" and sees a reflection of himself and his history. In her article on the ideology of womanhood in the nineteenth century, Judith Newton identifies a shift from 1798 to 1850, from Wordsworth's "Tintern Abbey" to Arnold's "The Buried Life," from the representation of woman as mirror for man to woman as man's refuge from the world.[31] Newton need not have gone to Arnold to articulate this change. Perhaps Wordsworth imagines himself as one of those war-wearied knights that Dora soothes in "The Triad," not wearied, perhaps, by direct participation in the world of commerce and manufacturing (although his ventures into popular publishing brought him close to that world), but needing support at a time when he felt increasingly at odds with the "progress" of his society. Rydal Mount became a haven from such forces. Whereas in "Tintern Abbey" William cannot see Dorothy's otherness through the lens of his egotism, in his later poetry Wordsworth is faced with an otherness that he shapes to his own desires, an otherness of passive Egyptian maids and secretly empowered goddesses who work for the good of men.

Wordsworth's view of women in his later poetry harmonizes with his increasingly formal and ceremonial attitude.[32] He is more concerned with the outward, often pictorial manifestations of tradition than he was earlier: he stations Dora before the tea urn and crowns Edith Southey queen of her hearth. Furthermore, religious orthodoxy converges with the ideology of women's piety. Woman's place is as set as the rituals of baptism, communion, and marriage in the *Ecclesiastical Sketches*. In his emphasis on custom and ceremony (but not in his emphasis on religious orthodoxy) Wordsworth anticipates Yeats's "A Prayer for My Daughter": "And may her bridegroom bring her to a house / Where all's accustomed, ceremonious" (73–74).[33] At Rydal Mount, custom and ceremony could and did flourish, with Wordsworth as paterfamilias and various women playing their allotted supporting roles in the romance of their household.

Conclusion:
Dora Wordsworth,
a Daughter's Story

My dear Sir,

I earnestly wish that the little volume here inscribed to you, in token of affectionate veneration, were pervaded by more numerous traces of those strengthening and elevating influences which breathe from all your poetry—'a power to virtue friendly'. I wish, too, that such token could more adequately convey my deep sense of gratitude for moral and intellectual benefit long derived from the study of that poetry—for the perpetual fountains of 'serious faith and inward glee' which I have never failed to discover amidst its pure and lofty regions—for the fresh green places of refuge which it has offered me in many an hour when

> The fretful stir
> Unprofitable, and fever of the world
> Have hung upon the beatings of my heart;

and when I have found in your thoughts and images such relief as the vision of your 'sylvan Wye' may, at similar times, have afforded to yourself.

> *Felicia Hemans, canceled Dedication to*
> Scenes and Hymns of Life, *1834*

Then I made her get a book, and read English to me for an hour by way of penance. I frequently dosed her with Wordsworth in this way and Wordsworth steadied her soon; she had difficulty in comprehending his deep, serene and sober mind; his language too was not facile to her; she had to ask questions; to sue for explanations; to be like a child and acknowledge me as her senior and director. Her instinct instantly penetrated and possessed the meaning of more ardent imaginative writers; Byron excited her; Scott, she loved; Wordsworth only, she puzzled at, wondered over, and hesitated to pronounce an opinion upon.

> *Charlotte Brontë,* The Professor *(1857)*

In chapter 5 much of the poetry and many of the letters quoted were concerned with or were inspired by Dora Wordsworth: as an infant, a child, a young woman. Dora emerges from these texts as a dutiful daughter who assumes a major role in her father's life and in the life of Rydal Mount: taking dictation, presiding at tea, visiting neighbors, threatening to become a scholar (see figure 6). Dora's letters and papers do not contradict this image so much as they reveal the difficulties inherent in assuming the domestic role and in her later attempt to modify the script. Dora's travel journal of 1828, quoted briefly in chapter 5, reveals much about Dora's character and her commitments. In her letters, too, Dora shows herself to be a generous and loving person, but a woman who sometimes feels her generosity and love stretched to the limit, as we shall see particularly in letters to Maria Jane Jewsbury and in one crucial letter that she wrote to Isabella Fenwick upon first visiting Tintern Abbey.[1]

But before looking at either the travel journal or at this group of letters, I would like to clarify Dora's perspective on gender. It is clear that Dora grew up in a household of talented, thinking women, but not women who sympathized with radical notions of gender or of equality between the sexes. From her early letters on and in her journals, for instance, Dorothy Wordsworth voices contempt for bluestockings and for anything that smacks of female literary careerism. In the 1820s, when Felicia Hemans presented herself at Rydal Mount, the women generally felt that she talked too much and thought too much of her own talents. Nor did they look kindly on Sara Coleridge's intense studies, even though Sara Coleridge never had ambitions for a literary career. Much later, Harriet Martineau was welcome at the Mount, in part, I think, because her eccentricities were so endearing that they cloaked her intellectual accomplishments.

Dora Wordsworth for the most part accepted the outlook of Rydal Mount, as her actions and comments make clear. In a letter to Susan Wordsworth (27 July ?1843), Dora describes a visit to the Mount by a Dr. Howe and his wife from Boston. Dora's response is both funny and revealing, for she first describes the doctor and then says that he came "with a horrid rude clever, radical woman of a wife Oh what a dislike I took to that woman." "Horrid rude clever"—all in one breath. Only add "radical" and the description is complete. Wordsworth himself, with characteristic disdain for Americans, writes to Miss Fenwick: "The Husband is an intelligent Man, and his Wife passes among Americans as a bright Specimen of the best they produce in female character" (*LY* 4:461).

Figure 6. *Dora Wordsworth*. Watercolor on ivory by Margaret Gillies. 1839.
By permission of the Wordsworth Trust, Dove Cottage, Grasmere, England.

I surmise that this horrid woman was none other than the feminist Julia Ward Howe, who visited Rydal Mount with her husband, an admirer of Wordsworth. No doubt Mrs. Hemans was meek in Dora's eyes in comparison to what she saw as this American virago. Dora had a generous spirit, but even her generosity was cooled by the spectacle of this woman, who perhaps presented many opinions about the woman "problem" that Dora found threatening. In this case, Wordsworth's description of Dora in "The Triad"—"Insight as keen as frosty star / Is to her charity no bar" (149–50)—misses the mark.

DORA ON THE RHINE: SUMMER, 1828

Dora's identification with the values of Rydal Mount did not shield her from controversy or prevent her from thinking and feeling for herself. Dora may never have succeeded as a student of German, but, as her journal of 1828 reveals, she became a keen and usually sympathetic observer of the human and natural scene. Dora made the most of her education: she read her father's poetry, and she read and thought about journals written by her aunt and mother. She was aware of the conventions of journal-writing and wanted to create vivid descriptions for her family to share. She was also aware of her responsibility in recording the journey "through Belgium, down the Meuse by boat, up the Rhine to Godesberg and back through Holland" (*Moorman* 2:435) as a memorial of time spent with her father and Coleridge.

In addition to the descriptions she includes in her journal, Dora hopes to bring home pencil sketches of interesting scenes. She expends a good bit of energy setting up her sketching apparatus, only to be disturbed by hordes of onlookers who break her concentration. This entry is typical: "I sat me down, soon a rabble was collected, my Father did his best to encourage me, & disperse the crowd but it was all in vain & not having nerve[?] to bear the idea of *positively blocking up* the causeway I rose in a fluster—anxious as I was to bring away one at least characteristic memorial of a Dutch Town" (82).

Although Dora is often frustrated, she does produce several sketches (which, unfortunately, have not been preserved with the manuscript). But even though we lack this visual record, in her journal Dora does indeed recreate the scenes in vivid, pictorial language. In fact, she characteristically thinks in compositional terms and frames each scene for a viewer, commenting on both the scene and her way of perceiving it: "Town beautiful vanishing from our sight—whilst in front exquisite views open upon us. Walls of rock on each side assuming grotesque forms. Now a Tower, now a Pillar—now rounded, now square"(16b). Dora says that she sees everything with an "English eye" (29), and she refers to Lake District colors and skies: "today has been quite a Lake colouring day" (41). As she composes her scenes with a disciplined eye, Dora uses such words as *frame* and *foreground* and refers to painterly techniques: "The Ruined Castle of Hammerstein on the ridge of a hill was very fine; it presented itself to us under favorable circumstances, backed by a wild sky one that Salvatore Rosa would have delighted in" (36).

What I have found most interesting about Dora's composition is that she highlights the human element and includes the sometimes rough and messy details of everyday life, a technique linked in chapter 1 to the picturesque and to women artists. Dora's scenes are not neatly compartmentalized. For instance, on the way to Ghent she sees this:

> Country very interesting—a tempting road through Avenues of trees to our left—women reaping, cloth bleaching—a flock of Sheep tended by their Shepherd & his Dog which would make a sweet picture—Banks deepen lowly Cottages sprinkled about—road on each bank & each through an avenue of trees—Water lilies abundant—a black & white Goat tottered close together on the steep bank.
>
> (7)

What is so striking about this entry is the way that Dora weaves together—really, pieces together like a quilt—the various elements she sees, adopting a technique that will be familiar to readers of Dorothy Wordsworth's journals. Dora's details come alive in a loosely unified composition, but the details have an integrity and poignancy of their own. Dora sees people at work (women reaping) and the material results of labor (cloth bleaching); she reveals the human dependency on nature and the interrelationship of the human and animal worlds in the "sweet picture" of the shepherd. Her final image of the tottering goats seems to suggest the precariousness of it all—yet she holds the scene together.

Dora is intrigued by perspective in more than a visual sense. Upon entering a village, she comments that "People become more humanized" (41) when you get close to them. She wants people to be human, to be individuals, and she tries to think beyond stereotypes. Dora also empathizes with the people she meets and focuses on their points of view. For instance, she describes an encounter that Wordsworth uses for his poem "The Jewish Family." Wordsworth invokes the "Genius of

Raphael" (1) to inspire his description of the beautiful children of this
impoverished woman. Wordsworth's poem is sympathetic and appreciative, yet he idealizes the family (a mother, a son, and two daughters),
viewing them as representatives of the Jewish diaspora:

> Two lovely Sisters, still and sweet
>   As flowers, stand side by side;
> Their soul-subduing looks might cheat
>   The Christian of his pride:
> Such beauty hath the Eternal poured
>   Upon them not forlorn,
> Though of a lineage once abhorred,
>   Nor yet redeemed from scorn.
>   (33–40)

Although Dora does not want to "anticipate Father's Poem by tran-
scribing my thoughts & feelings," she cannot resist noting "one affect-
ing thing. . . . When Mr. Coleridge told this Rachel how much he admired her Child—'Yes,' said she, 'she is beautiful (adding with a sigh)
but see these rags & misery—' pointing to its frock *wh* was made up of
a thousand patches" (49; also quoted in *PW* 2:525n). Whereas Wordsworth takes the perspective of the idealizing Christian viewing the family's otherness, Dora Wordsworth allows the woman to speak of her
misery and to reveal her awareness of the paradox that such a bereft
child could be so beautiful. Dora does not so much anticipate her father's poem as she complements his perspective. Her way of seeing seems
closer to Joanna Baillie's theory in her "Introductory Discourse": "The
Highest pleasure we receive from poetry, as well as from real objects
which surround us in the world, are derived from the sympathetic interest we all take in beings like ourselves" (6). Even in 1843, when
Wordsworth was recalling the scene for Isabella Fenwick, he focused on
the physical beauty and "intelligence of [the Jews'] countenances" as opposed to those of the German peasantry, rather than commenting on this
particular woman's plight. And yet one sentence in his note reveals her
devotion to her faith and its laws despite her destitute (and abandoned?)
state: "We had taken a little dinner with us in a basket, and invited them
to partake of it, which the mother refused to do, both for herself and
children, saying it was with them a fast-day; adding diffidently, that
whether such observances were right or wrong, she felt it her duty to
keep them strictly" (*PW* 2:525n).

Throughout her journal Dora Wordsworth is aware of the potential
for the poetic or artistic vision to obscure as well as clarify the material

scene. For instance, she describes the following scene around Coblentz when a storm was gathering:

> far too poetical a scene for me to write upon[—]a wild, glowing, yet subdued sky veiled in part by the rapidly advancing storm—a building of lurid white—nay of a color only heard of in enchanted Castles rising out of a river—behind it a field or lawn of a green which could only come from faery land and this seen under the arches of a noble massive & gloomy bridge—The falling rain too soon awoke us from our dream. We hastened on Shore—took shelter under a gate-way where fifty ragged Children—put to flight all bewitching or poetical imaginings—
>
> (37–38)

Dora Wordsworth can paint this picture of an enchanted castle in faery land in all its splendor, but the most interesting part of the passage occurs at the end, when the presence of "fifty ragged Children" brings the viewer back to earth. What strikes me is not only the contrast between the enchanted scene and the ragged children, but the fact that Dora recognizes the implicit suffering of the children and deliberately puts them in the picture so that her readers can see in this perspective too. Dora wants to inscribe—not transcend—the material world and its inhabitants, although she is moved by and comments on the religious art and architecture that she observes. Dora's spirituality, in other words, is grounded in empathic responses to the people and the world around her, not in renunciation or transcendence.

DORA AT TINTERN ABBEY: SPRING 1838

We recall that Dorothy Wordsworth was eager to subdue the waywardness of young Dora's character. Dora herself suggests that it was the discipline of school that finally taught her this control. When writing to her godchild Jemima Quillinan on Jemima's fourteenth birthday (6 October 1833), Dora thinks of herself at fourteen and writes that "school-discipline to me who till that time had been perfectly wild was as irksome as it was needful but when once broken in I found the life a very happy one & after an imprisonment of three years I was almost as loath to resume my liberty as I had been to part with it." It seems in this letter that Dora is initiating Jemima into the feminine role of nun-like imprisonment. Dora could be giving a personal commentary on "Nuns Fret Not," implying that she too had felt the weight of too much liberty.

But despite this seeming acceptance, Dora's letters of the period betray a sadness and a yearning. Dora's sense of loss is particularly apparent in her correspondence with Maria Jane Jewsbury, which continues until her friend's death in 1833. In these letters, the only group of Dora's letters published thus far, Dora writes intensely of her love for her friends and family. She refers to Sara Coleridge's marriage and new infant daughter and follows the difficult story of Edith Southey's plans to marry. But most telling is her response to Maria Jane Jewsbury's own marriage plans. Jewsbury had introduced herself to the Wordsworth family as an admirer of the poet and an aspiring "poetess" herself. She had become friendly with the whole family but was especially intimate with Dora. In a letter to Dora (12 March 1831) Jane (then thirty, three years older than Dora) wrote that she hoped to marry a poor clergyman named Mr. Fletcher, of whom her father disapproved but who was given a probationary period. Jane describes Mr. Fletcher as "one, who, if he realize his own temporal prospects, and satisfy my moral requirements— I shall certainly feel bound in honour and inclination to marry, some time after his probation is ended."[2] Some of the conflicts Jewsbury felt may have affected Dora Wordsworth quite personally: Maria Jane Jewsbury wanted her father's approval for her marriage, and she felt torn in leaving her widowed father and younger siblings for a life of her own. In the letter quoted above, she refers to her sister Geraldine as nearly nineteen and presumably capable of taking her place in the family. Thus Dora witnessed closely the wretchedness of her friend who desired to marry against the will of her father and who already had given the siblings "the best of me." By mid-October 1831 Jewsbury wrote of her impending marriage to Mr. Fletcher, who had accepted a chaplaincy with the East India Company in Bengal.[3]

In March 1831 Dora writes another letter to Jane. This document reveals her feelings on the prospect of her friend's marriage—the move to Bengal, which intensifies her unhappiness, is not yet in the picture. Rather than the more public stance of happiness at Jane's good fortune, Dora confides:

> You well know with what feelings your letter was seized & read; a thousand thousand thanks—for the first time in my life I have had to struggle against the feeling that distance & death only differ in name—when I had you by [m]y side I could not think so—now alas at times it weighs me to the ground—when I pass your door—when I throw myself on the sofa—when I stroll into the garden. I feel mournful stillness—sad & mournful as the stillness of death—This I know will wear [a]way, but the love & affection which

now call out the feeling will never fade [I think I m[a]y say never may I not?] I am perfectly calm & cheerful downstairs; my sadness I keep to myself—& indeed I do not nurse it—but endeavour to be thankful for the large portion of undeserved pleasure that has been granted to me—

When you left me I turned to the only fountain, whence pure hope, comfort, & consolation can be drawn—then I read your letter & then what do you think I had strength & courage to do—In compliance with your wish I burnt all your letters except those written to me during your illness these treasures I will never part with—by the time I had done this—Father & Mother were returned from their drive to Grasmere & found me bright as usual & ready to read to them which I did—But when I retired to my own room oh it was more than I had strength for—then I did give way & wept myself to sleep long before you had gone to rest—[4]

This letter suggests not only the degree of the love between the friends, but also the fact that their relationship is much closer even than Dora's with her immediate family. Much has been written about such intense female relationships—how common they actually were in nineteenth-century England and America.[5] While there might be genuine love and devotion felt for family (as there certainly was in Dora's case), this female friendship fulfills a need for intimacy that cannot be found in merely familial relationships. The kind of love Dora feels for her parents makes her want to protect them and thus to hide her grief: to be bright as usual downstairs but let the grief overflow in private. By burning the letters Dora makes sure that no one else will share Jane's intimacy—although Jane obviously preserved Dora's letters. And from the comments that Wordsworth makes to Quillinan on Jewsbury's death, it is clear that he either does not understand or does not acknowledge the depth of Dora's love for her:

Poor Mrs Fletcher (Miss Jewsbury that was) has found a grave in India— from the first we had a fore-feeling that it would be so. She was a bright Spirit, and her sparkling, of which she had at times too much, was settling gradually into a steady light. Her journal is to her friends very interesting, and I cannot but think that if she had survived, we should have had from her pen some account of Indian appearances and doings with which the public would have been both amused and instructed. She died of Cholera, but the particulars of her death have not reached her friends.

(LY 2:719, June 1834)

What is remarkable is the absence of any comment on Dora's loss, which must have been far greater than that of the public who could no longer hope for amusement and instruction from Jewsbury's pen. Indeed,

Wordsworth fails to exhibit any real feeling for Jewsbury's literary ambitions. But beyond that, either he betrays great insensitivity, or he is
simply oblivious to Dora's intense love.

When Dora contemplates Jane's marriage, even before she knows that
her friend's destination will be another continent, she anticipates the loss
of the frequent visits and shared feelings. Her language is extreme—she
is seized with emotions on receiving the letter; for the first time in her
life she connects death with distance. The stillness that Wordsworth had
valued for its spiritual consolation in *The White Doe* becomes for Dora
the dread of emptiness. The emotions Dora feels are closer to her father's
"Strange fits of passion," where the narrator associates death and loss
with his distance from Lucy's cottage and confides his story to "the
lover's ear alone." She writes to Jane using the language of love, and goes
on to say, "I wish I might just be alone for a few days—my heart sick-
ens at the thought of appearing joyous, my thoughts will turn to you I
feel what I have parted from, I know not if ever I shall again have those
eyes overflowing with love cast upon me—& that thought causes mine
to overflow with tears— . . . how I longed for you last Evening."[6]

Such erotic language was not unusual for female friends, but in
Dora's case it sounds particularly urgent, perhaps because Dora realizes
that with the loss of her female friends to marriage she too may have to
face the prospect of her father's disapproval if (when) she wants to
marry. (Dora had already received offers, but no one but Quillinan
would she consider.) In this sense, the intense language of her letters to
Jane may be her way of trying to maintain her life as a loving and dutiful child. She may realize, in other words, that she too may have to go
through a similarly painful family conflict if she is to marry, so she chan-
nels her desires in a safer direction. The love for a female friend, from
this perspective, represents less family conflict and strife because it does
not involve leaving home and forming a new household. It represents the
intimacies of girlhood, as Dora's later letter to her old school friend Mary
Calvert (?26 July 1841) from a newly discovered group of Dora's letters
at the Wordsworth Library makes clear. Dora writes to Mary, anticipating Mary's objections to her marriage to a Catholic: "Mr Quillinan
is to make me his before we leave Bath." Dora wants to treat Mary with
"frank affection as when we were school girls together [ ] & before that
to interchange thoughts with each other as freely as with our very selves."
But she knows, I think, that this time is no more.

Not that Edward Quillinan is ever far from Dora's thoughts in 1831.
Many of her letters are to Quillinan or to his daughters, Rotha and

Jemima. She writes to the girls with great affection, saying on 27 April 1832 that "I write to you now not because I have anything particular to write about but because writing to you is next best thing to talking to you." In a letter shortly following this one, Dora assures Edward "that as long as life is given to me your Darlings will have one friend who must always think of them with a Mother's [ ] & love them with a Mother's Love & whose only regret will be or rather is that her power of serving them falls so very short of her desire to serve" (26 June 1832). Quillinan had obviously asked a great deal from Dora in making this request, although they still seem to be coy regarding their mutual affections. Dora writes on 6 October 1833 that "when I was young even I never found any one disposed to flirt with me so now I have no reason to complain: as to petrified hearts those who have them may be envied & I congratulate you on your good fortune & only wish I were in like ease." Such indirection and irony is typical of Dora's correspondence with Quillinan during the early and mid 1830s, until Quillinan pushes the point in 1838.

In 1838 Dora Wordsworth's relationship with Edward Quillinan and with her parents reaches a crisis. By the spring of 1838, Dora has let her father know that she wanted to marry Quillinan, although, according to Alan Hill's note, Dora had written to Quillinan that "'My love for you is a spiritual Platonism such as a man might feel for a man or woman for woman . . . I wish for your own sake you were fairly married to someone else.' To this E. Q. replied from Rydal Mount on 8 Dec., calling her advice heartless: 'I am not spiritualized enough for you—you—frigid disagreeable thing! . . . it is a woodpecker's tap on a hollow tree in my ears: it is a squirt of lemon-juice in my eyes, and it is gall and wormwood on my tongue'" (LY 3:497n). Quillinan admits to having flirted with her in the past, but writes to Dora later in December 1837 that "I have had some troubles so severe as nothing but a rational and thoughtful and downright and resolute, though passionate, love for a good and virtuous girl could have given me fortitude to bear" (LY 3:549–50n). It is clear from this interchange that Quillinan was not easily refused, especially on platonic grounds. His letters have a passion and urgency that perhaps scared Dora and that certainly presented her emotions with a less ideal, romantic love than she felt for Jane.

To heighten her anxiety about marriage, Dora received this response from her father: "I take no notice of the conclusion of your Letter; indeed part of it I could not make out. It turns upon a subject which I shall never touch more either by pen or voice. Whether I look back or forward it is depressing and distressing to me, and will for the remainder of my life, continue to be so" (*LY* 3:549, 5 April 1838). After a lifetime of smooth affection, this is the way Wordsworth responds to Dora's request, invoking his law and his authoritative silence through the metonymy "by pen or voice."

The dispute between Dora and her parents over her desire to marry would finally be mediated by Isabella Fenwick, the family friend who was close to all concerned. This woman was clearly more important in Wordsworth's life than the editorial reduction of her to "Fenwick notes" would indicate. But before Miss Fenwick would actually help to make the marriage possible, she became the person to whom Dora revealed her private thoughts and frustrations, by pen and voice: "to you dearest Miss Fenwick I say nothing because my feelings be too deep for words but you will give me credit for feeling as I ought to one to whom I owe so much you can never know till hidden things are brought to light in another & happier world" (19 April 1838).

Of all the letters I have found from this period, Dora's unpublished letter of 19 April 1838 is the most revealing both of Dora's emotions and of her reading of her father's poetry. In this letter Dora talks of a trip to Tintern Abbey and its environs with her friends and cousins. Dora describes the day as a glorious mix of light and shade: "had my heart been in sunshine I too should have been in 'wild ecstasies'"—alluding, of course, to the passage in "Tintern Abbey" where the speaker blesses his sister and looks toward the time when her "wild ecstasies shall be matured / Into a sober pleasure" (138–39). Dora's allusion implies not only that she does not feel the sober pleasures of maturity but also that her heart prevents her from feeling the immediate pleasures of the scene. As Dora looks down on the ruins, she continues: "as it was this beauty was overpowering I could only weep & wish myself more worthy of such privilege I felt it was all to me 'as is a landscape to a blind man's eye.'" Here Dora distinguishes herself from her father, who had claimed that "These beauteous forms, / Through a long absence, have not been to me / As is a landscape to a blind man's eye" (22–24). Dora's letter is obviously filled with emotion, but she wants to feel consoled by the scene and by her memory of "Tintern Abbey." It almost seems that she wants to take Dorothy's place and to carry on the consoling vision, but she is unable to do so.

Dora's response also contrasts sharply with that of Mary, who visits Tintern Abbey and the Wye Valley with Joanna and Tom Hutchinson in May and June of 1812. This tour provides a dramatic setting for a se-

ries of love letters between William and Mary, for William remains in
London while Mary tours the Wye. Mary writes to her husband on
29 May:

> With a beating heart did I greet the Wye—O sylvan Wye thou Wanderer thro
> the Woods!—O what a verdant bed does it rest in where we first came in sight
> of it! I was most exceedingly delighted with this Ride—I dare say this Coun-
> try, indeed it must be so, looks far more beautiful than when the season is
> further advanced—when the leaves are in full perfection—[7]

Although Mary Wordsworth approaches the Wye Valley with reverence
for her husband's poem, she makes the interesting observation that the
valley must look even more beautiful in late spring than in midsummer,
when the valley is "clad in one green hue." This comment distinguishes
her vision to a certain extent from her husband's. She continues in her
next letter (2–3 June 1812): "O William what enchanting scenes have
we passed through—but you know it all—only I must say longings to
have you by my side have this day been painful to me beyond expression" (219). Mary accepts the spirit of "Tintern Abbey" and the authority of William's judgment, only wishing William were there to share
the experience.

William responds, in a most passionate letter of 3–4 June 1812, "I
think of you by the waters & under the shades of the Wye" (229):

> I received very expeditiously your sweet Letter from Hereford; That very
> evening, viz Tuesday, I had been reading at Lamb's the Tintern abbey, and
> repeated a 100 times to my self the passage ["]O Sylvan Wye thou Wanderer
> through the woods," thinking of past times, & Dorothy, dear Dorothy, and
> you my Darling.
>
> (227)

Completing this epistolary duet, William injects more sadness and sense
of loss into the scene by his repetition of the "O Sylvan Wye" and the
allusion to Dorothy. Whereas Mary evoked the emotion of seeing the
Wye River through the mediation of William's line, William lingers over
the passage that begins with the conditional thought that he does not
complete in "Tintern Abbey": "If this be but a vain belief . . ." Wordsworth's sadness in rereading this passage of his own poetry is poignantly
ironic if we recall that the Wordsworths' daughter Catharine died sud-
denly in June 1812, just after this correspondence, and in later years both
William and Mary would look back over these letters with bittersweet
memories, as Mary's later notations on the letters indicate.

Perhaps Dora's grief at Tintern Abbey is not only for herself but also for her Aunt Dorothy, who (as Wordsworth observed above) by this time was but a shadow of the young woman who had stood on the cliffs above the Wye Valley in 1798. In a letter dated (probably) March 1838, Dorothy Wordsworth wrote to her niece a letter that Dora must have received with great sadness. I quote it in full:

> They say I must write a letter—and what shall it be? News—news I must seek for news. My own thoughts are a wilderness—'not pierceable by power of any star'—News then is my resting-place—news! news!
> Poor Peggy Benson lies in Grasmere Church-yard beside her once-beautiful Mother. Fanny Haigh is gone to a better world. My Friend Mrs Rawson has ended her ninety and two years pilgrimage—and I have fought and fretted and striven—and am here beside the fire. The Doves behind me at the small window—the laburnum with its naked seed-pods shivers before my window and the pine-trees rock from their base.—More I cannot write so farewell! and may God bless you and your kind good Friend Miss Fenwick to whom I send love and all the best of wishes.—
>
> (LY 3:528)

Although the letter gives evidence of Dorothy's past life—from her imperfect allusion to *The Faerie Queene* to her keen description of the view from her window—the overwhelming feeling is of dislocation and sadness. For the Wordsworth family the image of Dorothy before the fire even in the warmest weather became a painful symbol of her derangement.[8]

Several reports by visitors to Rydal Mount reveal the family's response to the cruel irony of Dorothy's condition. The Duke of Argyle wrote a letter in September 1848 that describes Wordsworth reading "Tintern Abbey" aloud in the presence of Mary and Dorothy:

> The strong emphasis that he put on the words addressed struck me as almost unnatural at the time—'My dear, dear friend' ran the words,—'in thy wild eyes.' It was not till after the reading was over that we found out that the old paralytic and doited woman we had seen in the morning was the sister to whom T.A. was addressed, and her condition accounted for the fervour with which the old Poet read lines which reminded him of their better days. But it was melancholy to think that the vacant silly stare which we had seen in the morning was from the 'wild eyes' of 1798.
>
> (PW 2:517)

Dorothy's letter and this description indicate both Dorothy's physical and mental decline and its effect on the family. Fifty years after he stood with Dorothy above Tintern Abbey, the poet reenacts the scene and survives in the face of yet more drastic change. But Dorothy cannot hear his exhortations, nor has she continued to live the life that her brother imagined for her.

Dora Wordsworth was very likely thinking of her aunt during her visit to the Wye Valley and Tintern Abbey—and thinking that her father's exhortations were difficult to follow. In her letter to Miss Fenwick, Dora goes on to say that she and her party traveled to the abbey itself in a hailstorm, but then left their coach in the sunshine. Now it seems, Dora is on her own ground. She is no longer retracing the steps of 1798 and "Tintern Abbey," but does what her father had not recorded: she climbs the narrow steps of the abbey and looks out on the valley from this perspective. Although it is very cold, she does not hurry, "since I saw it thoroughly & felt it more than I had felt the glories of the Wye & [ ]cliffs." Dora confesses feeling more deeply while in the abbey, explaining that "maybe the sadness, the ruins, the desolation of the place were more in harmony with my own feelings." Perhaps Dora also connects the monastic past with the confinement she feels in her own life, a theme not introduced in "Tintern Abbey" but, as we have seen, evident in Wordsworth's later poetry. She is certainly not oppressed by the weight of too much liberty when she visits the abbey and finds the "courage to mount the narrow winding staircase." Ten years after the incident at Bruges, Dora seems to be far from the "Maiden" "Borne gaily o'er the sea, / Fresh from the beauty and the bliss / Of English liberty" (38–40).

Dora is not so downcast that she cannot reflect on her experience of visiting Tintern Abbey. In fact, she focuses after these descriptions not on her loneliness and grief but on the value of the trip. "The Wye is one of the first things of which I have heard so much that more than realized my expectations." Whereas Wordsworth frequently writes of unfulfilled expectations and "something evermore about to be" (1805 *Prelude*, 6:542), Dora takes stock of the event itself, emphasizing that neither her father's poem nor the prints that she had seen of the abbey and its surroundings had prepared her: "I was not prepared for such fine cliffs not cliffs of such extent. . . . The Abbey too was much finer—the prints I have seen give you no idea of its beauty tho' one cannot well say why for they are very correct when you come to compare them with their stormy 'archetype.'" What Dora achieves in this letter to Miss Fenwick is, paradoxically, a consolation based on her own experience, judgment, and feelings. By the end of the letter she is still unhappy, but she is not oppressed by thoughts of what she should feel or what would be correct to see. By sharing both her sorrow and her insight with her friend, Dora finds some strength. And an addendum to the letter explains that she has received an "affectionate" letter from her father in response to a "bold speaking out one of mine." In a moving reversal, Wordsworth's daughter changes the course of her own life and instructs the poet of household affections to look into his own heart.

THE CULTIVATION OF WOMEN

One year before Dora Wordsworth stood at Tintern Abbey and wondered about the direction of her own life, her father went on a tour of Italy with his old friend Crabb Robinson. A few years before this tour, Robinson recorded in his *Diary* that Wordsworth "returned with me to chambers and we spent several hours in reading his manuscript and I wrote from dictation—rather a trying task."[9] Perhaps Robinson should have learned from this, but, nevertheless, on the tour the friends had a brief falling out, with Robinson explaining that he "was forced to resist his too large demands on my good nature" (172). Based on this experience, Wordsworth decided while abroad that he would never again go on a long trip without a "female companion" (*Moorman* 2:527). When Wordsworth dedicated the *Memorials of a Tour in Italy, 1837* (1842) to Robinson, he thanked him

> For kindness that never ceased to flow,
> And prompt self-sacrifice to which I owe
> Far more than any heart but mine can know.

Robinson may have been honored by this dedication from a friend he truly loved and admired, but we know from his *Diary* that he felt the strain of playing the woman's part.

Robinson, who shrewdly referred to Dorothy Wordsworth, Mary Wordsworth, and Sara Hutchinson as Wordsworth's "three wives," understood what others have realized as well: that Wordsworth thrived within his circle of female supporters who made it possible for him to produce and continuously revise a great body of poetry. As we have seen, Wordsworth's poetry and his attempts to define himself as a poet over a long career were influenced by the actual women in his life, by his reluctant and often unconscious identification with suffering or abandoned women, by his perception of the proper feminine role, and by his uneasiness in the company of contemporary women writers. And according to many reports, Wordsworth was finally silenced as a poet by the loss of Dora three years before his own death—the loss he had most feared, the loss from which he could not recover.

Throughout his career Wordsworth sympathizes with female characters and cares deeply about the women in his life, but he is never really able to enter into another consciousness with what Keats referred to in a letter to George and Tom Keats (41, December 1817) as "negative capability." I do not agree, however, with those who say that Wordsworth was too masculine or too obsessed with his own egotistical sublimity, because such an analysis overlooks his identification with such figures as the banished Negro and Laodamia. Yet a certain blindness in Wordsworth's poetry prevents him from moving out of what is often an unconscious identification to a fuller awareness of those he imagines. Wordsworth continues to see others as the Other. Even in his moving and sympathetic poem on the Jewish family, for instance, he ultimately remains outside their experience, looking in this case from the perspective of the Christian seeing the Jewish child not in his historical plight but as an "exquisite Saint John" (24) who becomes an emblem of Wordsworth's own religious faith.

Wordsworth's poetic self-dramatization as Lear or Milton, as a father who desires "to curb" his daughter in "A Little Onward," proves prophetic of his dilemma with Dora. He adores her, as we have seen, but his love threatens to confine Dora and to deny her the passionate life that he has lived and the kind of happiness that has nurtured him. When Dora rebels, Wordsworth's first response is to silence her, in a way ironically reminiscent of Richard Norton's treatment of Emily in *The White Doe*. There is no space in Rydal Mount for this disruptive voice. And yet, under the intervention and mediation of others, Wordsworth relents.

Keats's characterization of Wordsworth as the poet of "the egotistical sublime" has certainly stuck, but his contemporaries made many contradictory observations of Wordsworth. Witnesses of his later life—in particular those, such as Isabella Fenwick and Crabb Robinson, who knew him well—all note that the poet himself embodies contradictory impulses. In 1845, Miss Fenwick tells Aubrey de Vere that "No degree of intimacy . . . can diminish your reverence for him, though you would discover a small . . . man in the midst of the great and noble man—he has in fact two natures, though the better one prevails."[10] Likewise, Harriet Martineau comments on Wordsworth's advice to charge her houseguests for meat: "The mixture of odd economics and neighborly generosity was one of the most striking things in the old poet."[11] A small man and a noble man; odd economics and generosity—it seems finally

best to acknowledge Wordsworth's contradictions and to view his imagination of women as a part of this odd mixture.

While Wordsworth was nurtured within his intimate family circle, the
women with whom he lived and worked plotted their lives around his
and cultivated their own gardens with varying degrees of success. They
also left a legacy for us as readers of Wordsworth—especially those of
us who have been trained to read like Dorothy in 1798 or 1802 ("ask
yourself in what spirit it was written") or Felicia Hemans in 1834, but
who also identify with Dora standing in Tintern Abbey or George Eliot
struggling with the Wordsworthian method of instruction. I hope that
this book has shown at least one way to admire the poet, to love the poetry, and yet to critique some of the assumptions about women upon
which Wordsworth's poetry and life were founded.

Notes

INTRODUCTION

1. *Romanticism and Feminism*, ed. Anne K. Mellor (Bloomington: Indiana University Press, 1988), appeared as I was beginning this project. After I completed the manuscript, Mellor's *Romanticism and Gender* (New York: Routledge, 1993), a comprehensive study of what Mellor terms "masculine romanticism" and "feminine romanticism," was published. My notes throughout and my list of secondary sources in the bibliography indicate the range of publications over the past five or six years.

2. Frederika Beatty, *William Wordsworth of Rydal Mount: An Account of the Poet and His Friends in the Last Decade* (London: J. M. Dent and Sons, 1939), 22.

3. I am, of course, borrowing the term "resisting reader" from Judith Fetterly, *The Resisting Reader: A Feminist Approach to American Fiction* (Bloomington: Indiana University Press, 1978).

4. John Jones, *The Egotistical Sublime: A History of Wordsworth's Imagination* (1954; rpt. London: Chatto and Windus, 1960).

5. Helen Darbishire, *The Poet Wordsworth* (1949; rpt. Westport, Conn.: Greenwood Press, 1980), 27.

6. Alice Comparetti, Introduction to *The White Doe of Rylstone* (Ithaca: Cornell University Press, 1940), 21. See also Edith C. Batho, *The Later Wordsworth* (Cambridge: Cambridge University Press, 1933), particularly 106–14.

7. Don H. Bialostosky, *Wordsworth, Dialogics, and the Practice of Criticism* (New York: Cambridge University Press, 1992), 117.

8. References to the two-part *Prelude* and to later versions of the poem are to the edition by Jonathan Wordsworth, M. H. Abrams, and Stephen Gill, *The Prelude, 1799, 1805, 1850* (New York: W. W. Norton, 1979).

9. References here and throughout to "Laodamia" and "A Little Onward . . ." are to the edition by Carl H. Ketcham, *Shorter Poems, 1807–1820, by William Wordsworth* (Ithaca: Cornell University Press, 1989).

10. Raymond Williams, *Keywords: A Vocabulary of Culture and Society* (New York: Oxford University Press, 1976), 81.

CHAPTER ONE. FROM THE SUBLIME TO THE BEAUTIFUL

1. See, for instance, Margaret Homans, in the first chapter of *Women Writers and Poetic Identity* (Princeton: Princeton University Press, 1980); Mary Jacobus, "The Law of/and Gender: Genre Theory and *The Prelude*," *Diacritics* 14 (1984): 47–57, later published in *Romanticism, Writing, and Sexual Difference* (Oxford: Clarendon Press, 1989); and Gayatri Chakravorty Spivak, "Sex and History in *The Prelude* (1805): Books Nine to Thirteen," *Texas Studies in Literature and Language* 23 (1981): 324–60; later published in *In Other Worlds: Essays in Culture and Politics* (New York: Methuen, 1987). More recently Diane Long Hoeveler, *Romantic Androgyny: The Women Within* (University Park: Pennsylvania State University Press, 1990), has seen Wordsworth and the other male Romantics as poets who appropriate the feminine. For a strong challenge to these views, see Susan J. Wolfson, "Dorothy Wordsworth in Conversation with William," in *R&F*, 139–66. See also Laura E. Haigwood, "Oedipal Revolution in the *Lyrical Ballads*," *Centennial Review* 33 (Fall 1989): 468–89.

2. Keats refers to "the wordsworthian [*sic*] or egotistical sublime" in the letter to Woodhouse, 27 October 1818, 157. (References to Keats's letters are from the edition by Robert Gittings, *Letters of John Keats* [New York: Oxford University Press, 1987]. Letters are identified by date and page number.) The movement from solitude to relationship is an important part of John Jones's argument in *The Egotistical Sublime*. Jones sees Wordsworth moving away from the sublimity of solitude in the course of his poetry; the gender distinctions, although not explicit in this pre-feminist work, are implicit in Jones's argument, as well as in his references to the attitudes of Coleridge, Keats, and Hazlitt toward Wordsworth (see pages 29, 47, and passim). More recently, Thomas A. Vogler has seen this move toward relationship in psychoanalytic terms, arguing that Wordsworth spent most of his life "in recovery of a primal relationship with an idealized maternal 'nature,'" whereas I see Wordsworth as moved by both a masculine and feminine nature. I would also disagree with Vogler's assumption that "She was a Phantom of delight" refers to Dorothy Wordsworth rather than Mary Wordsworth. See Vogler's " 'A Spirit, Yet a Woman Too!' Dorothy and William Wordsworth," in *Mothering the Mind: Twelve Studies of Writers and Their Silent Partners*, ed. Ruth Perry and Martine Watson Brownley (New York: Holmes and Meier, 1984), 243.

3. For an example of this argument, see David Simpson, "Figuring Class, Sex, and Gender: What Is the Subject of Wordsworth's 'Gipsies'?" in *South Atlantic Quarterly* 88 (Summer 1989): 541–67.

4. Wordsworth also follows Burke in linking the sublime to feelings of pain, but pain held in check by distance. Wordsworth knew Burke's aesthetic and political theory in both the *Enquiry* and the *Reflections on the Revolution in France.*

See James K. Chandler, *Wordsworth's Second Nature* (Chicago: University of Chicago Press, 1984), for an elaboration of Wordsworth's complicated relationship to Burke's thought. For a brief but incisive analysis of gender in Burke's poetics, see W. J. T. Mitchell, *Iconology: Image, Text, Ideology* (Chicago: University of Chicago Press, 1986), 129–31. Meena Alexander also touches on this gendered dichotomy in *Women in Romanticism: Mary Wollstonecraft, Dorothy Wordsworth, and Mary Shelley* (Savage, Md.: Barnes and Noble, 1989), 29–30. See, in addition, Mellor's discussion in *Romanticism and Gender*, especially "Domesticating the Sublime," 85–106. Although Burke is the much more likely direct source for Wordsworth, Kant also analyzes these qualities in *Observations on the Feeling of the Beautiful and the Sublime*, trans. John T. Goldthwait (Berkeley: University of California Press, 1960).

5. Without explicitly discussing issues of gender, Theresa M. Kelley, in *Wordsworth's Revisionary Aesthetics* (New York: Cambridge University Press, 1988), argues that a "rhetorical competition" between figures of the beautiful and the sublime forms the basis of Wordsworth's aesthetics. I have benefited throughout from Kelley's ideas and from her sense of the movement of Wordsworth's imagination from the sublime to the beautiful.

6. *William Wordsworth: Guide to the Lakes*, ed. Ernest de Selincourt (1906; rpt. New York: Oxford University Press, 1973), 35.

7. Edmund Burke, *A Philosophical Enquiry into the Origins of Our Ideas of the Sublime and Beautiful*, ed. James T. Boulton (Notre Dame: Notre Dame University Press, 1958), 63.

8. This is actually a description of Windermere, from Arthur Young's *Six Month Tour*, vol. 3, quoted in Thomas West, *A Guide to the Lakes in Cumberland, Westmorland and Lancashire* (1784; rpt. Oxford: Woodstock Books, 1989), 69.

9. See Ronald Paulson, *Representations of Revolution, 1789–1820* (New Haven: Yale University Press, 1983), especially chap. 3, 57–87.

10. See *Moorman* 1:438–42 on Wordsworth's financial anxieties, as well as Wallace Douglas, *Wordsworth: The Construction of a Personality* (Kent, Ohio: Kent State University Press, 1968). See also David Simpson, *Wordsworth's Historical Imagination* (New York: Methuen, 1987), for an analysis of Wordsworth's financial and familial problems.

11. Uvedale Price, *An Essay on the Picturesque as Compared with the Sublime and the Beautiful* (London: J. Robson, 1794), 47–49.

12. I am thinking, for instance, of Marjorie Levinson's chapter on "Tintern Abbey" in her *Wordsworth's Great Period Poems: Four Essays* (New York: Cambridge University Press, 1986).

13. The Norton editors note that Wordsworth wrote such an account, the "Discharged Soldier," in January–February 1798, which became lines 363–504 in book 4 of the 1805 *Prelude*. The editors also note that Wordsworth echoes both Cowper's "The Winter Evening" and *The Task*, as well as the card game in Pope's *The Rape of the Lock*.

14. I borrow Kurt Heinzelman's term for Rydal Mount: "that manor house whose many-acred grounds William himself laid out and landscaped into a private garden" (R&F, 57). He argues that the Wordsworths' radical ideas about

work and home at Grasmere became a "cult of domesticity" at Rydal Mount: "The Cult of Domesticity: Dorothy and William Wordsworth at Grasmere," in *R&F*, 52–78.

15. For a discussion of the possibilities of the female sublime in regard to later women writers, see Patricia Yaeger, "Toward a Female Sublime," in *Gender and Theory: Dialogues on Feminist Criticism*, ed. Linda Kauffman (Oxford: Basil Blackwell, 1989), 191–212.

16. See for instance, Robert Con Davis, "The Structure of the Picturesque: Dorothy Wordsworth's Journals," *The Wordsworth Circle* 9 (1978): 45–49.

17. Martin Price, "The Picturesque Moment," in *From Sensibility to Romanticism*, ed. Frederick W. Hilles and Harold Bloom (New York: Oxford University Press, 1965), 277. I am indebted to William Snyder and other members of the NEH seminar at the University of California, Los Angeles, in 1989, "Gender and English Romanticism," for lively and suggestive discussions on gender and aesthetic categories. See also Snyder's "Mother Nature's Other Natures: Landscape in Women's Writing," *Women's Studies* 21 (1992): 143–62, for a fine analysis of gender and the picturesque; my comments on this subject are influenced by Snyder's thinking.

CHAPTER TWO. WORDSWORTH AND THE POETIC VOCATION

1. William Wordsworth and Dorothy Wordsworth, *The Letters of William and Dorothy Wordsworth*. Vol. 1: *The Early Years, 1787–1805*, ed. Ernest de Selincourt, rev. Chester L. Shaver (Oxford: Clarendon Press, 1967), 122.

2. See, for instance, Jon P. Klancher, *The Making of English Reading Audiences, 1790–1832* (Madison: University of Wisconsin Press, 1987), for a Marxist critique of this presumed change from a concern with "consumption" to a preoccupation with "reception" (137–50).

3. Peter J. Manning analyzes Wordsworth's construct of the "People" in "*The White Doe of Rylstone, The Convention of Cintra*, and the History of a Career," in his *Reading Romantics: Texts and Contexts* (New York: Oxford University Press, 1990), 165–94.

4. Morris Eaves, "Romantic Expressive Theory and Blake's Idea of Audience," *PMLA* 95 (1980): 790–91; later published in *William Blake's Theory of Art*, 171–204 (Princeton: Princeton University Press, 1982).

5. Except where noted, I refer to the 1800 text of the Preface. The 1802 version with various changes added over the years is identified as "1850" by Owen and Smyser; I follow their notation.

6. I discuss this at length in "'A History / Homely and Rude': Genre and Style in Wordsworth's 'Michael,'" *SEL* 29 (1989): 622–36.

7. Mary Wollstonecraft, *A Vindication of the Rights of Woman*, ed. Carol H. Poston (New York: W. W. Norton, 1975).

8. I am referring, of course, to Harold Bloom's *The Anxiety of Influence: A Theory of Poetry* (New York: Oxford University Press, 1973).

9. Wollstonecraft, *Vindication*, 183.

10. This is from R. S. Mackenzie's *Life of Charles Dickens*, 1870, quoted in Markham L. Peacock, Jr., *The Critical Opinions of William Wordsworth* (Baltimore: Johns Hopkins University Press, 1950), 243.

11. See Bradford Keyes Mudge, "The Man with Two Brains: Gothic Novels, Popular Culture, Literary History," *PMLA* 107 (January 1992): 92–104, for an extended discussion of the cultural implications of the rise of the novel and of the growing number of women as readers and writers.

12. See also Mary Poovey, *The Proper Lady and the Woman Writer* (Chicago: University of Chicago Press, 1984).

13. Virginia Woolf, *A Room of One's Own* (1929; rpt. New York: Harcourt Brace, 1957), 51.

14. Cora Kaplan makes this point in "Wild Nights: Pleasure/Sexuality/Feminism," in *Sea Changes: Culture and Feminism* (London: Verso, 1986), 47, in contrasting the male author's freedom with Wollstonecraft's repression of sexuality and pleasure in the *Vindication*.

15. Marlon B. Ross, *The Contours of Masculine Desire: Romanticism and the Rise of Women's Poetry* (New York: Oxford University Press, 1989), 26.

16. J. G. A. Pocock, *Virtue, Commerce, and History: Essays on Political Thought and History, Chiefly in the Eighteenth Century* (New York: Cambridge University Press, 1985), 114.

17. See Simpson, *Wordsworth's Historical Imagination* (New York: Methuen, 1987), 63–67.

18. Donald H. Reiman, ed., *The Romantics Reviewed*, 9 vols. (New York: Garland, 1972), 2:432–36.

19. *Women Writers Project Newsletter* 1, no. 1 (Spring 1990): 2.

20. Stuart Curran, "The I Altered," in *R&F*, 185–207.

21. See Ross, *Contours of Masculine Desire*, especially chap. 6, 187–231.

22. "Now it is remarkable that, excepting the nocturnal Reverie of Lady Winchilsea, and a passage or two in the Windsor Forest of Pope, the poetry of the period intervening between the publication of Paradise Lost and the Seasons does not contain a single new image of external nature; and scarcely presents a familiar one from which it can be inferred that the eye of the Poet had been steadily fixed upon his object, much less that his feelings had urged him to work upon it in the spirit of genuine imagination" (*PrW* 3:73).

23. I am indebted to Catherine Burroughs for first introducing me to Baillie's "Introductory Discourse" in 1989 during the NEH seminar "Gender and British Romanticism." My text for Baillie is *The Dramatic and Poetical Works of Joanna Baillie* (1851; rpt. New York: Georg Olms Verlag, 1976).

24. Stuart Curran mentions the importance of this work in "The I Altered," and Marlon Ross draws attention to several general parallels between Baillie's "Discourse" and Wordsworth's Preface in his brief biographical essay, "Joanna Baillie," in the *Dictionary of Literary Biography*, vol. 93, ed. John R. Greenfield (Detroit: Gale Research, 1990), 3–15, and in *The Contours of Masculine Desire*, 257–59.

25. Mary Wordsworth, *The Letters of Mary Wordsworth, 1800–1855*, ed. Mary E. Burton (1958; rpt. Westport, Conn: Greenwood Press, 1979), xxv.

26. See, again, Simpson's "Figuring Class, Sex, and Gender," 541–67, and John Barrell's "The Uses of Dorothy: 'The Language of the Sense' in 'Tintern

Abbey,' " in *Poetry, Language, and Politics* (New York: St. Martin's, 1988), 137–67.

27. I am thinking of Margaret Homans's analysis at the beginning of *Bearing the Word: Language and Female Experience in Nineteenth Century Women's Writing* (Chicago: University of Chicago Press, 1986). I borrow Homans's term, "scene of instruction," throughout.

28. Carolyn G. Heilbrun, *Writing a Woman's Life* (New York: Ballantine Books, 1988), 43.

29. See Lenore Davidoff and Catherine Hall, *Family Fortunes: Men and Women of the English Middle Class, 1780–1850* (Chicago: University of Chicago Press, 1987), 348–53 and passim.

30. Kelley, *Wordsworth's Revisionary Aesthetics*, 61.

31. Hoeveler, *Romantic Androgyny*, 96.

32. On the formation of the 1800 edition of *Lyrical Ballads* in relation to "Michael" and "Christabel," see Susan Eilenberg, " 'Michael,' 'Christabel,' and the Poetry of Possession," *Criticism* 30 (Spring 1988): 205–24.

33. *Early Years*, 314.

34. See Carol Gilligan, *In a Different Voice: Psychological Theory and Women's Development* (Cambridge: Harvard University Press, 1982). In Gilligan's terms, an abstract principle overrides a feminine ethic of care based on compromise.

35. See, for instance, Peter J. Manning's "*Michael*, Luke, and Wordsworth," in *Reading Romantics*, 35–52.

36. Ross, *Contours of Masculine Desire*, 87–111.

37. *Early Years*, 367.

38. *Collected Letters of Samuel Taylor Coleridge*, ed. Earl Leslie Griggs, 6 vols. (Oxford: Clarendon Press, 1956–71), 2:1013.

CHAPTER THREE. WORDSWORTH'S FRENCH REVOLUTION

1. David V. Erdman, "Wordsworth as Heartsworth; or, Was Regicide the Prophetic Ground of Those 'Moral Questions'?" in *The Evidence of the Imagination: Studies of Interactions Between Life and Art in English Romantic Literature*, ed. Donald H. Reiman, Michael C. Jaye, and Betty T. Bennett (New York: New York University Press, 1978), 15. Not all recent students of Wordsworth have seen the connection between his revolutionary and his sexual politics. For instance, in *Wordsworth and Coleridge: The Radical Years* (Oxford: Clarendon Press, 1988), Nicholas Roe mentions Annette Vallon briefly, but does not focus on this relationship.

2. Dorothy Wordsworth, *The Journals of Dorothy Wordsworth*, ed. Mary Moorman (2d ed. New York: Oxford University Press, 1976), 127.

3. Moorman (1:565) attributes seven sonnets to Calais, but Reed assigns with fairly strong certainty five sonnets to this period: "Calais, August, 1802" ("Is it a Reed that's shaken by the wind"), "Composed by the Sea-Side, near Calais, August, 1802" ("Fair Star of Evening, Splendor of the West"), "It is a Beauteous Evening," "To a Friend, Composed near Calais" ("Jones! when from Calais southward you and I"), and "Calais, August 15th, 1802" ("Festivals have I seen

that were not names"). As to the two others attributed by Moorman, Reed acknowledges that it is possible that "To Toussaint L'Ouverture" may belong to the trip, but concludes that "On the Extinction of the Venetian Republic" "does not seem on balance certainly assignable to this month" (Mark L. Reed, *Wordsworth: The Chronology of the Middle Years, 1800–1815* [Cambridge: Harvard University Press, 1975], 190).

4. See Irene Tayler, "By Peculiar Grace: Wordsworth in 1802," in *Evidence of the Imagination*, 119–41.

5. David V. Erdman, *Blake: Prophet Against Empire—A Poet's Interpretation of the History of His Own Times* (1954; rpt. Garden City, New York: Doubleday, 1969), 74–76.

6. Dorothy Wordsworth, *Journals*, 152.

7. My text for this and all quotations from Wordsworth's poetry in this chapter (with the exception of the versions of the channel-crossing sonnet first called "The Banished Negroes") is *William Wordsworth*, ed. Stephen Gill, Oxford Authors series (New York: Oxford University Press, 1984), which provides the earliest version of each poem.

8. In thinking of Wordsworth's conception of the dynamics of the sonnet form in relation to Milton, I have learned from Janel M. Mueller, "On Genesis in Genre: Milton's Politicizing of the Sonnet in 'Captain or Colonel,'" *Renaissance Genres*, ed. Barbara K. Lewalski, 213–40, Harvard Studies in English 14 (Cambridge: Harvard University Press, 1986).

9. Kurt Heinzelman discusses Wordsworth's relationship to Milton in a similar context in "The Cult of Domesticity," 63–65 and passim. My work on these sonnets was originally published at the same time as " 'The weight of too much liberty': Genre and Gender in Wordsworth's Calais Sonnets," *Criticism* (Spring 1988): 189–203.

10. Lee M. Johnson, *Wordsworth and the Sonnet*, Anglistica 19 (Copenhagen: Rosenkilde and Bagger, 1973), 48–49.

11. J. Hillis Miller, "The Still Heart: Poetic Form in Wordsworth," *New Literary History* 2 (Winter 1971): 303.

12. *Selections from the Poetical Works of Edmund Spenser*, ed. S. K. Heninger, Jr. (Boston: Houghton-Mifflin, 1970), lines 291–95.

13. Spivak, "Sex and History in *The Prelude*," 326.

14. On this subject see Jacobus, "The Law of/and Gender," as well as Deborah Kennedy's "Revolutionary Tales: Helen Maria Williams's *Letters from France* and William Wordsworth's 'Vaudracour and Julia,'" *The Wordsworth Circle* 21 (Summer 1990): 109–14.

15. See, for instance, Markham L. Peacock Jr., *The Critical Opinions of William Wordsworth* (Baltimore: Johns Hopkins University Press, 1950), 187–88. Also, Manning discusses what I find to be Wordsworth's more typical, indirect biblical references in "Wordsworth's Intimations Ode and Its Epigraphs," in *Reading Romantics*, 68–84.

16. *The Interpreter's Dictionary of the Bible*, ed. George Arthur Buttrick et al., 5 vols. (Nashville: Abingdon Press, 1962), 1:21–22. See also the *Theological Dictionary of the New Testament*, ed. Gerhard Kittel, trans. Geoffrey W. Bromiley, 10 vols. (Grand Rapids: William B. Eerdmans, 1965),

3:824–26, for readings of the term. I thank T. W. Lewis for his help with these sources.

17. Phyllis Trible, *God and the Rhetoric of Sexuality* (Philadelphia: Fortress Press, 1978), 69.

18. Charlotte Brontë, *Shirley*, ed. Andrew and Judith Hook (Harmondsworth, England: Penguin, 1985), 376.

19. In comparing Wordsworth's persona to the lover-speaker in the Petrarchan tradition, I am thinking of this lyric tradition in the terms developed by Nona Fienberg in "The Emergence of Stella in *Astrophil and Stella*," *SEL* 25 (1985): 5–19.

20. Dorothy Wordsworth, *Journals*, 153.

21. Reed, *Wordsworth: The Middle Years*, 191.

22. A related sonnet in protest of the French government is "To Toussaint L'Ouverture." For the political background of Wordsworth's treatment of this well-known historical figure see C. L. R. James, *The Black Jacobins: Toussaint L'Ouverture and the San Domingo Revolution*, 2d ed. (1938; rpt. New York: Random House, 1963). Toussaint L'Ouverture was betrayed by the French, brought to Europe, and imprisoned on 24 August 1802 at Fort de Joux in the French Alps, where he died of cold and starvation on 7 April 1803.

23. I have constructed this 1803 text from the notes provided by Jared Curtis in the Cornell Wordsworth. See *Poems, in Two Volumes, and Other Poems, 1800–1807*, ed. Jared Curtis (Ithaca: Cornell University Press, 1983).

24. *Recueil général, annoté, des lois, décrets, ordannances, etc. 1789–1830*, 16 vols. (Paris: A l'administration du journal des notaires et des avocats, 1836), 9:361. I thank David Combe of the Tulane University Law Library for his help in finding the ordinance.

Not much has been written on this edict. Shelby T. McCloy, *The Negro in France* (1961; rpt. New York: Haskell House, 1973), mentions briefly that "the census was required by the law of July 2, 1802, which specified that every Negro or mulatto, other than those serving in the French army or navy, who arrived at a seaport was to be put in a depot and sent to the colonies as soon as possible. Negroes and mulattoes of foreign crews, if found on French soil, were likewise to be reported and placed in the depots" (126).

William B. Cohen, *The French Encounter with the African: White Response to Blacks, 1530–1880* (Bloomington: Indiana University Press, 1980), argues that the ordinance was in line with prerevolutionary racist paranoia about blacks. He quotes an official document from 1777: "The Negroes are multiplying every day in France. They marry Europeans, the houses of prostitutes are infected by them; the colours mix, the blood is changing . . . these slaves, if they return to America, bring with them the spirit of freedom, independence and equality, which they communicate to others" (111).

25. For a discussion of the reporting in the British press, see Robin Blackburn, *The Overthrow of Colonial Slavery, 1776–1848* (New York: Verso, 1988), 251–52: "The British press, which would have been happy to celebrate his [Toussaint's] execution in 1796, gave harrowing accounts of his imprisonment and death."

26. Alan Liu, *Wordsworth: The Sense of History* (Palo Alto: Stanford University Press, 1989), 476.

27. See Mary Jacobus, "Geometric Science and Romantic History, or Wordsworth, Newton, and the Slave Trade," in her *Romanticism, Writing and Sexual Difference*, 77.

28. On the British abolition of the slave trade (1807) and slavery (1838), see James Walvin, *England, Slaves, and Freedom, 1776–1838* (Jackson: University Press of Mississippi, 1986).

29. See Alan Richardson's "Colonialism, Race, and Lyric Irony in Blake's 'The Little Black Boy,'" *Papers on Language and Literature* 26 (1990): 233–48. Wordsworth was familiar with abolitionist discourse. He corresponded with James Montgomery, and the abolitionist Thomas Clarkson and his wife Catherine were, for a while, neighbors of his in the Lake District. Catherine Clarkson became one of Dorothy Wordsworth's lifelong friends and correspondents. Allusions to Thomas Clarkson's work for the abolitionist cause are scattered throughout the letters of the Wordsworth family. In *Thomas Clarkson, the Friend of Slaves* (1936; rpt. Westport, Conn.: Negro Universities Press, 1970), especially the later chapters, Earl Leslie Griggs discusses the relationship between the Wordsworths and the Clarksons.

30. See McCloy, *The Negro in France*, 64–85.

31. See Richardson, "Colonialism, Race, and Lyric Irony," 237–39 and passim; and Moira Ferguson, *Subject to Others: British Women Writers and Colonial Slavery, 1670–1834* (New York: Routledge, 1992).

32. Barbara Bush, *Slave Women in Caribbean Society, 1650–1838* (Bloomington: Indiana University Press, 1990), 14. Bush also suggests that in Holloway's (sometimes mistaken for Blake's) engraving of the slave Joanna from John Stedman's *Narrative*, the one bare breast "hint[s] at the alleged sensuality of African women" (16).

33. According to the *OED*, Malthus used the word *intercourse* with a sexual connotation in 1798: "An illicit intercourse between the sexes." We have already seen how Wordsworth uses this and related words in the Preface in sexually charged ways.

34. See Hugh Honour, *The Image of the Black in Western Art*, 2 parts (Cambridge: Harvard University Press for the Menil Foundation, 1989). Honour is specific about the history of the painting, although Jean-Pierre Cuzin, *French Painting in the Louvre* (New York: Scala, 1982), 92, simply states that the painting was purchased by the Louvre in 1818. I thank Elise Smith for bringing Benoist's painting to my attention.

35. Stephen Gill, *William Wordsworth: A Life* (Oxford: Clarendon Press, 1989), 340, records this passage from Mary Wordsworth's journal. Although Wordsworth says in his letters that he is more impressed with the Jardin des Plantes (7 October 1820 to Lord Lonsdale, *MY* 2:642) than with the artworks of the Louvre, Dorothy Wordsworth makes a point of assessing their location in relation to the Louvre: "The only inconvenience is our distance from the Louvre etc, but I am so strong that to me it is nothing" (to Catherine Clarkson, 2:645). They obviously went to the "Louvre etc" frequently.

36. Honour, *Image of the Black*, 2:6–12.

37. In *Wordsworth's Interest in Painters and Pictures* (Wellesley, Mass.: Wellesley Press, 1945), Martha Hale Shackford provides evidence to show that Wordsworth had a long-standing interest in portrait painting and, because of the human interest in the subject, even preferred it to landscape painting.

38. Honour, *Image of the Black*, 2:12, 22. In a footnote, Honour states that "It has been suggested that the bare breast symbolizes Liberty and that the head drapery 'two meters long' shows that the subject cannot be a slave" (2:248).

39. See especially Mary Wollstonecraft's *Vindication of the Rights of Woman* (1792) for this connection. Nancy Moore Goslee, in "Slavery and Sexual Character: Questioning the Master Trope in Blake's *Visions of the Daughters of Albion*," *ELH* 57 (Spring 1990): 101–28, provides an analysis of the "master trope" of slavery for racial and sexual oppression in the *Vindication* and *Visions*, revealing the problems in conflating racial and gender oppression.

40. See Jacobus, "Geometric Science and Romantic History," 73.

CHAPTER FOUR. IMPASSIONED WIVES AND
CONSECRATED MAIDS

1. For a history of Wordsworth's reputation as a conservative in the nineteenth century, see James Chandler's " 'Wordsworth' After Waterloo," in *The Age of William Wordsworth: Critical Essays on the Romantic Tradition*, ed. Kenneth R. Johnston and Gene W. Ruoff (New Brunswick: Rutgers University Press, 1987), 84–111.

2. Erdman, "Wordsworth as Heartsworth," 15.

3. Donald H. Reiman, "The Poetry of Familiarity: Wordsworth, Dorothy, and Mary Hutchinson," in *The Evidence of the Imagination*, 170, and cf. especially 164–71; Jean Hagstrum follows this notion in chap. 3 of *The Romantic Body: Love and Sexuality in Keats, Wordsworth, and Blake* (Knoxville: University of Tennessee Press, 1985).

4. A version of "Laodamia" was probably completed in October 1814 and revised by February 1815 for publication in the *Poems* (Reed, *Wordsworth: The Middle Years*, 578). My text for "Laodamia" is from the Cornell Wordsworth, reading text 2; all references to variants are also to the Cornell edition. For Wordsworth's notes to the poem, I have used *PW*.

5. For a listing of Wordsworth's echoes of these works, see W. A. Heard's essay in *The Poetical Works of William Wordsworth*, ed. William Knight, 8 vols. (New York: Macmillan, 1896), 6:10–15. Wordsworth himself acknowledges his debts to Virgil, Euripides, and Pliny's *Natural History* in his note to "Laodamia" (*PW* 2:272).

6. See *Moorman* 2:330–34 and Robert Gittings and Jo Manton, *Dorothy Wordsworth* (Oxford: Clarendon Press, 1985), 204–10. On the subject of Dorothy's anxiety, see Mary Wordsworth's letter to her regarding the trip to France (Mary Wordsworth, *Letters*, 25).

7. See William Wordsworth and Mary Wordsworth, *The Love Letters of William and Mary Wordsworth*, ed. Beth Darlington (Ithaca: Cornell University Press, 1981).

8. Geoffrey Hartman, "Words, Wish, Worth: Wordsworth," in *Deconstruction and Criticism,* ed. Harold Bloom et al., 177–216 (New York: Old Seabury Press, 1979).

9. I see the conflicts as more diverse and complicated than does Richard D. McGhee, who argues that Wordsworth tempers romantic passion with classical forms: "'Conversant with Infinity': Form and Meaning in Wordsworth's 'Laodamia,'" *Studies in Philology* 68 (July 1971): 357–69. Lawrence Lipking's brief discussion of "Laodamia" in *Abandoned Women and Poetic Tradition* (Chicago: University of Chicago Press, 1988), is excellent, but in his argument that Wordsworth focuses on Laodamia's fate from a male point of view, Lipking does not see Wordsworth's complicated identification with his character.

10. See Herbert Read, *Wordsworth* (London: Faber and Faber, n.d.), 149.

11. See *Wordsworth's Historical Imagination,* 4–6 and passim. Simpson identifies this dynamic conflict working in much of Wordsworth's poetry, but he does not consider the question of gender in the paradigm.

12. Samuel Johnson, "Life of Milton," in *Lives of the English Poets,* intro. by Arthur Waugh, 2 vols. (1906; rpt. New York: Oxford University Press, 1967), 1:108.

13. Mary Wordsworth, *Letters,* 23.

14. *Heroides and Amores,* with Latin text and trans. Grant Showerman, 2d ed., rev. G. P. Goold (Cambridge: Harvard University Press, 1977): "hanc specto teneoque sinu pro coniuge vero, / et, tamquam possit verba referre, queror" (lines 157–58).

15. See *Iphigenia in Aulis,* trans. Charles R. Walker, in *Euripides IV,* ed. David Grene and Richard Lattimore (Chicago: University of Chicago Press, 1958), 224: "Squatting they played at draughts, / Delighting in trickery."

16. George Eliot, *The Mill on the Floss,* ed. Gordon S. Haight (Oxford: Clarendon Press, 1980), 437–38.

17. See Gilligan, *In a Different Voice,* 128–50.

18. See the Cornell edition, 151–52, for a full transcription of the revisions in these lines.

19. See Peter M. Sacks, *The English Elegy: Studies in the Genre from Spenser to Yeats* (Baltimore: Johns Hopkins University Press, 1985), for connections between mourning and eroticism in "Adonais" and other elegies. Sacks analyzes Freud's "Mourning and Melancholia" (1917) in relation to elegiac conventions.

20. Reiman, ed., *Romantics Reviewed,* 2:523.

21. See, for instance, Wordsworth's letter to Coleridge (19 April 1808, *MY* 1:221–23) and the letter to Francis Wrangham (18 January 1816, *MY* 2:276); see also Isabella Fenwick's notes on *The White Doe* in *PW* 3:543.

22. Reiman, ed., *Romantics Reviewed,* 2:454–58.

23. See Manning's brilliantly argued "*The White Doe of Rylstone, The Convention of Cintra,* and the History of a Career," in his *Reading Romantics,* 165–94. Although I have used the Cornell text, I wrote on the publication history of *The White Doe* before I had access to Dugas's introduction.

24. Thomas Dunham Whitaker, *The History and Antiquities of the Deanery of Craven in the County of York,* 3d ed. (London: Cassell, Petter, and Galpin, 1878), 525.

25. For an extended discussion of the cultural implications of embroidery, see Rozsika Parker, *The Subversive Stitch: Embroidery and the Making of the Feminine* (1984; rpt. New York: Routledge, 1989).

26. See Lionel Trilling's discussion of Wordsworthian "wise passiveness" as an activity in "Wordsworth and the Iron Time," in *Wordsworth: A Collection of Critical Essays,* ed. M. H. Abrams (Englewood Cliffs, N.J.: Prentice-Hall, 1972), 65. In *Wordsworth's Heroes* (Berkeley: University of California Press, 1985), Willard Spiegelman argues that "the poem concerns types of heroic behavior, one active, the other passive, and refuses to acknowledge the superiority of either" (168). I think that Wordsworth does value the passive as superior, but its association with the feminine complicates the matter.

27. James A. W. Heffernan, *Wordsworth's Theory of Poetry: The Transforming Imagination* (Ithaca: Cornell University Press, 1969), 215. In the introduction to the Cornell edition, Kristine Dugas also accepts the poem as "an idealized account" (5) of suffering and loss; she does not critique Wordsworth's treatment of Emily.

28. Geoffrey Hartman makes this connection in *Wordsworth's Poetry, 1787–1814* (New Haven: Yale University Press, 1964), 329. Barbara Gates develops the connection between Emily's grief and Wordsworth's grief over the loss of his brother in "Wordsworth's Symbolic Doe: The Power of History in the Mind," *Criticism* 17 (Summer 1975): 234–45.

29. See *Early Years,* 539 and following. Beginning with Wordsworth's response to Richard Wordsworth's letter on 11 February 1805, the family correspondence focuses on this tragedy.

30. See, for instance, John Danby, *The Simple Wordsworth: Studies in the Poems, 1797–1807* (1960; rpt. London: Routledge and Kegan Paul, 1971), 131–35, and Manning, *Reading Romantics,* 188–90 and passim.

31. Reed, *Wordsworth: The Middle Years,* 24.

32. On the topic of 1815 as a time in which the fears and oppositions of the 1790s were intensified, see, again, James K. Chandler's "'Wordsworth' After Waterloo."

33. Sara Ruddick, *Maternal Thinking: Toward a Politics of Peace* (New York: Ballantine Books, 1990).

34. "Speech to the Troops at Tilbury" (1588), in *The Female Spectator: English Women Writers Before 1800,* ed. Mary R. Mahl and Helene Koon (Old Westbury, N.Y.: Feminist Press, 1977), 48. Joan Kelly points out that Elizabeth reinforces the notion that she is "'an exception to the Law of Nature'": "Early Feminist Theory and the *Querelle des Femmes,*" in *Women, History, and Theory* (Chicago: University of Chicago Press, 1984), 88.

35. See Jeffrey's negative comment in *Romantics Reviewed* (2:455), as well as that of Josiah Conder, who dislikes the "mystical elements" (2:370).

36. See, for instance, Sonia Hofkosh, "The Writer's Ravishment: Women and the Romantic Author—The Example of Byron," in *R&F,* 93–114.

37. Reiman, ed., *Romantics Reviewed,* 2:370.

38. John Jones makes this point in *The Egotistical Sublime,* 154. For an extended discussion of the politics of form and presentation, see Manning, "Tales

and Politics: *The Corsair, Lara*, and *The White Doe of Rylstone*," in *Reading Romantics*, 195–215.

39. See Byron's dedication to Thomas Moore in *Byron: Poetical Works*, ed. Frederick Page, corrected by John Jump (New York: Oxford University Press, 1970), 277.

40. See Kelley, *Wordsworth's Revisionary Aesthetics*, 151–52. My text is the Cornell edition.

41. For a convincing study of the father's tyrannous hold on Matilda, another motherless female character, see Reeve Parker, "Reading Wordsworth's Power: Narrative and Usurpation in *The Borderers*," *ELH* 54 (Summer 1987): 299–331: "For all its apparent benevolence and innocence, the relationship has strong if shadowy elements of untoward and tormenting bondage—indeed of punitive tyranny and enslavement to passion" (304). I have argued that Richard Norton's actions place abstract honor over family. Parker sees a similar narrative in *The Borderers*: "the usurpation of his baronial domains is the emblematic result of abdicating domestic responsibilities (a familiar topos of quest chivalry), abdication that likewise places his family at risk" (309).

42. Reed, *Wordsworth: The Middle Years*, 24.

43. See *PW* 5:227–29 for the canceled narrative.

CHAPTER FIVE. WORDSWORTH AS PATERFAMILIAS

1. Peter Manning, "Wordsworth at St. Bees: Scandals, Sisterhoods, and Wordsworth's Later Poetry," *ELH* 52 (Spring 1985): 33–58; included in *Reading Romantics*, 273–99.

2. Hartley Coleridge, *The Letters of Hartley Coleridge*, ed. Grace Evelyn Griggs and Earl Leslie Griggs (New York: Oxford University Press, 1936), 196 (21 August 1836).

3. Dora Wordsworth, *The Letters of Dora Wordsworth*, ed. Howard P. Vincent (Chicago: Packard, 1944), 45 (1 December 1828). In this volume Vincent has collected the correspondence of Dora Wordsworth to Maria Jane Jewsbury. Other letters written by Dora to which I refer are from the unpublished collection in the Wordsworth Library, Grasmere.

4. In *Ambitious Heights: Writing, Friendship, Love—The Jewsbury Sisters, Felicia Hemans, and Jane Welsh Carlyle* (New York: Routledge, 1990), 61–68, Norma Clarke offers a more astringent reading of Wordsworth's treatment of his "four wives," Mary, Dorothy, Sara, and Dora.

5. See Batho, *The Later Wordsworth*, 90.

6. See *Moorman* 2:527 for a description of the trip.

7. *R&F*, 53. Heinzelman's is a wonderfully suggestive analysis of the idea of labor in the Grasmere years, but the title of the essay, "The Cult of Domesticity: Dorothy and William Wordsworth at Grasmere," is confusing because, according to Heinzelman's definition, the cultic qualities of domesticity arise after the Grasmere years.

8. In 1826, Wordsworth did purchase a tract adjacent to Rydal Mount that later became known as Dora's Field, in order to forestall his landlady from evicting him. See *Moorman* 2:421–22.

9. Frederika Beatty notes the custom in *William Wordsworth of Rydal Mount,* 93–94.

10. See Davidoff and Hall, *Family Fortunes,* chap. 8, especially 357–70.

11. M. Jeanne Peterson, *Family, Love, and Work in the Lives of Victorian Gentlewomen* (Bloomington: Indiana University Press, 1989).

12. Introduction to *Letters of Dora Wordsworth,* 11. The travel journal is *Journal of a Few Months' Residence in Portugal, and Glimpses of the South of Spain,* 2 vols. (London: Edward Moxon, 1847).

13. Hartley Coleridge, *Letters,* 112 (30 August 1830).

14. John Dryden, "To the Pious Memory of the Accomplisht Young Lady Mrs Anne Killigrew, Excellent in the Two Sister-Arts of Poesie, and Painting, An Ode" (1686 text), in *Eighteenth Century English Literature,* ed. Geoffrey Tillotson et al. (New York: Harcourt Brace, 1969), lines 13–15.

15. Geoffrey Hartman, "Words, Wish, Worth: Wordsworth," 204–5.

16. Barbara Johnson, "Gender and the Yale School," in *Speaking of Gender,* ed. Elaine Showalter (New York: Routledge, 1989), 47.

17. This collection was first published as *Ecclesiastical Sketches* in 1822; it was renamed *Ecclesiastical Sketches in a Series of Sonnets* in 1832; and the *Ecclesiastical Sonnets in Series* in 1837. See de Selincourt's note, *PW,* 3:341.

18. *Letters of Dora Wordsworth,* 93.

19. See Jeffrey C. Robinson, "A Later Poem by Wordsworth to 'Emma,'" *Philological Quarterly* 64 (Summer 1985): 411.

20. Quoted in Elizabeth Gaskell, *The Life of Charlotte Brontë,* ed. Alan Shelston (Harmondsworth, England: Penguin, 1975), 173.

21. Bradford Keyes Mudge's admirable book, *Sara Coleridge, a Victorian Daughter: Her Life and Essays* (New Haven: Yale University Press, 1989), certainly reveals the tensions Sara Coleridge experienced in trying to make this fit.

22. For a discussion of Wordsworth's contributions to annuals and anthologies, see N. Stephen Bauer, "Wordsworth and the Early Anthologies," *The Library* 27 (March 1972): 37–45. I am grateful to Richard Sha for this reference.

23. Nina Auerbach, *Woman and the Demon: The Life of a Victorian Myth* (Cambridge: Harvard University Press, 1982), 34.

24. See also Mellor's brief but incisive interpretation of this ship in terms of gender in *Romanticism and Gender,* 168–69.

25. Carol T. Christ, "The Feminine Subject in Victorian Poetry," *ELH* 54 (Summer 1987): 395.

26. For such readings see, for instance, Margaret Homans's *Bearing the Word,* 120, 126, and Marlon Ross's "Naturalizing Gender: Woman's Place in Wordsworth's Ideological Landscape," *ELH* 53 (Summer 1986): especially 392–96.

27. Anne K. Mellor allowed me to read her paper in progress, "Felicia Hemans, Domestic Ideology, and the Graves of a Household," which helped me think about Hemans and domesticity. She has now elaborated these ideas in *Romanticism and Gender,* 123–43.

28. *The Poetical Works of Felicia Hemans*, ed. William M. Rossetti (London: Ward Lock and Co., 1878).

29. See Robert Bernard Martin, *Tennyson: The Unquiet Heart* (New York: Oxford University Press, 1980), 200.

30. Edith C. Batho, *The Later Wordsworth*, says that "It would seem that he knew the *Poems by Two Brothers* of 1826, possibly also Timbuctoo of 1829 and the *Poems* of 1830" (33).

31. Judith Newton, "Making—and Remaking—History: Another Look at Patriarchy," in *Feminist Issues in Literary Scholarship*, ed. Shari Benstock, 124–40 (Bloomington: Indiana University Press, 1987).

32. On the greater emphasis on formality and ceremony in Wordsworth's later poetry, see Jones, *The Egotistical Sublime*, especially chap. 4, as well as Manning's "Wordsworth at St. Bees."

33. William Butler Yeats, *The Collected Poems of W. B. Yeats* (New York: Macmillan, 1956).

CONCLUSION. DORA WORDSWORTH: A DAUGHTER'S STORY

1. All of the letters other than those to Jewsbury are from the unpublished collection at the Wordsworth Library, Grasmere. The Jewsbury letters are from *Letters of Dora Wordsworth*. The first epigraph for this conclusion is taken from *LY* 2:706n; Wordsworth had asked Hemans to tone down the dedication, which finally read: "To William Wordsworth, Esq., In token of deep respect for his character, and fervent gratitude for moral and intellectual benefit derived from reverential communion with the spirit of his Poetry, this Volume is affectionately inscribed by Felicia Hemans." Passages from Dora Wordsworth's "Journal of a Tour of the Continent 1828" (DCMS 110) are identified by page number. The body of the manuscript is just under one hundred handwritten pages. The letter of 19 April 1838 is particularly difficult to read in parts, because it is written on the front and back of the sheets and is cross-written on both sides.

2. *Letters of Dora Wordsworth*, 81.

3. In *Ambitious Heights*, Norma Clarke focuses on the relationship from Jewsbury's point of view and emphasizes the importance of Jewsbury's literary ambitions as distinguishing Jane from Dora (61–68); but I would still argue that Dora's friendship is more than a consolation prize for the young poet who initially wanted a friendship with Wordsworth. Maria Jane Jewsbury was to die of cholera in India on 4 October 1833.

4. *Letters of Dora Wordsworth*, 84.

5. See the article that initiated the discussion, Carroll Smith-Rosenberg's "The Female World of Love and Ritual: Relations Between Women in Nineteenth-Century America," *Signs: Journal of Women in Culture and Society* 1 (Autumn 1975): 1–29. Although Smith-Rosenberg confines her argument to nineteenth-century America, many of the conditions, such as the blurring of the roles of mother and daughter, can be found in Britain in general and in the Wordsworth household in particular. Perhaps even more relevant is Lillian Faderman's *Surpassing the Love of Men: Romantic Friendship and Love Between*

Women from the Renaissance to the Present (New York: William Morrow, 1981), especially the chapter on nineteenth-century England entitled "Kindred Spirits," 157–77.

6. *Letters of Dora Wordsworth*, 83–85.

7. Wordsworth and Wordsworth, *Love Letters*, 197–98.

8. Mellor offers an interesting analysis of Dorothy Wordsworth's decline in *Romanticism and Gender*, especially 165–68.

9. *The Diary of Henry Crabb Robinson*, ed. Derek Hudson (New York: Oxford University Press, 1967), 141 (23 March 1835).

10. Beatty, *William Wordsworth of Rydal Mount*, 97–98.

11. Harriet Martineau, *Autobiography*, 3d ed., 2 vols. (London: Smith, Elder, 1877), 2:235.

Select Bibliography

PRIMARY SOURCES

Baillie, Joanna. *The Dramatic and Poetical Works of Joanna Baillie*. 1851; rpt. New York: Georg Olms Verlag, 1976.

Burke, Edmund. *A Philosophical Enquiry into the Origins of Our Ideas of the Sublime and Beautiful*. Ed. James T. Boulton. Notre Dame: Notre Dame University Press, 1958.

Byron, George Gordon, Lord. *Byron: Poetical Works*. Ed. Frederick Page, corrected by John Jump. New York: Oxford University Press, 1970.

Coleridge, Hartley. *The Letters of Hartley Coleridge*. Ed. Grace Evelyn Griggs and Earl Leslie Griggs. New York: Oxford University Press, 1936.

Coleridge, Samuel Taylor. *Collected Letters of Samuel Taylor Coleridge*. Ed. Earl Leslie Griggs, 6 vols. Oxford: Clarendon Press, 1956–71.

Gaskell, Elizabeth. *The Life of Charlotte Brontë*. Ed. Alan Shelston. Harmondsworth, England: Penguin, 1975.

Hemans, Felicia. *The Poetical Works of Felicia Hemans*. Ed. William M. Rossetti. London: Ward Lock and Co., 1878.

Johnson, Samuel. "Life of Milton." In *Lives of the English Poets*, 2 vols., intro. by Arthur Waugh, 63–134. 1906; rpt. New York: Oxford University Press, 1967.

Keats, John. *John Keats: Complete Poems*. Ed. Jack Stillinger. Cambridge: Harvard University Press, 1982.

———. *Letters of John Keats*. Selected and ed. Robert Gittings. New York: Oxford University Press, 1987.

Martineau, Harriet. *Autobiography*. 3d ed., 2 vols. London: Smith, Elder, 1877.

Milton, John. *John Milton: Complete Poems and Major Prose*. Ed. Merritt Y. Hughes. 1957; rpt. Indianapolis: Odyssey Press, 1976.

Price, Uvedale. *An Essay on the Picturesque as Compared with the Sublime and the Beautiful*. London: J. Robson, 1794.

Robinson, Henry Crabb. *The Diary of Henry Crabb Robinson*. Ed. Derek Hudson. New York: Oxford University Press, 1967.

Shelley, Percy Bysshe. *Shelley's Poetry and Prose*. Ed. Donald H. Reiman and Sharon B. Powers. New York: W. W. Norton, 1977.

Spenser, Edmund. *Selections from the Poetical Works of Edmund Spenser*. Ed. S. K. Heninger, Jr. Boston: Houghton-Mifflin, 1970.

Tennyson, Alfred, Lord. *The Poems of Tennyson*. 3 vols. Ed. Christopher Ricks. Berkeley: University of California Press, 1987.

Tillotson, Geoffrey, et al. *Eighteenth Century English Literature*. New York: Harcourt Brace, 1969.

West, Thomas. *A Guide to the Lakes in Cumberland, Westmorland and Lancashire*. 1784; rpt. Oxford: Woodstock Books, 1989.

Wollstonecraft, Mary. *A Vindication of the Rights of Woman*. Ed. Carol H. Poston. New York: W. W. Norton, 1975.

Wordsworth, Dora. *Journal of a Few Months' Residence in Portugal, and Glimpses of the South of Spain*. 2 vols. London: Edward Moxon, 1847.

———. "Journal of a Tour of the Continent 1828." Dove Cottage Manuscript (DCMS 110). The Wordsworth Trust, Grasmere, England.

———. *The Letters of Dora Wordsworth*. Ed. Howard P. Vincent. Chicago: Packard, 1944.

———. Unpublished Letters. Dove Cottage Manuscripts. The Wordsworth Trust, Grasmere, England.

Wordsworth, Dorothy. *The Journals of Dorothy Wordsworth*. Ed. Mary Moorman. 2d ed. New York: Oxford University Press, 1976.

Wordsworth, Mary. *The Letters of Mary Wordsworth, 1800–1855*. Ed. Mary E. Burton (1958; rpt. Westwood, Conn: Greenwood Press, 1979).

Wordsworth, William. *The Borderers by William Wordsworth*. Ed. Robert Osborn. Ithaca: Cornell University Press, 1982.

Wordsworth, William. *The Critical Opinions of William Wordsworth*. Ed. Markham L. Peacock, Jr. Baltimore: Johns Hopkins University Press, 1950.

———. *Poems, in Two Volumes, and Other Poems, 1800–1807*. Ed. Jared Curtis. Ithaca: Cornell University Press, 1983.

———. *The Poetical Works of William Wordsworth*. Ed. William Knight. 8 vols. New York: Macmillan, 1896.

———. *The Poetical Works of William Wordsworth*. Ed. Ernest de Selincourt and Helen Darbishire. 5 vols. Oxford: Clarendon Press, 1940–49.

———. *The Prelude, 1799, 1805, 1850*. Ed. Jonathan Wordsworth, M. H. Abrams, and Stephen Gill. New York: W. W. Norton, 1979.

———. *The Prose Works of William Wordsworth*. 3 vols. Ed. W. J. B. Owen and Jane Worthington Smyser. Oxford: Clarendon Press, 1974.

———. *Shorter Poems, 1807–1820, by William Wordsworth*. Ed. Carl H. Ketcham. Ithaca: Cornell University Press, 1989.

———. *The White Doe of Rylstone; or The Fate of the Nortons by William Wordsworth*. Ed. Kristine Dugas. Ithaca: Cornell University Press, 1988.

————. *William Wordsworth*. The Oxford Authors Series. Ed. Stephen Gill. New York: Oxford University Press, 1984.

————. *William Wordsworth: Guide to the Lakes*. Ed. Ernest de Selincourt. 1906; rpt. New York: Oxford University Press, 1973.

Wordsworth, William, and Dorothy Wordsworth. *The Letters of William and Dorothy Wordsworth*. Vol. 1: *The Early Years, 1787–1805*. Ed. Ernest de Selincourt. Revised by Chester L. Shaver. Oxford: Clarendon Press, 1967.

————. *The Letters of William and Dorothy Wordsworth*. Vol. 2: *The Middle Years*. Part 1: *The Middle Years, 1806–1811*. Ed. Ernest de Selincourt. Revised by Mary Moorman. Oxford: Clarendon Press, 1969.

————. *The Letters of William and Dorothy Wordsworth*. Vol. 2: *The Middle Years*. Part 2: *The Middle Years, 1812–1820*. Ed. Ernest de Selincourt. Revised by Mary Moorman and Alan G. Hill. Oxford: Clarendon Press, 1970.

————. *The Letters of William and Dorothy Wordsworth*. Vols. 4–7: *The Later Years, 1821–1853*. 4 parts. Ed. Ernest de Selincourt. Revised by Alan G. Hill. Oxford: Clarendon Press, 1967–88.

Wordsworth, William, and Mary Wordsworth. *The Love Letters of William and Mary Wordsworth*. Ed. Beth Darlington. Ithaca: Cornell University Press, 1981.

Yeats, William Butler. *The Collected Poems of W. B. Yeats*. New York: Macmillan, 1956.

SECONDARY SOURCES

Alexander, Meena. *Women in Romanticism: Mary Wollstonecraft, Dorothy Wordsworth, and Mary Shelley*. Savage, Md.: Barnes and Noble, 1989.

Auerbach, Nina. *Woman and the Demon: The Life of a Victorian Myth*. Cambridge: Harvard University Press, 1982.

Barrell, John. "The Uses of Dorothy: 'The Language of the Sense' in 'Tintern Abbey.'" In *Poetry, Language, and Politics*, 137–67. New York: St. Martin's, 1988.

Batho, Edith C. *The Later Wordsworth*. Cambridge: Cambridge University Press, 1933.

Beatty, Frederika. *William Wordsworth of Rydal Mount: An Account of the Poet and His Friends in the Last Decade*. London: J. M. Dent and Sons, 1939.

Bialostosky, Don H. *Wordsworth, Dialogics, and the Practice of Criticism*. New York: Cambridge University Press, 1992.

Blackburn, Robin. *The Overthrow of Colonial Slavery, 1776–1848*. New York: Verso, 1988.

Bush, Barbara. *Slave Women in Caribbean Society, 1650–1838*. Bloomington: Indiana University Press, 1990.

Buttrick, George Arthur, et al., eds. *The Interpreter's Dictionary of the Bible*. 5 vols. Nashville: Abingdon Press, 1962.

Chandler, James K. "'Wordsworth' After Waterloo." In *The Age of William Wordsworth: Critical Essays on the Romantic Tradition*, ed. Kenneth R. Johnston and Gene W. Ruoff, 84–111. New Brunswick: Rutgers University Press, 1987.

————. *Wordsworth's Second Nature.* Chicago: University of Chicago Press, 1984.

Christ, Carol T. "The Feminine Subject in Victorian Poetry." *ELH* 54 (Summer 1987): 385–401.

Clarke, Norma. *Ambitious Heights: Writing, Friendship, Love—The Jewsbury Sisters, Felicia Hemans, and Jane Welsh Carlyle.* New York: Routledge, 1990.

Cohen, William B. *The French Encounter with the African: White Response to Blacks, 1530–1880.* Bloomington: Indiana University Press, 1980.

Comparetti, Alice. Introduction to *The White Doe of Rylstone.* Ithaca: Cornell University Press, 1940.

Curran, Stuart. "The I Altered." In *R&F,* 185–207.

Cuzin, Jean-Pierre. *French Painting in the Louvre.* New York: Scala, 1982.

Danby, John. *The Simple Wordsworth: Studies in the Poems, 1797–1807.* 1960; rpt. London: Routledge and Kegan Paul, 1971.

Darbishire, Helen. *The Poet Wordsworth.* 1949; rpt. Westport, Conn.: Greenwood Press, 1980.

Davidoff, Lenore, and Catherine Hall. *Family Fortunes: Men and Women of the English Middle Class, 1780–1850.* Chicago: University of Chicago Press, 1987.

Davis, Robert Con. "The Structure of the Picturesque: Dorothy Wordsworth's Journals." *The Wordsworth Circle* 9 (Winter 1978): 45–49.

Douglas, Wallace. *Wordsworth: The Construction of a Personality.* Kent, Ohio: Kent State University Press, 1968.

Eaves, Morris. "Romantic Expressive Theory and Blake's Idea of Audience." *PMLA* 95 (1980): 790–91.

Eilenberg, Susan. "'Michael,' 'Christabel,' and the Poetry of Possession." *Criticism* 30 (Spring 1988): 205–24.

Erdman, David V. *Blake: Prophet Against Empire—A Poet's Interpretation of the History of His Own Times.* 1954; rpt. Garden City, N.Y.: Doubleday, 1969.

————. "Wordsworth as Heartsworth; or, Was Regicide the Prophetic Ground of Those 'Moral Questions'?" In *The Evidence of the Imagination: Studies of Interactions Between Life and Art in English Romantic Literature,* ed. Donald H. Reiman, Michael C. Jaye, and Betty T. Bennett, 12–41. New York: New York University Press, 1978.

Faderman, Lillian. *Surpassing the Love of Men: Romantic Friendship and Love Between Women from the Renaissance to the Present.* New York: William Morrow, 1981.

Ferguson, Moira. *Subject to Others: British Women Writers and Colonial Slavery, 1670–1834.* New York: Routledge, 1992.

Fetterly, Judith. *The Resisting Reader: A Feminist Approach to American Fiction.* Bloomington: Indiana University Press, 1978.

Fienberg, Nona. "The Emergence of Stella in *Astrophil and Stella.*" *SEL* 25 (1985): 5–19.

Gates, Barbara. "Wordsworth's Symbolic Doe: The Power of History in the Mind." *Criticism* 17 (Summer 1975): 234–45.

Gill, Stephen. *William Wordsworth: A Life.* Oxford: Clarendon Press, 1989.

Gilligan, Carol. *In a Different Voice: Psychological Theory and Women's Development*. Cambridge: Harvard University Press, 1982.

Gittings, Robert, and Jo Manton. *Dorothy Wordsworth*. Oxford: Clarendon Press, 1985.

Goslee, Nancy Moore. "Slavery and Sexual Character: Questioning the Master Trope in Blake's *Visions of the Daughters of Albion*." *ELH* 57 (Spring 1990): 101–28.

Griggs, Earl Leslie. *Thomas Clarkson, the Friend of Slaves*. 1936; rpt. Westport, Conn.: Negro Universities Press, 1970.

Hagstrum, Jean. *The Romantic Body: Love and Sexuality in Keats, Wordsworth, and Blake*. Knoxville: University of Tennessee Press, 1985.

Haigwood, Laura E. "Oedipal Revolution in the Lyrical Ballads." *Centennial Review* 33 (Fall 1989): 468–89.

Hartman, Geoffrey. "Words, Wish, Worth: Wordsworth." In *Deconstruction and Criticism*, ed. Harold Bloom et al., 117–216. New York: Old Seabury Press, 1979.

————. *Wordsworth's Poetry, 1787–1814*. New Haven: Yale University Press, 1964.

Heffernan, James A. W. *Wordsworth's Theory of Poetry: The Transforming Imagination*. Ithaca: Cornell University Press, 1969.

Heilbrun, Carolyn G. *Writing a Woman's Life*. New York: Ballantine Books, 1988.

Heinzelman, Kurt. "The Cult of Domesticity: Dorothy and William Wordsworth at Grasmere." In *R&F*, 52–78.

Hoeveler, Diane Long. *Romantic Androgyny: The Women Within*. University Park: Pennsylvania State University Press, 1990.

Hofkosh, Sonia. "The Writer's Ravishment: Women and the Romantic Author— The Example of Byron." In *R&F*, 93–114.

Homans, Margaret. *Bearing the Word: Language and Female Experience in Nineteenth Century Women's Writing*. Chicago: University of Chicago Press, 1986.

————. *Women Writers and Poetic Identity*. Princeton: Princeton University Press, 1980.

Honour, Hugh. *The Image of the Black in Western Art*. 2 parts. Cambridge: Harvard University Press for the Menil Foundation, 1989.

Jacobus, Mary. "Geometric Science and Romantic History, or Wordsworth, Newton, and the Slave Trade." In *Romanticism, Writing, and Sexual Difference*. Oxford: Clarendon Press, 1989.

————. "The Law of/and Gender: Genre Theory and *The Prelude*." *Diacritics* 14 (1984): 47–57.

————. *Romanticism, Writing, and Sexual Difference*. Oxford: Clarendon Press, 1989.

James, C. L. R. *The Black Jacobins: Toussaint L'Ouverture and the San Domingo Revolution*. 2d ed. 1938; rpt. New York: Random House, 1963.

Johnson, Barbara. "Gender and the Yale School." In *Speaking of Gender*, ed. Elaine Showalter, 45–55. New York: Routledge, 1989.

Johnson, Lee M. *Wordsworth and the Sonnet*. Anglistica 19. Copenhagen: Rosenkilde and Bagger, 1973.

Jones, John. *The Egotistical Sublime: A History of Wordsworth's Imagination.* 1954; rpt. London: Chatto and Windus, 1960.

Kaplan, Cora. "Wild Nights: Pleasure/Sexuality/Feminism." In *Sea Changes: Culture and Feminism,* 31–56. London: Verso, 1986.

Kelley, Theresa M. *Wordsworth's Revisionary Aesthetics.* New York: Cambridge University Press, 1988.

Kelly, Joan. "Early Feminist Theory and the *Querelle des Femmes.*" In *Women, History, and Theory,* 65–109. Chicago: University of Chicago Press, 1984.

Kennedy, Deborah. "Revolutionary Tales: Helen Maria Williams's *Letters from France* and William Wordsworth's 'Vaudracour and Julia.'" *The Wordsworth Circle* 21 (Summer 1990): 109–14.

Klancher, Jon P. *The Making of English Reading Audiences, 1790–1832.* Madison: University of Wisconsin Press, 1987.

Levinson, Marjorie. *Wordsworth's Great Period Poems: Four Essays.* New York: Cambridge University Press, 1986.

Lipking, Lawrence. *Abandoned Women and Poetic Tradition.* Chicago: University of Chicago Press, 1988.

Liu, Alan. *Wordsworth: The Sense of History.* Palo Alto: Stanford University Press, 1989.

McCloy, Shelby T. *The Negro in France.* 1961; rpt. New York: Haskell House, 1973.

McGhee, Richard D. "'Conversant with Infinity': Form and Meaning in Wordsworth's 'Laodamia.'" *Studies in Philology* 68 (July 1971): 357–69.

Mahl, Mary R., and Helene Koon. *The Female Spectator: English Women Writers Before 1800.* Old Westbury, N.Y.: Feminist Press, 1977.

Manning, Peter J. *Reading Romantics: Texts and Contexts.* New York: Oxford University Press, 1990.

Martin, Robert Bernard. *Tennyson: The Unquiet Heart.* New York: Oxford University Press, 1980.

Mellor, Anne K. *Romanticism and Gender.* New York: Routledge, 1993.

Mellor, Anne K., ed. *Romanticism and Feminism.* Bloomington: Indiana University Press, 1988.

Miller, J. Hillis. "The Still Heart: Poetic Form in Wordsworth." *New Literary History* 2 (Winter 1971): 297–310.

Mitchell, W. J. T. *Iconology: Image, Text, Ideology.* Chicago: University of Chicago Press, 1986.

Moorman, Mary. *William Wordsworth: A Biography.* Volume 1: *The Early Years, 1770–1803.* New York: Oxford University Press, 1957.

———. *William Wordsworth: A Biography.* Volume 2: *The Later Years, 1803–1850.* New York: Oxford University Press, 1965.

Mudge, Bradford Keyes. "The Man with Two Brains: Gothic Novels, Popular Culture, Literary History." *PMLA* 107 (January 1992): 92–104.

———. *Sara Coleridge, a Victorian Daughter: Her Life and Essays.* New Haven: Yale University Press, 1989.

Mueller, Janel M. "On Genesis in Genre: Milton's Politicizing of the Sonnet in 'Captain or Colonel.'" In *Renaissance Genres,* ed. Barbara K. Lewalski, 213–40. Harvard Studies in English 14. Cambridge: Harvard University Press, 1986.

Newton, Judith. "Making—and Remaking—History: Another Look at Patri-archy." In *Feminist Issues in Literary Scholarship*, ed. Shari Benstock, 124–40. Bloomington: Indiana University Press, 1987.

Page, Judith W. "'A History / Homely and Rude': Genre and Style in Wordsworth's 'Michael.'" *SEL* 29 (1989): 622–36.

———. "'The weight of too much liberty': Genre and Gender in Wordsworth's Calais Sonnets." *Criticism* (Spring 1988): 189–203.

Parker, Reeve. "Reading Wordsworth's Power: Narrative and Usurpation in *The Borderers*." *ELH* 54 (Summer 1987): 299–331.

Parker, Rozsika. *The Subversive Stitch: Embroidery and the Making of the Fem-inine*. 1984; rpt. New York: Routledge, 1989.

Paulson, Ronald. *Representations of Revolution, 1789–1820*. New Haven: Yale University Press, 1983.

Peacock, Markham L., Jr. *The Critical Opinions of William Wordsworth*. Bal-timore: Johns Hopkins University Press, 1950.

Peterson, M. Jeanne. *Family, Love, and Work in the Lives of Victorian Gentle-women*. Bloomington: Indiana University Press, 1989.

Pocock, J. G. A. *Virtue, Commerce, and History: Essays on Political Thought and History, Chiefly in the Eighteenth Century*. New York: Cambridge Uni-versity Press, 1985.

Poovey, Mary. *The Proper Lady and the Woman Writer*. Chicago: University of Chicago Press, 1984.

Price, Martin. "The Picturesque Moment." In Frederick W. Hilles and Harold Bloom, eds. *From Sensibility to Romanticism*. New York: Oxford University Press, 1965.

Read, Herbert. *Wordsworth*. London: Faber and Faber, n.d.

Reed, Mark L. *Wordsworth: The Chronology of the Early Years, 1770–1799*. Cambridge: Harvard University Press, 1967.

———. *Wordsworth: The Chronology of the Middle Years, 1800–1815*. Cam-bridge: Harvard University Press, 1975.

Reiman, Donald H. "The Poetry of Familiarity: Wordsworth, Dorothy, and Mary Hutchinson." In *The Evidence of the Imagination: Studies of Interac-tions Between Life and Art in English Romantic Literature*, ed. Donald H. Reiman, Michael C. Jaye, and Betty T. Bennett, 142–77. New York: New York University Press, 1978.

Reiman, Donald H., ed. *The Romantics Reviewed*. 9 vols. New York: Garland, 1972.

Richardson, Alan. "Colonialism, Race, and Lyric Irony in Blake's 'The Little Black Boy.'" *Papers on Language and Literature* 26 (1990): 233–48.

Robinson, Jeffrey C. "A Later Poem by Wordsworth to 'Emma.'" *Philological Quarterly* 64 (Summer 1985): 411.

Roe, Nicholas. *Wordsworth and Coleridge: The Radical Years*. Oxford: Claren-don Press, 1988.

Ross, Marlon B. *The Contours of Masculine Desire: Romanticism and the Rise of Women's Poetry*. New York: Oxford University Press, 1989.

———. "Joanna Baillie." In the *Dictionary of Literary Biography*, vol. 93, ed. John R. Greenfield, 3–15. Detroit: Gale Research, 1990.

————. "Naturalizing Gender: Woman's Place in Wordsworth's Ideological Landscape." *ELH* 53 (Summer 1986): 391–410.

Ruddick, Sara. *Maternal Thinking: Toward a Politics of Peace.* New York: Ballantine Books, 1990.

Sacks, Peter M. *The English Elegy: Studies in the Genre from Spenser to Yeats.* Baltimore: Johns Hopkins University Press, 1985.

Shackford, Martha Hale. *Wordsworth's Interest in Painters and Pictures.* Wellesley, Mass.: Wellesley Press, 1945.

Simpson, David. "Figuring Class, Sex, and Gender: What Is the Subject of Wordsworth's 'Gipsies'?" *South Atlantic Quarterly* 88 (Summer 1989): 541–67.

————. *Wordsworth's Historical Imagination.* New York: Methuen, 1987.

Smith-Rosenberg, Carroll. "The Female World of Love and Ritual: Relations Between Women in Nineteenth-Century America." *Signs: Journal of Women in Culture and Society* 1 (Autumn 1975): 1–29.

Snyder, William. "Mother Nature's Other Natures: Landscape in Women's Writing." *Women's Studies* 21 (1992): 143–62.

Spiegelman, Willard. *Wordsworth's Heroes.* Berkeley: University of California Press, 1985.

Spivak, Gayatri Chakravorty. "Sex and History in *The Prelude* (1805): Books Nine to Thirteen." *Texas Studies in Literature and Language* 23 (1981): 324–60.

Tayler, Irene. "By Peculiar Grace: Wordsworth in 1802." In *Evidence of the Imagination: Studies of Interactions Between Life and Art in English Romantic Literature,* ed. Donald H. Reiman, Michael C. Jaye, and Betty T. Bennett, 119–41. New York: New York University Press, 1978.

Theological Dictionary of the New Testament. 10 vols. Ed. Gerhard Kittel. Trans. Geoffrey W. Bromiley. Grand Rapids: William B. Eerdmans, 1965.

Trible, Phyllis. *God and the Rhetoric of Sexuality.* Philadelphia: Fortress Press, 1978.

Trilling, Lionel. "Wordsworth and the Iron Time." In *Wordsworth: A Collection of Critical Essays,* ed. M. H. Abrams, 45–66. Englewood Cliffs, N.J.: Prentice-Hall, 1972.

Vogler, Thomas A. "'A Spirit, Yet a Woman Too!' Dorothy and William Wordsworth." In *Mothering the Mind: Twelve Studies of Writers and Their Silent Partners,* ed. Ruth Perry and Martine Watson Brownley, 239–58. New York: Holmes and Meier, 1984.

Walvin, James. *England, Slaves, and Freedom, 1776–1838.* Jackson: University Press of Mississippi, 1986.

Whitaker, Thomas Dunham. *The History and Antiquities of the Deanery of Craven in the County of York.* 3d ed. London: Cassell, Petter, and Galpin, 1878.

Williams, Raymond. *Keywords: A Vocabulary of Culture and Society.* New York: Oxford University Press, 1976.

Wolfson, Susan J. "Dorothy Wordsworth in Conversation with William." In *R&F,* 139–66.

Woolf, Virginia. *A Room of One's Own*. 1929; rpt. New York: Harcourt Brace, 1957.

Yaeger, Patricia. "Toward a Female Sublime." In *Gender and Theory: Dialogues on Feminist Criticism*, ed. Linda Kauffman, 191–212. Oxford: Basil Blackwell, 1989.

Index

Abandonment, in Wordsworth's life and art, 5–6
Abolitionism, 71–72, 173nn. 28–30
Abraham, 63, 65–66, 70, 96
Adam (first man), 84, 137
"Address to My Infant Daughter" (Wordsworth), 119, 120–22, 123, 126
Adeline Mowbray (Opie), 34–35
"Adonais" (Shelley), 91, 175n. 19
Aeneid (Virgil), 79, 86
"Alastor" (Shelley), 46
Anderson, Robert, 40
Antigone, 123, 125
Argyle, Duke of, 160
Aristotle, 35
Arnold, Matthew, 65, 103, 145
Arthur, King, 135, 137, 139–40, 142, 144
Audience: "consumption" vs. "reception" by, 30; gender of, 5, 7, 29, 31, 44, 51–52, 142; reform of, 29-30; relationship with artist, 29–31, 41, 103–4; tastes corrupted, 32, 33–35, 37, 42, 43; tastes vindicated, 42–43
Auerbach, Nina, 139
Austen, Jane, 45
The Authors of England (Chorley), 143

Bacon, Francis, 99
Baillie, Joanna, 7, 39; on artist/audience relationship, 41; on individual genius, 41; influence of, 40–41; on public taste, 42–43; sympathetic perspective of, 41, 152

Ballads, as genre for women, 35
"The Banished Negroes" (Wordsworth), 54, 77, 79, 163; on mysteries of gender and race, 68, 71–73, 75–76; protest of racial injustice, 68–76
Barrell, John, 44
Batho, Edith C., 5, 179n. 30
Bathsheba (Hardy's character), 45
Battle of Waterloo, 80, 99
Beatty, Frederika, 112
Beaumont, Lady, 118, 140
Beaumont, Sir George, 75
Beauty: as consolation for loss, 158, 161; of domestic poetry, 114–15; familiarity of, 18–19, 20; gendered roles of, 13, 14, 19, 24–26, 28; idealization of, 26, 28; and the picturesque, 20–21; playful images of, 28; and repudiation of "action" poetry, 104; and sublimity, 6, 15–24, 125, 167n. 5; as tempering influence, 47
Benoist, Marie-Guillemine, 73–74, 75
Bialostosky, Don H., 6
Bible, King James, 32, 65
Biographia Literaria (Coleridge), 53
Blackburn, Robin, 172–73
Black people: European stereotypes about, 72, 173n. 32; exclusion from France, 68-76, 172n. 24; paranoia about, 69, 172n. 24; portraiture of, 75, 174n. 38
Blackwood's Magazine, 3
Blake, William, 4, 127, 174n. 39; and Milton, 61, 126; on occupation of

191

Compositor: BookMasters, Inc.
Text: 10/13 Sabon
Display: Sabon
Printer and Binder: Thomson-Shore, Inc.